Tyndale New Commen

Volume 10

TNTC

Ephesians

Tyndale New Testament Commentaries

Volume 10

Series Editor: Eckhard J. Schnabel
Consulting Editor: Nicholas Perrin

Ephesians

An Introduction and Commentary

Darrell L. Bock

An imprint of InterVarsity Press
Downers Grove, Illinois

InterVarsity Press, USA
P.O. Box 1400
Downers Grove, IL 60515-1426, USA
ivpress.com
email@ivpress.com

Inter-Varsity Press, England
36 Causton Street
London SW1P 4ST, England
ivpbooks.com
ivp@ivpbooks.com

InterVarsity Press®, USA, is the book-publishing division of InterVarsity Christian Fellowship/USA® and a member movement of the International Fellowship of Evangelical Students. Website: intervarsity.org.

Inter-Varsity Press, England, is closely linked with the Universities and Colleges Christian Fellowship, a student movement connecting Christian Unions throughout Great Britain, and a member movement of the International Fellowship of Evangelical Students. Website: uccf.org.uk.

First published 2019

USA ISBN 978-0-8308-4298-8 (print)
USA ISBN 978-0-8308-5737-1 (digital)
UK ISBN 978-1-78359-894-6 (print)
UK ISBN 978-1-78359-895-3 (digital)

Set in Garamond 11/13pt
Typeset in Great Britain by CRB Associates, Potterhanworth, Lincolnshire
Printed in the United States of America ∞

InterVarsity Press is committed to ecological stewardship and to the conservation of natural resources in all our operations. This book was printed using sustainably sourced paper.

Library of Congress Cataloging-in-Publication Data
Names: Bock, Darrell L., author.
Title: Ephesians : an introduction and commentary / Darrell L. Bock.
Description: Downers Grove : InterVarsity Press, 2019. | Series: Tyndale New
    Testament commentaries ; VOLUME 10 | Includes bibliographical references.
Identifiers: LCCN 2019007988 (print) | LCCN 2019012624 (ebook) | ISBN
    9780830857371 (eBook) | ISBN 9780830842988 (pbk. : alk. paper)
Subjects: LCSH: Bible. Ephesians—Commentaries.
Classification: LCC BS2695.53 (ebook) | LCC BS2695.53 .B63 2019 (print) | DDC
    227/.5077—dc23
LC record available at https://lccn.loc.gov/2019007988

British Library Cataloguing-in-Publication Data
A catalogue record for this book is available from the British Library.

P 25 24 23 22 21 20 19 18 17 16 15 14 13 12 11 10 9 8 7 6 5 4 3 2 1
Y 39 38 37 36 35 34 33 32 31 30 29 28 27 26 25 24 23 22 21 20 19

CONTENTS

GENERAL PREFACE

The Tyndale Commentaries have been a flagship series for evangelical readers of the Bible for over sixty years. Both the original New Testament volumes (1956–1974) as well as the new commentaries (1983–2003) rightly established themselves as a point of first reference for those who wanted more than is usually offered in a one-volume Bible commentary, without requiring the technical skills in Greek and in Jewish and Graeco-Roman studies of the more detailed series, and with the advantage of being shorter than the volumes of intermediate commentary series. The appearance of new popular commentary series demonstrates that there is a continuing demand for commentaries that appeal to Bible study leaders in churches and at universities. The publisher, editors and authors of the Tyndale Commentaries believe that the series continues to meet an important need in the Christian community, not least in what we call today the Global South, with its immense growth of churches and the corresponding need for a thorough understanding of the Bible by Christian believers.

In the light of new knowledge, new critical questions, new revisions of Bible translations, and the need to provide specific guidance on the literary context and the theological emphases of the individual passage, it was time to publish new commentaries in the series. Four authors will revise their commentary that appeared in the second series. The original aim remains. The new commentaries are neither too short nor unduly long. They are exegetical and thus root the interpretation of the text in its historical context. They do not aim to solve all critical questions, but they are written with an awareness of major scholarly debates which may be treated in the Introduction, in Additional Notes or in the commentary itself. While not specifically homiletic in aim, they want to help readers to understand the passage under consideration in such a way that they begin to see points of relevance and application, even though the commentary does not explicitly offer these. The authors base their exegesis on the Greek text, but they write for readers who do not know Greek; Hebrew and Greek terms that are discussed are transliterated. The English translation used for the first series was the Authorized (King James) Version, while the volumes of the second series mostly used the Revised Standard Version; the volumes of the third series use either the New International Version (2011) or the New Revised Standard Version as primary versions, unless otherwise indicated by the author.

An immense debt of gratitude for the first and second series of the Tyndale Commentaries was owed to R. V. G. Tasker and L. Morris, who each wrote four of the commentaries themselves. The recruitment of new authors for the third series proved to be effortless, as colleagues responded enthusiastically to be involved in this project, a testimony both to the larger number of New Testament scholars capable and willing to write commentaries, to the wider ethnic identity of contributors, and to the role that the Tyndale Commentaries have played in the church worldwide. It continues to be the hope of all those concerned with this series that God will graciously use the new commentaries to help readers understand as fully and clearly as possible the meaning of the New Testament.

Eckhard J. Schnabel, Series Editor
Nicholas Perrin, Consulting Editor

AUTHOR'S PREFACE

The epistle to the Ephesians is about a dynamic community. Such a community is what stands behind the writing of this commentary. I taught this epistle in a basic exegesis course at Dallas Theological Seminary for well over twenty years. The interaction with students and their enthusiasm to get serious about the study of the Greek text kept this study from becoming old. My thanks go to the many students who taught me much as we discussed this letter, as well as to the New Testament Department where I have served for more than thirty-five years. These are some of the best colleagues one could spend a career working alongside.

I also must express appreciation to my team past and present at the Hendricks Center. My more recent work on cultural engagement has sought to encourage the application of much of what this letter calls for from believers. So my thanks go to Bill Hendricks, Pam Cole, Kymberli Cook, Amanda Stidham, Mikel Del Rosario, Heather Zimmerman and Carol Rosell, all of whom have taught me much about faith in practice. Special thanks go to Peter Green, who read over this manuscript and made many helpful observations about it in terms of content and clarity. I have used the New English Translation (NET) or Revised Standard Version (RSV) in most cases. In other places, the translation is my own.

I am grateful for the invitation of Eckhard Schnabel to participate in this series and for giving me the choice to work on this great epistle. It was a risk on his part to let this mostly Jesus and Gospels person work on a piece from Paul.

Once again, I must thank my wife of well over forty years, Sally Bock. She has been a great life partner and during these years has experienced many an hour when I have been at my computer working on one commentary or another.

So I offer this treatment of a wonderful short epistle whose impact far outweighs its length. No words are adequate to summarize its content and value, but perhaps this commentary will encourage its readers to the good works God prepared beforehand by his grace that we might walk in them (Eph. 2:10).

Darrell L. Bock

ABBREVIATIONS

1QH	*Thanksgiving Hymns*
1QM	*War Scroll*
1QS	*Rule of the Community*
AB	Anchor Bible
AGJU	Arbeiten zur Geschichte des antiken Judentums und des Urchristentums
Ant.	Josephus, *Antiquities of the Jews*
2 Apoc. Bar.	*2 Baruch*
BDAG	*A Greek–English Lexicon of the New Testament and Other Early Christian Literature*, ed. W. Bauer, F. W. Danker, W. F. Arndt and F. W. Gingrich, 3rd edn (Chicago: University of Chicago Press, 2000)
BDB	*Hebrew and English Lexicon of the Old Testament*, ed. F. Brown, S. R. Driver and C. A. Briggs, rev. and corrected edn (Oxford: Clarendon Press, 1959)
BECNT	Baker Exegetical Commentary on the New Testament
BibSac	*Bibliotheca Sacra*
b. Yeb.	*Babylonian Talmud, Yebamoth*
CD	*Damascus Document*
EEC	Evangelical Exegetical Commentary
HALOT	*The Hebrew and Aramaic Lexicon of the Old Testament*, ed. L. Koehler, W. Baumgartner and J. J. Stamm, translated and edited under the supervision of M. E. J. Richardson, 5 vols. (Leiden: Brill, 1994–2000)

HTKNT	Herders theologischer Kommentar zum Neuen Testament
HTS	*Hervormde Teologiese Studies*
ICC	International Critical Commentary
JETS	*Journal of the Evangelical Theological Society*
JSNT	*Journal for the Study of the New Testament*
JTS	*Journal of Theological Studies*
Jub.	*Jubilees*
LXX	Septuagint (Greek translation of the Old Testament)
m. 'Abot	*Mishnah, 'Abot*
m. Peah	*Mishnah, Peah*
MT	Masoretic Text
NCBC	New Century Bible Commentary
NICNT	New International Commentary on the New Testament
NT	New Testament
NTL	New Testament Library
OT	Old Testament
RNT	Regensburger Neues Testament
SBLMS	Society of Biblical Literature Monograph Series
SNTSMS	Society of New Testament Studies Monograph Series
Tg. Pss	*Targum of Psalms*
TNTC	Tyndale New Testament Commentaries
TrinJ	*Trinity Journal*
T. Sol.	*Testament of Solomon*
War	Josephus, *The Jewish War*
WBC	Word Biblical Commentary
WTJ	*Westminster Theological Journal*
WUNT	Wissenschaftliche Untersuchungen zum Neuen Testament
ZECNT	Zondervan Exegetical Commentary on the New Testament

Bible versions

| ESV | English Standard Version (2007) |
| NASB | New American Standard Bible (1995) |

NET	New English Translation (2005)
NIV	New International Version (2011)
NLT	New Living Translation (1996)
NRSV	New Revised Standard Version (1989)
RSV	Revised Standard Version (1971 New Testament Second Edition)

SELECT BIBLIOGRAPHY

Commentaries on Ephesians

Abbott, T. K. (1897), *A Critical and Exegetical Commentary on the Epistles to the Ephesians and Colossians*, ICC (Edinburgh: T&T Clark).

Arnold, Clinton E. (2010), *Ephesians*, ZECNT (Grand Rapids, MI: Zondervan).

Barth, Markus (1974), *Ephesians*, 2 vols., AB (Garden City, NY: Doubleday).

Baugh, S. M. (2016), *Ephesians*, EEC (Bellingham, WA: Lexham Press).

Best, Ernest (1998), *Ephesians*, ICC (Edinburgh: T&T Clark).

Bruce, F. F. (1984), *The Epistle to the Colossians, to Philemon, and to the Ephesians*, NICNT (Grand Rapids, MI: Eerdmans).

Ernst, Josef (1974), *Die Briefe an die Philipper, an Philemon, an die Kolosser, an die Epheser*, RNT (Regensburg: Pustet).

Foulkes, Francis (1989), *Ephesians*, 2nd edn, TNTC (Leicester: Inter-Varsity Press; Downers Grove, IL: InterVarsity Press).

Fowl, Stephen (2012), *Ephesians: A Commentary*, NTL (Louisville, KY: John Knox Press).

Gnilka, Joachim (1982), *Der Epheserbrief*, 3rd edn, HTKNT (Freiburg: Herder).

Hoehner, Harold (2002), *Ephesians: An Exegetical Commentary* (Grand Rapids, MI: Baker).

Kuruvilla, Abraham (2015), *Ephesians* (Eugene, OR: Cascade).

Lincoln, Andrew T. (1990), *Ephesians*, WBC (Dallas, TX: Word).

Mitton, C. Leslie (1976), *Ephesians*, NCBC (London: Marshall, Morgan & Scott).

Robinson, J. Armitage (1904), *Commentary on Ephesians*, 2nd edn, repr. 1979 (Grand Rapids, MI: Kregel).

Schnackenburg, Rudolph (1991), *The Epistle to the Ephesians: A Commentary* (Edinburgh: T&T Clark).

Snodgrass, Klyne (1996), *Ephesians*, NIV Application Commentary (Grand Rapids, MI: Zondervan).

Thielman, Frank (2010), *Ephesians*, BECNT (Grand Rapids, MI: Baker).

Witherington, Ben (2007), *The Letters to Philemon, the Colossians, and the Ephesians: A Socio-Rhetorical Commentary on the Captivity Epistles* (Grand Rapids, MI: Eerdmans).

Other commentaries, books, monographs and articles

Arnold, Clinton E. (1989), *Ephesians: Power and Magic: The Concept of Power in Ephesians in Light of Its Historical Situation*, SNTSMS 63 (Cambridge: Cambridge University Press).

Balch, D. (1981), *Let Wives Be Submissive: The Domestic Code in 1 Peter*, SBLMS 26 (Chico, CA: Society of Biblical Literature).

Barnard, Jody A. (2009), 'Unity in Christ: The Purpose of Ephesians', *Expository Times* 120, pp. 167–172.

Bartchy, Scott (1973), *ΜΑΛΛΟΝ ΧΡΗΣΑΙ: First-Century Slavery and the Interpretation of 1 Corinthians 7:21* (Missoula, MT: Scholars).

Baugh, S. M. (1992), '"Savior of All People": 1 Tim 4:10 in Context', *WTJ* 54, pp. 331–340.

Bedale, S. (1954), 'The Meaning of κεφαλή in the Pauline Epistles', *JTS* 5, pp. 211–215.

Bock, Darrell L. (1994), '"The New Man" as Community in Colossians and Ephesians', in C. H. Dyer and Roy Zuck (eds.), *Integrity of Heart, Skillfulness of Hands: Biblical and Leadership Studies in Honor of Donald K. Campbell* (Grand Rapids, MI: Baker), pp. 157–167.

Calvin, John (1548–1556; 1965 edn), *The Epistles of Paul to the Galatians, Ephesians, Philippians, Colossians*, ed. David W. Torrance and Thomas F. Torrance, tr. T. H. L. Parker (Grand Rapids, MI: Eerdmans).

Cohick, Lynn H. (2012), 'Tyranny, Authority, Service: Leadership and Headship in the New Testament', *Ex Auditu* 28, pp. 74–89.

Collins, John (2007), 'What Does πληροῦσθε ἐν πνεύματι Mean?', *Presbyterion* 33, pp. 12–30.

Darko, Daniel (2015), 'What Does It Mean to Be Saved? An African Reading of Ephesians 2', *Journal of Pentecostal Theology* 24, pp. 44–56.

Ferda, Tucker S. (2012), '"Sealed with the Holy Spirit" (Eph 1, 13–14) and Circumcision', *Biblica* 93, pp. 557–579.

Foster, Robert L. (2007), '"A Temple in the Lord Filled to the Fullness of God": Context and Intertextuality (Eph. 3:19)', *Novum Testamentum* 49, pp. 85–96.

Gibson, Jack (2011), 'Ephesians 5:21–33 and the Lack of Marital Unity in the Roman Empire', *BibSac* 168, pp. 162–177.

Gosnell, Peter W. (2006), 'Honor and Shame as a Unifying Motif in Ephesians', *Bulletin for Biblical Research* 16, pp. 105–128.

Harris, W. Hall (1996), *Descent of Christ: Ephesians 4:7–11 and Traditional Hebrew Imagery*, AGJU 32 (Leiden: Brill; repr. Grand Rapids, MI: Baker).

Harrison, J. R. (2003), *Paul's Language of Grace in Its Greco-Roman Context*, WUNT 2/172 (Tübingen: Mohr Siebeck).

Hartog, Paul (2008), 'Polycarp, Ephesians, and Scripture', *WTJ* 70, pp. 255–275.

Healy, Mary (2011), 'St. Paul, Ephesians 5, and Same-Sex Marriage', *Homiletic and Pastoral Review* (May), pp. 12–21.

Immendörfer, Michael (2017), *Ephesians and Artemis*, WUNT 436 (Tübingen: Mohr Siebeck).

Keener, Craig (2009), 'One New Temple in Christ (Ephesians 2:11–22; Acts 21:27–29; Mark 11:17; John 4:20–24)', *Asian Journal of Pentecostal Studies* 12, pp. 75–92.

Keown, Mark (2016), 'Paul's Vision of a New Masculinity (Eph 5:21 – 6:9)', *Colloquium* 48, pp. 47–60.

Klingbeil, Gerald A. (2006), 'Metaphors and Pragmatics: An Introduction to the Hermeneutics of Metaphors in the Epistle to the Ephesians', *Bulletin for Biblical Research* 16, pp. 273–293.

Lunde, Jonathan, and John Dunne (2012), 'Paul's Creative and Contextual Use of Isaiah in Ephesians 5:14', *JETS* 55, pp. 87–110.

Martin, Troy W. (2012), 'Performing the Head Role: Man Is the Head of the Woman (1 Cor 11:3 and Eph 5:23)', *Biblical Research* 57, pp. 69–80.

Merkle, Benjamin L. (2017), 'The Start of Instruction to Wives and Husbands: Ephesians 5:21 or 5:22?', *BibSac* 174, pp. 179–192.

Metzger, Bruce (1994), *A Textual Commentary on the Greek New Testament*, 2nd edn (New York, NY: United Bible Societies).

Mouton, Elna (2014), '"Ascended Far above All the Heavens": Rhetorical Functioning of Psalm 68:18 in Ephesians 4:8–10', *HTS Teologiese Studies/Theological Studies* 70, pp. 1–9.

———— (2014), 'Reimaging Ancient Household Ethos? On the Implied Rhetorical Effect of Ephesians 5:21–33', *Neotestamentica* 48, pp. 163–185.

Murphy-O'Connor, Jerome (2008), *St. Paul's Ephesus: Texts and Archaeology* (Collegeville, MN: Liturgical Press).

Pereira, G. C. (2013), 'Ephesians: An Ecclesiology of Identity and Responsibility in Light of God's Cosmic Plan and a Canonical View of God's People', *Scriptura* 112, pp. 1–12.

Schwindt, Rainer (2002), *Das Weltbild des Epheserbriefes*, WUNT 148 (Tübingen: Mohr Siebeck).

Sherwood, Aaron (2012), 'Paul's Imprisonment as the Glory of the *Ethnē*: A Discourse Analysis of Ephesians 3:1–13', *Bulletin for Biblical Research* 22, pp. 97–112.

Smillie, Gene R. (1997), 'Ephesians 6:19–20: A Mystery for the Sake of Which the Apostle Is an Ambassador in Chains', *TrinJ* NS 18, pp. 199–222.

Suh, Robert H. (2007), 'The Use of Ezekiel 37 in Ephesians 2', *JETS* 50, pp. 715–733.

Taylor, Richard A. (1991), 'The Use of Psalm 68:18 in Ephesians 4:8 in Light of the Ancient Versions', *BibSac* 148, pp. 319–336.

Tracy, Steven R. (2008), 'What Does "Submit in Everything" Really Mean? The Nature and Scope of Marital Submission', *TrinJ* NS 29, pp. 285–312.

Trebilco, Paul (2004), *The Early Christians in Ephesus from Paul to Ignatius*, WUNT 166 (Tübingen: Mohr Siebeck).

Turner, Max (2006), 'Human Reconciliation in the New Testament with Special Reference to Philemon, Colossians and Ephesians', *European Journal of Theology* 16, pp. 37–47.

Wenkel, David H. (2007), 'The "Breastplate of Righteousness"
     in Ephesians 6:14', *Tyndale Bulletin* 58, pp. 275–287.
Winter, Bruce (2003), *Roman Wives, Roman Widows: The Appearance
     of New Women and the Pauline Communities* (Grand Rapids, MI:
     Eerdmans).
Yorke, Gosnell L. (2007), 'Hearing the Politics of Peace
     in Ephesians: A Proposal from an African Postcolonial
     Perspective', *JSNT* 30, pp. 113–127.
Yule, G. Udny (1944), *The Statistical Study of Literary Vocabulary*
     (Cambridge: Cambridge University Press).

INTRODUCTION

1. The importance of Ephesians

This little epistle packs much power. It is a circular letter sent to the Asia Minor region of the early church that reviews core themes of the gospel: the programme of God; the church; the mystery, hope, riches and power of the gospel rooted in grace, not works of the law; and a gospel whose result is reconciliation.[1] The result of all this divine activity is a call to live a distinctive life in the world and in our key social relationships in marriage, within family and through the household.[2] The epistle is a capsule of Paul's apostolic

---

1. For an instructive metaphor map of the book, in which imagery involving the body, position and family dominates, see Klingbeil, 'Metaphors', pp. 273–293. The importance of the church and identity in the letter is reinforced through such a map.

2. It is important to see the role of honour and shame in all of this as ancient culture was more about honour and shame than a guilt-oriented

teaching because it touches on many of these themes, expressing them in very focused and summarized forms. For example, salvation by grace that produces a quality life appears in Ephesians 2:8–10, and another core theme that is a result of the gospel, reconciliation bringing Jew and Gentile together into unity, shows up in 2:11–22. The letter originally served as an exhortation to a region of the church about what salvation is and what to do with that salvation as a result. It examines where the church as a community should be headed, with a crucial reminder that God in his grace has already given them all they need to get there. As such, reconciliation and being equipped to serve others becomes a central focus. Jody Barnard suggests this as the theme of the letter: 'We may confidently affirm that Ephesians was written to promote unity, particularly between Jew and Gentile, to affirm the supremacy of Christ over every power, and to remind believers of their privileges in Christ.'[3] But the epistle is about more than this. Its second half urges a life lived drawing on this new 'in Christ' identity, relying on Christ's power and strength. The result entails a distinctive quality of existence carried out in a dark world where the main challenge is spiritual. The uniqueness of this Christ-rooted approach to life points to its being from God and testifies to him. Believers are to see themselves both individually *and* corporately. In fact, how they live distinctively together in their believing, multi-ethnic community is the most powerful testimony they can give to show God is present. The letter is about gospel doctrine, enablement and exhortation to living wedded together in as crisp a fashion as we see anywhere in the New Testament. In short, it is a gem well worth the study.

2. Destination(s)

It might be better to speak of *destinations* (plural) for this letter. The question is tied to a textual issue in the first verse. There are

---

(note 2 *cont.*) approach: Gosnell, 'Honor and Shame', pp. 105–128. Position, identity, corporate role and corporate perceptions drive a culture structured around such values.

3. Barnard, 'Unity', p. 171.

important manuscripts that omit the phrase 'in Ephesus'. These include p⁴⁶, ℵ and B, but p⁴⁶ does so with a unique wording as it omits the phrase *tois hagiois ousin kai* while the majuscules have the article *tois* placed right before *ousin*. This is an awkward construction either way and most literally means 'to the saints who are and' (p⁴⁶) or 'saints those who are and' (ℵ, B). The two majuscules do get corrected later to include a reference to Ephesus, as the phrase most naturally does expect a place name to complete it (Phil. 1:1; 2 Cor. 1:1; Rom. 1:7). Origen also excludes Ephesus, as does Basil with Jerome, giving evidence of the uncertainty of the text. Interestingly, despite the omission, Origen and Basil still see the letter as sent to Ephesus. A problem for omitting the phrase is the awkward *kai* ('and') that lingers in our manuscript evidence where a place name is lacking. So there is an indication that very early in the passing on of this text a variation emerged. The only question is in what direction it went, whether from 'Ephesus' to a blank, or the other way around.

Those who see the letter as lacking a specific address also note the general themes of the letter, its impersonal tone with a lack of personal greetings, and a lack of any indication of a specific cause for the letter. Yet the geographic distribution of including a reference to Ephesus favours its originality.[4] The way Ignatius addresses the Ephesians in his letter from the early second century seems to assume a knowledge of this epistle. Yet the other factors should not be ignored. This is not a localized letter in terms of its approach to issues. So it makes sense to see the letter as an encyclical, intended for the churches in the entire region. That could explain the nature of the contents as well as the manuscript history. There is precedent for this as the letter to the Colossians also was intended for circulation to other sites (Col. 4:16). In fact, some even suggest that the Colossians reference to a letter to Laodicea may be a reference to this Ephesians letter. So it is likely that this letter was addressed originally to Ephesus, but also was intended for the house churches of the region. This generalized set of destinations explains the survey themes of the letter and led to its character as an

---

4. Hoehner, pp. 144–148; Schwindt, *Weltbild*, pp. 55–62.

overview of key early Christian teaching.[5] It can also explain why the letter lacks personal greetings, because the scope of the letter went beyond one specific location.[6]

So a view emerges that sees the letter addressed to Ephesus as a hub, but intended for wider circulation in the province of Asia. Ephesus was the third or fourth largest city of the Roman Empire after Rome, Alexandria and possibly Antioch of Syria, as well as being the capital city of the province of Asia since the time of Augustus. The estimated population at the time was 200,000–250,000.[7] It is estimated that the Jewish population in Ephesus was between 5 and 10%, meaning 10,000–25,000.[8] They had been present since the third century and many had Roman citizenship (Josephus, *Ant.* 12.125). Jews present in the city often experienced persecution for their faith, something the references in Josephus describe (e.g. *Ant.* 16.45). In addition to all of this, the emperor's cult was present. That political dimension was limited to some degree by the emphasis on Artemis in Ephesus, but Roman power and presence was everywhere. This meant that the bringing together of Jews and Gentiles into one group would be a challenge since the worship of deities and the honouring of the emperor were considered civil duties, with the expectation of participation in the celebrations tied to such duties, not to mention the habits that had been developed out of them in everyday life.

These factors raise the question of the city's general character as a backdrop to the letter's reception. Ephesus was a famous city on what is today the west coast of modern Turkey and was tied to the

5. Thielman, p. 11, calls this 'the most general letter in the Pauline corpus'.

6. Although it should be noted that another circular letter, Colossians, does have some personal greetings to a church Paul is said not to have directly planted. The one important difference is that Colossians has a dispute it is resolving, while Ephesians has no such controversy. The greater tension might make a personal word an important pastoral element in Colossians.

7. For studies on Ephesus, see Trebilco, *Early Christians* (for population, p. 17); and Murphy-O'Connor, *St. Paul's Ephesus*.

8. Trebilco, *Early Christians*, pp. 50–51.

Aegean Sea. In the first century it was not difficult to reach the seaport, although today that port has silted up completely. Roads ran to it from the north, east and south. As such a large city, it was a major trading centre in the region. It housed one of the wonders of the ancient world, the temple to Artemis, which was a site of pilgrimage whose temple site was once connected to the Anatolian goddess Kybele, but was now converted to the worship of a Graeco-Roman deity also known as Diana. The temple area was about the size of a full American football field, from one end zone to another, or comparable to a European soccer pitch. This made it the largest structure in the ancient world. For comparison, the Parthenon in Athens was one quarter of its size. It has been argued that Paul shows much evidence of the influence of this setting on his themes in the letter.[9] Artemis was seen as the 'Queen of Heaven' and described as 'Lady-Lord' and 'Saviour' and the one who controlled the underworld. So it is transparent that claiming the same for the Messiah, as does Ephesians 1:15–23, would challenge her sovereignty. The many gods of the Graeco-Roman world had a welcome place in this city, with Arnold noting up to fifty deities being worshipped there.[10] It had been under Roman control since 133 BC. This worship was a key part of the city's economy, as Acts 19 indicates. Magic also attracted itself to the city. Another key location in the city was the outdoor theatre. In its current visible configuration, the theatre's remains can hold around 20,000 spectators. In Paul's time the theatre was much smaller, but was still a substantial venue, holding several thousand. So Ephesus was a prominent regional city, a fact that fits a letter written to the region for which it was a hub. It also was a city with much religious activity where transcendent beings were respected.[11] It is no wonder Paul spoke of a battle that was ultimately spiritual (Eph. 6:12).

---

9. Immendörfer, *Ephesians*, is a careful look at this religious background along with a careful treatment of the evidence of inscriptions about Artemis, noting two dozen possible allusions to this context. He speaks of indirect polemic against this cult.

10. Arnold, p. 33.

11. On this background, see Arnold, *Ephesians: Power and Magic*.

3. Issues tied to authorship: comparison with Colossians

The letter most like Ephesians in the New Testament is Colossians. More than one-third of Colossians overlaps with Ephesians, with Foulkes putting the number at 75 of 155 verses being involved.[12] Most of it involves conceptual overlaps rather than exact verbal correspondence, with some of these a fusion of contexts (e.g. Eph. 2:1–5 with Col. 2:13; 3:6). The one example of a long overlap is Ephesians 6:21–22 and Colossians 4:7–8, with thirty-two consecutive words. Anyone reading the two letters can see a level of connection unlike in any other pair of Pauline letters. However, there is enough variation to point not so much to a copying as to an overlap that is thematically and conceptually parallel.

Shared themes include Christ as Lord of creation, being raised with Christ, Christ as head of the body, the idea of mystery, the hostility of principalities and powers, the old and new self, and a list of virtues and vices tied to household codes. The debate over the sequencing of these two letters (i.e. which came first) is unresolved, with scholars opting in either direction, although the idea of Ephesians being second is more common.[13] A few differences also exist as Colossians is clearly written to deal with a specific problem, while Ephesians has no such focus. Colossians has personal greetings that Ephesians lacks. The net result is that so much of this

---

12. Mitton, p. 11; Lincoln, p. xlviii, says 34% of Colossians' words are in Ephesians and 26.5% of Ephesians' words are in Colossians; Foulkes, p. 23. Hoehner, p. 31, contests these numbers, arguing for 10% in the case of Ephesians and closer to 15% for Colossians. This appears to take into consideration overlapping contextual factors as well as mere overlaps in vocabulary, and also use of things like conjunctions and pronouns, prepositions and proper nouns, where some repetition is not so surprising.

13. Mitton, pp. 11–13, sees Colossians written first, as does Lincoln, pp. xlviii–lv, while Best, pp. 20–25, esp. p. 24, opts for Ephesians on an assumption of one author being responsible for both letters. Best later (p. 36) prefers two letters written by two distinct students of Paul, which leaves open the issue of sequence.

discussion is unclear in terms of the direction of usage that it cannot be a key to helping us understand the discussion over authorship.[14]

Mitton claims that two features of the two letters' relationship point to non-Pauline authorship.[15] First is the way unrelated words in Colossians are combined in Ephesians. Second, Ephesians uses the same words as Colossians but with different meanings. Among the terms noted here are mystery, reconciliation, head and stewardship. This first objection is based on the idea, not only that Colossians was the first letter written, but also that word combinations are somehow rigidly fixed even when contexts change. Both premises are subject to challenge, especially the latter. The second feature is part of the discussion on theological differences in how Ephesians uses terms; this will be treated in detail below when authorship is discussed directly. The debate there is whether this is an author working with his own thought or a Pauline follower who knows Paul's words but not his meanings. Since most regard the discussion on theological differences as a key to the authorship question, along with the ecclesiastical frame of the development of offices, we await our evaluation until both issues can be treated together.

4. Issues tied to authorship: comparison with other New Testament materials

This additional comparison with other New Testament works matters because some claim that the Ephesians material that overlaps with other New Testament materials shows a later

---

14. Of course, the options as sequencing relates to authorship are: (1) both letters are Pauline and sequence is less important between the letters than distinct settings; (2) a Pauline letter (usually seen as Colossians) has been used by a follower of Paul as a basis for Ephesians; or (3) both letters come from followers of Paul, with debate over whether there is one follower responsible for both letters, or two distinct authors.

15. Mitton, p. 12. Compare the discussion in Foulkes, pp. 23–28.

perspective than existed in Paul's time, so that the author cannot be Paul.[16] As these comparisons have an impact on the larger discussion about authorship, we summarize the discussed links here to set up the authorship discussion below.[17] The topic often includes historical claims about the development of formal structures in the early church, often called Early Catholicism. It is claimed that this phrase describes the emerging of offices and structures in the late first century, with literary pointers to this more developed ecclesiastical structure present in Ephesians. It is claimed that such structures postdate a lack of structure in the earliest church and so preclude Paul as the author. This kind of argumentation is often circular, since the later dates and settings of these other works are also disputed. If those other works are in fact early, the basis for later changes disappears. A decision depends on how and how quickly one sees the development of church office and structure in the early church. Generally, traditional views see this development as taking place much sooner than those modern critics who challenge such ancient authorial claims.

When it comes to the use of other Pauline letters by the author of Ephesians the observation is made that there often is a conflation of terms from more than one letter with a fresh interpretation of

---

16. Foulkes, pp. 28–37, has a walk through these arguments. He works through five groups of material: (1) other Pauline materials; (2) 1 Peter; (3) Luke–Acts; (4) Johannine literature; and (5) Hebrews.

17. Mitton, pp. 13–18. Best, pp. 25–27, limits himself to other Pauline epistles and concludes that the author knew Romans, 1 Corinthians, parts of Philemon and some parts of 2 Corinthians, while on the rest we cannot be sure. None of this precludes a Pauline dating. The debate turns on whether the presumed later author adapted and developed teaching in such a way as to disclose clearly that he as another, later author was at work. The only example Best raises for such development in overlaps is Eph. 2:6 and 1 Cor. 4:8, which he says clash. This involves a difference in perspective on realized eschatology, in which 1 Cor. 4 seems to reject what Eph. 2 accepts. Eph. 2 pictures salvation as complete, while 1 Cor. 4 seems to deny this idea. We will look at this under theological differences in the authorship discussion.

the emerging combination (e.g. Eph. 3:7 with Rom. 5:5 and 1 Cor. 3:10; Eph. 1:13–14 with 2 Cor. 1:22 and Gal. 3:14).[18] The claim is that no other letter of Paul does this. A factor minimized in this claim is that Ephesians is a unique letter of the 'Pauline collection' because it is not addressed to a specific problem in a specific location. Its generalized and summary form makes it distinct. Its tendency to overlap most with Romans, another doctrinal summary letter, actually fits with a writer working with his own material in summary. In other words, the key here is not that there are overlaps with distinct emphases, but whether the differences in nuance are substantive enough to point to another author. That question awaits the theological differences discussion.

When we turn to non-Pauline materials, we move into claims about the lateness of this material. Here the works that are said to reflect a later view are 1 Peter, Luke–Acts, John and Hebrews. The dates of these other works are also debated, except for John, which is seen by many to be late first century. So the argument here is rather circular.

Among the themes overlapping with 1 Peter are doxological elements, household codes, Christ's exaltation, warfare imagery, a hidden gospel disclosed, the purpose of God, lusts in the world, guile, and people of God themes tied to temple imagery. These are so general it is hard to speak of direct borrowing, and it is more likely that they reflect an ethos emerging in the church in the midst of a challenging culture, a pressure that was intensifying in the 60s as Neronian persecution focused in Rome was stepped up and worry about its potential spread grew in the church, not to mention local pressure that existed in Ephesus because of the influence of the Artemis cult, as Acts 19 shows.[19]

Themes tied to the church also have conceptual overlaps in the Pauline section of Acts, which makes no mention of any letters of Paul. Paul's speech in Acts 20 to the Ephesian elders alone has three

---

18. Mitton, p 13.

19. It is interesting that Mitton, pp. 17–18, argues for 1 Peter having copied Ephesians here, a point that would mean this connection cannot help us with the author issue.

points of contact: to the counsel of God, humility and the grace of God. This combination of conceptual connection but no mention of letters is less than surprising if these two works are early, but harder to explain if either or both are late.

Generic themes also show up that have ties to Johannine material and to Hebrews: light and darkness, life and death, love, knowledge and being in Christ for John; while exaltation, the cleansing of the church, atonement and access to God through Christ are tied to Hebrews.[20] None of these is specific enough or exclusive enough to these works to help us with the authorship question.

What we do see in this tour through other materials is how well Ephesians fits into the general teaching themes of the early church, even though it cannot help us much with the question of authorship.

5. Authorship and date

Among the more debated issues tied to the letter is the question of authorship. The traditional association of the letter with Paul comes from its greeting (1:1) and a side reference in the body (3:1). This view stood unchallenged until the late eighteenth to mid-nineteenth century when Evanson (1792), Usteri (1824), De Wette (1826, 1843) and Baur (1845) all raised questions about the tie to Paul.[21] The earliest testimony to Pauline authorship comes from Irenaeus (*Against Heresies* 1.3.1 and 1.3.4 citing Eph. 2:2 and 1:10 from Paul), Clement of Alexandria (*Miscellanies* 1.8.41 tying Eph. 4:14 to

---

20. Foulkes, pp. 35–36.

21. Gnilka, p. 13; Barth I, pp. 37–38, notes four approaches: (1) Pauline; (2) initiated by Paul in notes on themes or dictation of core ideas; (3) not Pauline; and (4) unable to be decided. He takes the view that although Pauline authorship cannot be definitely proven, it is 'still possible to uphold its authenticity' (p. 41, reinforced on p. 49). He rightly notes how the emphasis on unity and Gentiles belonging in the church fits with the kinds of disputes Paul adjudicates on in his undisputed epistles like Romans, Galatians and the Corinthian correspondence. Gnilka opts for a pseudonymous work (pp. 13–21), as does Ernst, pp. 254–263.

the apostle) and Tertullian (*Against Marcion* 3.5 and 14 citing Eph. 5:31–32 as from the apostle and Eph. 6:14–17 as from Paul). These early remarks come from the end of the second and beginning of the third century.[22] Beyond issues already noted above with regard to literary relationships, three types of argument are made against Pauline authorship: (1) vocabulary and style; (2) theological differences; and (3) historical relationships (which we have only introduced above). We have already noted that a claimed dependence on Colossians, though likely, is inconclusive for the authorship question. As we shall see, the second category of theological differences may be the most subjective in attributing to an author a certain stagnancy of thought, yet it is the one often claimed to be the most decisive in a decision against Pauline authorship, so it will get the closest examination. We discuss the three key categories one at a time.

a. Vocabulary and style

The issue of vocabulary comes in two ways: (1) the unique words Ephesians contains; and (2) the use of words in ways that are distinct from Paul's use elsewhere. There are forty-one terms that are unique to Ephesians and eighty-four terms in Ephesians that are not found elsewhere in Paul but are found in the rest of the New Testament.[23] On the surface this looks revealing, until one does comparisons. Galatians is a letter universally tied to Paul that is only slightly shorter than Ephesians. Its unique and Pauline numbers are thirty-five and ninety respectively. So merely counting is not persuasive.

More potentially significant are words used with a different sense or different words from those Paul normally uses with the same sense as his common terms. There are not many of them: 'devil' instead of 'Satan',[24] 'heavenly places' for 'heaven(s)', the idea of fullness applied to the church, mystery, inheritance, possession,

---

22. Arnold, p. 47, n. 100; Hoehner, pp. 3–4.

23. Hoehner, p. 24, who also makes the comparison with Galatians.

24. This term does appear in the Pastorals, but those who reject the Pastorals as Pauline do not count these uses.

stewardship, to sum up and to save.[25] Hoehner notes that Galatians has eighteen unique expressions and no-one challenges Paul's authorship of that letter.[26] Barth concludes his discussion of this area saying, 'There is no reason to assume that he was limited to one possible meaning for a given noun or verb, or with an understanding of the gospel that he had formed at an earlier period.'[27] This raises a key idea: profound writers are capable of developing their own ideas and nuance in complex discussion. Paul fits that category of writer.

When it comes to style, a series of features said to be out of line with Paul also gets noted. These include the proportion of long sentences, the use of certain prepositions in ways distinct from their use in other letters, the ratio of verbs to nouns, and complex phrases involving genitives. There are also factors that make Ephesians unique. They include the fact that this is an epistle without a specific church problem to discuss, but which operates more as a theological summary with the use of an array of traditional forms, including blessing, doxology, two prayers, household codes and liturgical material. Best recognizes the difficulty of using this part of the discussion as a standard when he says, 'The variety of conclusions arises from both the choice of statistical method and the literary factors highlighted, and means that the certainty for which those who have used this method hoped has not yet been fully realized.'[28] In other words, the varied conclusions show that this area is not decisive either. Hoehner makes the observation that the sample size of these works is too small to be considered a worthy sample by statisticians.[29] In sum, this category does not yield a clear conclusion about authorship.

---

25. Barth I, pp. 4–5. Some note common terms missing from the book, but negative evidence is normally not persuasive.
26. Hoehner, p. 26.
27. Barth I, p. 5.
28. Best, p. 32.
29. Hoehner, p. 27, cites Yule, *Statistical*, p. 281, who says that good individual samples must be around 10,000 words. Hoehner notes that this is something not true of Romans, the longest Pauline letter (7,094 words), or of Ephesians (2,429 words).

b. Theological differences

A long list of theological differences is raised when one discusses the authorship of this letter. Ernest Best has a representative list in his section on the thought of the letter.[30] The following is a numbered list with some reaction as we proceed through it. Some of these do have touch points with Colossians, a link we note with an asterisk.

(1*, 2) First, Ephesians covers the universal church rather than local congregations with the head being Christ, as opposed to focusing on a single individual congregation. Second, the church is central in this comparison, not Christ. These two observations belong together. The moment Paul thinks about a collection of churches and who heads it all up, the second shift comes with it naturally as the combination of congregations are placed in a focused network with a single head. The shift itself is not so great nor problematic for a single author once one recognizes that the topic is not the individual congregation but the church as a universal entity, a natural shift in a letter written in a general theological context rather than being about a specific local problem. This idea is latent as well elsewhere in Paul, as 1 Corinthians 1:2 speaks of 'the church of God . . . in Corinth' next to the idea of 'all those in every place who call on the name of our Lord'.[31]

(3) Ephesians stresses unity in 4:4–6 without a note about the Eucharist, which is the basis of the unity of believers in Paul's letters (1 Cor. 10:16–17 and 11:17–23). This is an argument from silence and also assumes that Paul would think of only one basis of unity. In 1 Corinthians, the specific problem of the abuse of the Supper is the concern as a violation of the assumed unity of the church. In Ephesians it is the reverse concern for unity as a whole that is driving what Paul says.

---

30. See Best, pp. 32–35, for this entire discussion. See also Schnackenburg, pp. 26–29, who regards this as a key reason for pseudonymity.

31. Hoehner, p. 53, also notes 1 Cor. 12:13 and Paul's reference to persecuting the church of God, which is about actions involving more than one local church (1 Cor. 15:9; Gal. 1:13; Phil. 3:6).

(4) There is a shift in the foundation of the church, in that Ephesians has the apostles and prophets as part of the foundation, with Jesus the cornerstone, while in Paul's letters, it is Christ alone (Eph. 2:20; 1 Cor. 3:11). But is this divide really so great? First Corinthians 3:10 and 9:2 speak of the apostles as builders who establish local congregations on the foundation of Jesus, with this being the sign of being an apostle, an office or role that is tied to the establishing of the building.[32] This difference is simply the choice of a distinct metaphor making the same point. The foundation is a development of the image of the church as a temple that is rooted in the Corinthian correspondence. As the church aged in life and history, the role of the New Testament apostles and prophets emerged as more significant in what Jesus had started. Jesus is still central as he continues to be the one in whom the building is built (Eph. 2:22). So we need to ask a few questions to understand this difference in emphasis: is this a move that requires another writer, or is it one that grows out of the passage of time? And does it simply reflect a step back to look at churches as a whole versus a local church? The deepening of the complexity of the imagery does not necessitate another author, but is merely a shift of perspective to a wider view since multiple churches are in view.

(5) The role given to Israel is no longer central as it is in Paul. Best himself notes that 1 Thessalonians 2:14–16 is similar and the argument is another one from silence. Would the same argument apply if we were reading only 1 Corinthians? The use of an argument from silence on a theme tells us nothing for this discussion. Here the shift to reconciliation has probably had an impact on how Israel is discussed.

(6)* Of the events of Jesus' life, the ascension receives more attention than the incarnation, death and resurrection. This is a fresh distinctive of the letter. It also is a natural move once one considers what the consequence of resurrection is. Again, is this a reflection of thought development or does it require another mind?

(7)* The eschatology of Ephesians is more realized as dying with Christ is absent but being raised with Christ is present (cf. Col. 3:1).

---

32. Foulkes, p. 38.

The idea of being raised with Christ is present in Romans 6:4–6 and is the culmination of this Christological act of salvation. We must be careful how we speak of the difference with realized eschatology, that is, the idea that part of God's promise tied to salvation is realized now, with more to come later. Such is the nature of Christian hope that either end of the process can be emphasized or both can be mentioned, depending on the concern addressed. The resulting difference in emphasis does not reveal a distinct theology. When in the Corinthian letter Paul complains of salvation not yet completed (1 Cor. 4:8), it is the lack of a completely realized eschatology that he is complaining about, not the beginning of realization. So is this such a big difference?

(8) While Paul is a unique recipient of revelation in Galatians, in Ephesians the apostles and prophets are also recipients. Again, the change in setting is key. In Galatians it is Paul's teaching and authority that is being challenged, so his authority for speaking is important. Here there is no such controversy, so Paul's qualifications are not in play and an emphasis on these is not needed.

(9) Reconciliation is now between people in Ephesians 2:11–22 as opposed to between God and people in Colossians and the other Pauline letters. Christ's central role is still in place as he is the basis for peace, one that is assumed with God and whose result between people is now highlighted. This is again a very natural move of perspective. Is this a development or does it require another mind?

(10)* The vocabulary of this move between people involves the use of a double compound for 'reconciliation' in Ephesians and Colossians (*apokatallassō* in Col. 1:20, 22 of the 'all things' in v. 20) instead of the normal verb Paul uses (*katallassō*, Rom. 5:10; 2 Cor. 5:18, 19, 20) so that the use has a different sense. The Colossians 1:20 text is interesting in speaking of the reconciliation of all things, opening up reconciliation in all directions. Might it be that the shift in the term used is related to the expansion of the angle of reconciliation and that the compound reflects that expansion? The use of the compound in Colossians 1:20 might suggest a development.

(11, 12, 13)* As already noted, there is a greater emphasis in Ephesians on Christ's authority over the cosmos, although this is not unknown in the undisputed Paulines (Rom. 8:19–24; Phil. 2:9–11). Future expectation gets less attention. And there is no mention of the parousia. As Best notes, the future is still in view (Eph. 1:12, 18; 2:12; 4:4), and silence on a theme in a given letter proves nothing.

(14*, 15) There is more emphasis on powers than in the earlier Paulines, and no mention of an underworld. The former observation is correct. First Corinthians 10:20–21 does note the presence of demons. One potential reading of Ephesians 4:9, a passage whose exact meaning is debated, assumes an underworld. If that is not the point of this text, then this is another argument from silence.

(16) Salvation by grace through faith without works recasts the terms of a standard Pauline theme with works being used additionally in a positive sense in Ephesians 2:10. Again, we are in a development mode so that the question is whether this is a work of Paul's mind or one requiring a different author.

(17) The transitoriness of the world is not present in the letter. This is another argument from silence. The metaphor has shifted to speaking about being brought into a new place in Christ, but that point is merely a variation on the 'in Adam'/'in Christ' contrast that has roots in Romans 5.

(18) Absent also is the idea of believers being weak and in need of grace, but Ephesians stresses the need to be filled with the Spirit. However, Ephesians 5:18 assumes such a view as it builds on Ephesians 2:1–10, which does express an inability without what God provides. Is this difference as great as implied, even as it is another argument from silence?

(19, 20, 21) The internal struggle of faith like that in Romans 7:7–25 also is missing. Nor is there any indication of struggle over the role of the law, nor appeal to *Heilsgeschichte* – that is, salvation history. This is yet more application of arguments from silence. In such a short letter, should we expect themes noted elsewhere necessarily to appear here?

(22) Certain terms are used in a fresh way in the epistle: *oikonomia*, *mystērion* and *plērōma*. There is a small total number of the uses of these terms in a small sample size, a point Hoehner already examined in detail.[33]

---

33. See discussion above on vocabulary and style.

(23) Best claims it is in the ethical area that the differences are the most significant. He argues that the household code in Ephesians 5 – 6 assumes homes made up only of believers. He asks, in effect, why is there no engagement with the presence of non-believers from the world as in 1 Peter? However, that issue was already covered in the material in Ephesians 4:17 – 5:21, the entire section that precedes the code.

(24) There is no missionary impulse in Ephesians. But the prayer request in Ephesians 6:19 appears to be aware of this impulse.

(25) Best claims that Paul shows no concern for all believers standing in equal relationship to God as we see in 1 Corinthians 12:13 or Galatians 3:28, but cares only about the relationship of Jews to Gentiles. This is another argument from silence. Would we disqualify Romans as Pauline on the basis of this kind of theme argument? Is choosing a distinct angle of impact of the 'in Christ' experience really a persuasive argument for another author?

(26, 27) There is no mention of singleness, and marriage is assumed as a good, in contrast to 1 Corinthians 7. There is also no discussion of how a celibate person should behave. However, 1 Corinthians 7 discusses part of a specific problem about choosing to get married or remain celibate, while Ephesians is about those who are already in such a marriage relationship. In addition, interpretations that see a negative attitude towards marriage are questionable, since Paul only prefers singleness and does not reject marriage outright. The call to avoid sexual immorality covers the issue of celibacy, so it is not directly but indirectly addressed.

(28) Best claims that the ethical discussion in Ephesians lacks the eschatological depth of the discussion in 2 Corinthians 8:9; 1 Thessalonians 5:8; or Romans 12:11–14. This observation is fair but ignores that the material in Ephesians utilizes lists influenced by more traditional ethical materials that this audience would appreciate. This is enough to accomplish his goals here. Again, if we were discussing Galatians or 1 Corinthians, would this particular argument be persuasive?

(29) The writing assumes the readers do not know Paul (Eph. 3) and there is a decided lack of interpersonal communication unlike in other Paulines. Yet one wonders if a non-Pauline author would describe Paul (his hero) as 'least of all the saints' as is present in

Ephesians 3:8.[34] If, as I shall suggest, the letter is one intended to communicate Paul's legacy into the future to those he does not know, the lack of personal greeting makes sense. So as we come to the end of such a list, what do we see? We see a minimizing of the distinct context of Ephesians as a general letter, a heavy appeal to arguments from silence, and an insistence that the fertile theological mind of Paul could not produce a letter that contains such moves with a simple and traceable trajectory. In sum, a closer look at the details here shows that the case for theological difference is not as strong as some assume, especially when many treat the question as resolved in favour of a distinct author. In the end, it boils down to whether one thinks one person can make the array of moves present here. With Best, we agree that the assessment is whether their cumulative effect points to a distinct author or not.[35] For him, it does. For us, we doubt such a conclusion. Too many of the points are arguments from silence. They minimize the general character of this letter not written to issues that posed specific problems. Such a general letter did not require pushing specific formulations in the light of specific problematic concerns. This difference permitted a broader overview of larger themes.[36]

c. Historical relationships

There are two issues here: (1) the nature of church structure and offices; and (2) the issue of how Jew and Gentile are seen in relationship to church membership. The first involves a claim that a form of more ecclesiastical structure reflects an Early Catholicism,

---

34. Foulkes, p. 40.
35. Best, p. 36.
36. In making these points, I have not even raised the potential impact of a secretarial role in the letter, a factor that some who defend Pauline authorship also raise (e.g. Baugh, pp. 2–8). A secretary through whom Paul wrote might explain some of these differences, but I prefer to present the case without this being a factor since its presence and the way it might affect the composition of the letter's content is not certain.

a later form of community life. The claim is that this reality is more reflective of a late-first-century, post-Pauline time frame. The second argues that the conditions in which Gentiles enter the church are no longer a subject of controversy as they were in Paul's time but are a given.[37] A further factor also often noted is that Ephesians lacks any kind of personal elements common in Paul's letters. In fact, in Ephesians 3 there is an assumption that many may not have heard in detail about Paul.

The lack of personal notes may reflect the fact that this letter has a regional goal, such that many of the churches that received the letter would not have had a past connection to Paul. Granted, the fact that Colossians, another circulating letter whose recipients Paul also lacked contact with, does have some personal notes makes this observation less than certain. The general tone of the letter may suggest a far wider circulation, which could explain the lack of personal remarks.

The general approach of the letter may also explain why no controversy is indicated on the Jew–Gentile issue. This letter stays above disputes and simply presents the church's position as the author sees it. It fits the tone of a theological summary that is designed to present the ideal of the church hovering above any specific polemical concerns. This ethical and ethnic equality of Jewish and Gentile believers is the result of Jesus' work of grace. In fact, such was a basic goal of Jesus' work. This equality is the point of focus that fits quite naturally where letters like Romans and Galatians take us in the end. As such, it does not betray a view of a particular time period. Finally, we may be dealing with a letter designed to be a legacy letter, a kind of last-testament statement by Paul about what he and the community he is a part of share together in terms of belief, since he does not know if he will live or die (Phil. 1:22). This means he does not want to enter into disputes but to discuss what the church's position is. This point of view may also explain the lack of greeting, since it may be the goal for him to leave a work that postdates his life such that readers who encounter the letter may well be people he knows will not have known him. It also

---

37. Mitton, p. 5.

may explain his use of Colossians and a sequence in which this is the last of his prison epistles.

The issue of church structure is tied in part to the theological perspective that highlights a universal church and the way apostles and prophets are portrayed, a point already covered in section b above. It also is part of a circular argumentation. The development in church structure is late, so epistles mentioning such are late, despite the claims of such sources that these offices were in play earlier. The only way one dismisses the sources' claims is to argue that the structures they point to are in fact later than the claims. The idea that a charismatic church would function without offices also being present is an unsubstantiated assumption that supposes a particular line of development for the church.

If the above points apply, then claims made on the basis of historical considerations also yield nothing that requires an author other than Paul.

d. Summary on authorship

There are many factors that complicate the judgment about authorship of this letter beyond the areas tied to literary considerations, vocabulary and style, theological differences and historical relationships. The possible influence of a secretary on features tied to expression, the general character of the letter, its regional nature, its possible testamentary point of view and the incorporation of traditional materials are factors that have an impact on what is a judgment call. How much difference is enough to point to an author separate from Paul? The call is admittedly hard to pin down, yet nothing in what we have discussed points clearly to a distinct author more than to Paul working with his own thought.[38]

---

38. Given a choice for Pauline authorship, there is no need to go into detail about issues tied to pseudonymity. That is much discussed in detail in other introductions to the letter. For a position in its favour, see Lincoln, pp. lix–lxxiii, and for one that argues against its presence in early Christianity, see Hoehner, pp. 38–49. Arnold, p. 49, notes that there are no examples of acceptable pseudepigraphical letters in Judaism, while Hoehner (p. 43) notes that the *Epistle to Jeremy* is a homily, not a letter,

Weighing all these factors suggests that this letter is more likely to be from Paul than from someone trying to imitate him or even represent him. Given Pauline authorship and a prison setting, a date in the early 60s becomes likely, for reasons we now turn to show.

6. Purpose, date and setting

The authorship discussion yields an interesting result at this point as efforts to describe a setting for a writer distinct from Paul have struggled to describe an appropriate context for such a later writing. Mitton notes, 'One of the chief reasons why scholars hesitated to ascribe Ephesians to a post-Pauline writer was the difficulty of suggesting any occasion in the post-Pauline Church which would be likely to produce such a writing.'[39] Lincoln also sees the issue for those who hold to a non-Pauline author, saying,

> For such scholars, Ephesians, however, proves a source of frustration. It simply does not contain references to a specific setting or problems, and therefore other external data cannot be brought to bear in the same way as other letters to build up a more detailed picture of the particular situation being addressed.[40]

Contrast this with the simple, more traditional description of J. Armitage Robinson on a Pauline context:

> we find him in confinement at the great centre of the world's activity writing to expound to the Gentile Christians of Asia Minor what is his final conception of the meaning and aim of Christian revelation . . . His mind is free, and ranges over the world – past, present and future. With a large liberty of thought he commences his great argument

---

and the *Letter to Aristeas* does not qualify as it was never accepted as authoritative by Jewish rabbis.
39. Mitton, p. 25. Those who hold to this view argue for a date in the AD 80–100 range.
40. Lincoln, p. lxxiv.

'before the foundation of the world', and carries it on to 'the fullness
of times', embracing in its compass 'all things in heaven and on earth'.[41]

Although made before much of the debate about authorship, this
summary states well the setting the letter claims to possess. Once
the arguments for a later date are seen as problematic and a late
setting is also not clear, one can see Ephesians fitting well into
a reflective prison setting in Rome in the early 60s, with time to
summarize what is central to the faith in the new, entire community.
There is evidence that this letter did not take long to garner respect
in the church as a sacred text. Polycarp seems to treat it as Scripture
in the early second century, showing a growing canonical awareness
very early on in the church.[42]

By speaking of a testament as the genre (see section 5c above),
it is not intended to say that this is a final testament, as there is no
mention of impending death. Rather, it is a testament of core theological teaching that is a summary testimony of Paul's unique insight
into the mystery about Gentiles in the church and reconciliation,
a point he will raise in Ephesians 3:2–13.

There are five key themes that underline this overview of
Christian teaching at the time.[43] (1) Paul opens the letter with the
sovereignty of God and also expounds the supremacy and centrality
of Christ, in whom all things are summed up and from whom
are all heavenly blessings. (2) This leads to a development of a
community's identity in Christ, considered both at a corporate and
at an individual level. This is an important theme for cultures where
individualism reigns supreme, as the connection of people to one
another who share the faith means we are not great independent
individuals, but that our identity is inseparably connected to Christ
and to those who share his name. (3) This linkage is possible
because of the reconciliation God has brought through Christ to
Jew and Gentile, removing the deep hostility that historically existed
between the two groups. (4) The move also places all believers in an

---

41. Robinson, pp. 10–11.
42. Hartog, 'Polycarp', pp. 255–275.
43. Arnold, pp. 41–46, notes the last four of these.

intense spiritual battle with powerful evil forces, forces from which
Christ rescued them and from which Christ's gifts now protect
them if they walk in faithfulness with the Spirit. (5) So there is a call
to live a lifestyle that fits that identity in Christ as opposed to the
old connection to Adam. This Christ-rooted lifestyle stands in
cultural contrast to the normal way of Gentile living. A reading of
this marvellous epistle is designed to set the table for a fruitful
Christian walk for the universal church, for individual churches and
for individual believers, reminding them of their Spirit-rooted
connection to each other for the sake of the world by means of the
grace and gifts of God through Christ.

ANALYSIS

1. **PRAISE FOR GOD'S WORK IN CHRIST AND PRAYER FOR AN UNDERSTANDING OF GOD'S POWER (1:1 – 2:22)**
   A. Greeting (1:1–2)
   B. Praise for God's plan and work in Christ (1:3–14)
   C. Prayer for understanding of God's power (1:15 – 2:22)
      i. Prayer for understanding of their hope, riches and especially power (1:15–23)
      ii. Power for new life by grace (2:1–10)
      iii. A new life of reconciliation of Jew and Gentile (2:11–22)

2. **PAUL'S CALLING IN THE MYSTERY TO MINISTER TO THE GENTILES CULMINATES IN PRAYER FOR STRENGTH AND A BENEDICTION OF GOD'S CAPABILITY (3:1–21)**
   A. Paul's calling to minister the mystery for Gentiles (3:1–13)
   B. Paul's prayer for strengthening (3:14–19)
   C. Paul's benediction of God's capability (3:20–21)

3. THE CHURCH IN THE WORLD (4:1 – 6:24)
  A. The walk (4:1 – 6:9)
- i. Walk in unity (4:1–16)
- ii. Walk unlike the Gentiles, in holiness (4:17–32)
- iii. Walk in love (5:1–6)
- iv. Walk in light (5:7–14)
- v. Walk in the Spirit (5:15–21)
- vi. Walk in core relationships (5:22 – 6:9)
  - a. Wives and husbands (5:22–33)
  - b. Children and parents (6:1–4)
  - c. Slaves and masters (6:5–9)

  B. The armour of God (6:10–20)

  C. Closing remarks (6:21–24)

COMMENTARY

1. PRAISE FOR GOD'S WORK IN CHRIST AND PRAYER FOR AN UNDERSTANDING OF GOD'S POWER (1:1 – 2:22)

It is often the case that an outline of Ephesians separates chapter 1 from chapter 2, as well as making the common observation that the letter reflects Paul's typical style of laying down doctrine and then applying it. Paul follows this doctrinal structure in Ephesians 1 – 3, while dealing with application in Ephesians 4 – 6. However, a conceptual separation of chapter 1 from chapter 2 obscures an important connection in Paul's doctrinal argument. The description of how God brings new life in Christ by grace with its result of reconciliation *is* the illustration of God's power that Paul prays the Ephesians might grasp in Ephesians 1:15–23. Salvation is rooted in God's power and aims at a reconciliation that is not just between an individual and God but between groups, giving them access to God. Appreciating this reshaping of how we see the world is one of Paul's goals. The fact that believers are linked to each other in Christ and as a group share access to God's unlimited power is why Paul launches into praise of God's work. The note of doctrine, worship and prayer sets the spiritual tone of the letter.

A. Greeting (1:1-2)

Context
The spiritual note of the letter comes right at the start with Paul's greeting. Paul states that he is the sender of this missive, while grounding his communication in the connection his recipients have to God our Father and the Lord Jesus Christ. This relationship means that the Ephesians are part of the special, set-apart people ('saints') of God. The description of the Ephesians as also being faithful reminds us of what begins this connection: an ongoing trust in Christ that opens up access to the power that fuels the new life. Grace and peace surround the Ephesians, and so Paul greets them noting these two core blessings that come from God. In this opening, Paul has taken a standard greeting (sender, recipients, note of greeting) and has sanctified it because life is not just about people, but also about their connection to God.

Comment
1. *Paul* is the author of this letter. He is a commissioned leader (*apostle*) who came to that apostleship *by the will of God* (Gal. 1:15). The allusion here is to the calling on the Damascus road (Acts 9). The term *apostle* means a commissioned, authorized messenger, a 'sent one'. Paul opens Romans 1:1; Galatians 1:1; 1 Corinthians 1:1; 2 Corinthians 1:1; Colossians 1:1; 1 Timothy 1:1; 2 Timothy 1:1; and Titus 1:1 noting his apostleship as well. Another common self-referential opening is as a 'slave' of Jesus (Rom. 1:1; Phil. 1:1; Titus 1:1). The raised Jesus transformed the former chief persecutor of the church into the premier theologian of the early church. The theology he developed was not his creation, as the core of high Christology and faith was sufficiently in place to make possible his change of view about the church when Jesus confronted him on the Damascus road. When Jesus appeared to him, Paul suddenly realized what the apostles and the church had been preaching about: a raised and exalted Jesus was reality. That theology had emerged in the events tied to the life of the one Paul now called Lord. It took the presence of such a high Christology for him to understand what Jesus' appearing to him meant. Paul developed what the depth of faith involved and now summarizes it for the Ephesians. It is rooted

in Paul's own awareness that he had done nothing to deserve the ministry God had graciously given to him (1 Cor. 15:9; Gal. 1:13–15; 1 Tim. 1:12–16). When Paul speaks of God's grace, it is because he understands that salvation is not earned, but is simply received by faith as the gift it is. Paul will develop what this apostleship means in Ephesians 3:1–13.

Paul's reference to himself as an *apostle* does not make him one of the Twelve, but is a description of his encounter with Jesus and of his calling to a significant role in the church, one he shared with figures like Barnabas, James, the Lord's brother, and Apollos (Acts 14:4, 14; 1 Cor. 15:7; Gal. 1:19; 1 Cor. 4:6, 9). These apostles functioned like a combination of missionary and church emissary. Paul was a church planter and edifier. His ministry to the Ephesians in Acts 19 shows this part of his role. Later he had left the church in the leaders' hands as he headed to Jerusalem and then to Rome, where he arrived as a prisoner whose fate would be determined there (Acts 20:17–38). Now, from that Roman prison, he sends a letter to Ephesus and the wider region to solidify their understanding of what it means to know God and his grace.

The recipients in Ephesus and beyond[1] are described with two key terms: *saints* and *faithful in Christ Jesus*. A saint is one set apart as not common, called to be used by God. In the Old Testament, a variety of items were described as set apart: a nation (Exod. 19:6), a specific place (Exod. 3:5), the temple (1 Chr. 29:3), the Sabbath (Exod. 31:14–15), as well as people (Exod. 22:31). In our time, sainthood is often seen as earned, but to Paul, anyone in Christ is a saint, set apart and made holy by God, not by that person's own work, and brought to new life to serve God. This results in all believers being priests (1 Pet. 2:9), not as professional clergy but as fellow ministers for the cause of God. This sainthood is one of the great benefits of being a recipient of God's grace. It also reflects a responsibility to act like one who has received this calling.

---

1. The idea that this is a circular letter to the region, with Ephesus as the hub, was treated with the textual problem of Eph. 1:1 in the Introduction.

These Ephesians are also faithful (cf. Col. 1:2). This word can refer to one who has faith (active) or one who is faithful (passive, so referring to the product of an active faith). The active sense alone cannot be meant as that would be awkward in the syntax of the sentence. The point is not about simply having faith, but about the responsiveness built into faith. One who trusts also responds out of that trust. So faith is not absent from what Paul is saying here, but more than that is present. In a sense faith begins and drives the Christian walk, so it is hard to point to one meaning over another here. Those who are in Christ trust him and live in the light of that initiating faith from day to day. This is one of the reasons why they can be said to be 'in Christ'. They have trusted Christ not merely for an initial moment but for their very spiritual lives. So their lives are found to be *in Christ Jesus*. In the Messiah who is Jesus, they have been brought into a new life and a new community, set apart to serve God.

2. Paul's greeting expands on the normal Greek greeting that simply said, in effect, 'welcome' or 'hello'.[2] Instead, Paul mentions two spiritual benefits that run through his recipients' entire relationship to God: grace and peace. The wording is common in Paul (Rom. 1:7; 1 Cor. 1:3; 2 Cor. 1:2; Gal. 1:3; Phil. 1:2; 2 Thess. 1:2; Phlm. 3). The repetition and use by other Christian writers point to a common liturgical use of the phrase (1 Pet. 1:2; 2 Pet. 1:2; Rev. 1:4). *Grace* is tied to the entire activity of God growing out of Christ's work. Grace as a gift is rooted in God's mercy and comes with no sense of my entitlement or being owed anything. *Peace* is the Hebrew concept of *shalom* (Gen. 29:6), referring to well-being. Paul's wish is for the Ephesians to experience this in fullness. The fact that this grace and peace come as a blessing equally from *God our Father and the Lord Jesus Christ* shows the cooperation that exists between them in salvation. Hebrew greetings often referred to mercy and peace, so this is an adaptation of that kind of greeting (Jude 2; *Jub.* 12:29; *2 Apoc. Bar.* 78:2). It is almost a cause-and-effect greeting, with grace being the context, which results in peace. God's acceptance of them frees them to live at peace. The intimacy of the

---

2. BDAG, pp. 873–874.

blessing is noted in its originating from *our* Father, alongside the authority of such gifts being mediated through the Lord Jesus who serves as the anointed one (*Christ*) of the kingdom.

Theology

A theology of pastoral care emerges from the greeting. Paul commends the Ephesians for their faithfulness even as he turns to exhort them. The challenge of a pastor is to encourage his or her people to grow. Paul reminds them of their secure position in Christ, having been set apart to God. Paul requests grace and peace for them, something their connection to God and Christ can supply.

B. Praise for God's plan and work in Christ (1:3–14)

Context

The opening note of blessing of God works through what God has done in Christ, what the goal of that plan is and what believers have received as a result. God has given believers every heavenly blessing in Christ as part of a plan he has worked out to sum up all things in Christ. So believers are chosen, fully adopted children of God, redeemed and forgiven recipients of grace with access to wisdom and understanding. Those who believe in Jesus as Messiah and Saviour are God's own possession, have hope in Christ and are sealed with the Spirit of God as a guarantee of their coming full redemption. In other words, Paul is rejoicing in all God has done for those who are his. His desire is for the Ephesians to appreciate the rich treasure trove they possess. This presence of a note of praise is distinct from Paul's normal pattern, which is to follow his greeting with thanksgiving and a prayer. The prayer for the community will follow this note of praise. The other interesting feature of this exclamation of blessing, called a *berakah* or a eulogy (in a positive sense), is its length. It is one long sentence of 202 words, a literal string of quite extended praise. All of this describes part of a plan God worked out for believers before the creation. Their place, with all its benefits, has been reserved for them since eternity.

This honouring of God serves as an introduction, an overture, to the entire letter. Reconciliation is at the base of the church. Such reconciliation reflects a way of life that is distinctive about

Christians. It is a crucial goal in salvation. It stands prominent among the array of blessings that are rooted in the salvation that comes in Christ. So in the body of the letter Paul will turn from what salvation gives to what it means for our walk and identity. The fact that the church, reconciliation and the distinctive ways of living are not mentioned here at the start does not disqualify the note of praise from setting up such themes, acting as the theological base for the development Paul will present. Paul will move from faithfulness to the blessings and what they contain, creating a transition to these larger themes.

Comment

3. The opening word, *blessed*, serves to point to a note of praise to God (Gen. 9:26; Exod. 18:10; 1 Sam. 25:32; 1 Chr. 29:10). Gnilka calls this the theme verse of the unit.[3] If this were a psalm, we would be thinking of a praise psalm, where God is acclaimed and then the reasons for that acclamation follow. That is very much what we have here. When we say a blessing, we are giving a note of praise, speaking well of someone.[4] It is a declaration and acclamation, not a mere wish. When we receive a blessing, we are the beneficiaries of an act of bestowal from someone who has done something worthy and beneficial. This verse has both ideas. We praise God for what he has done and we are the recipients of those actions. It is the *God and Father of our Lord Jesus Christ* who is praised. He is the initiator of the plan. All things flow from him. He is the one who *has blessed us in Christ with every spiritual blessing.* We have received all heaven has to offer in salvation, a blessing rooted in eternity past, participated in now and connected with an eternal future that remains for those who share in it. It also is a blessing that comes from beyond, a transcendent form of life that God supplies to those who trust him.

The verse has reference to blessing three times: we bless God, God blesses and we have received blessing from him. Paul opens with a cascade of appreciation. These blessings are *spiritual*: they

---

3. Gnilka, p. 60.
4. BDAG, p. 322.

touch the deepest part of a person, the part that drives a person and his or her way of seeing and acting. They are also spiritual because they come from and through the Spirit of God who energizes the image of God residing deep within us. These spiritual benefits come from heaven and are found in Christ. For Paul, there is nowhere else such spiritual treasure can be found.

The way Paul makes this point is in three consecutive clauses, each introduced by the preposition *en*. We have been blessed *with* (or 'in regard to') every spiritual blessing *in* heaven and *in* Christ. A threefold structure dominates this theme verse. In the note of praise as a whole, three divine agents also will be named: the Father, the Christ and the Holy Spirit. The Father is the source of blessing. The Son is the one in whom blessing is mediated. The Spirit is the one who is given both as enablement and as a down payment of more to come. The unit proceeds with the election by the Father (vv. 4–6), the redemption by the Son (vv. 7–12) and the seal of the Spirit (vv. 13–14). Each subunit ends with the refrain 'to the praise of his glory'.

4. The journey into blessing began in eternity past, in the choice made in Christ for us to be holy and blameless. God the Father chose those who belong to him from *before the foundation of the world*. This was a programme designed from before the creation, rooted in the mind and character of God. An array of terms in these verses shows God's initiation and direction of his plan: 'predestining', 'pleasure' and 'will' in verse 5; 'will', 'good pleasure' and 'set forth' in verse 9; and 'claimed', 'predestined', 'purpose' and 'will' in verse 11.[5] God's directive action is in view throughout this call to praise. The basis for how it works is hidden in the recesses of his person and revealed in Christ. It is all appreciated through the Spirit. There is an echo of his choice of Israel (Deut. 7:6–8). There was nothing Israel did to generate his choice of them, and the same is true of us. There is no entitlement in grace. It is a gift graciously given, undeserved.

The link to verse 3 is that God blessed us *even as* he elected us. This election is a choice to pick someone out for oneself. It makes

---

5. Lincoln, pp. 22–23.

God a relational God, interested not just in submission but in relationship with those he created. That election took place *in him*, in Christ, the one who mediates all the blessings of salvation (all of Gal. 3). The remark suggests pre-existence for Christ (Col. 1:15).[6] This connection stands in contrast to merely being in the world, in Adam (Rom. 5:12–21). It is what makes the church a specially called group. They are the 'in Christ' people. Their position in Christ leaves them *holy* and *blameless* because the work of Christ, which is about to be described in verses 7–11, has cleared the way for them to be set apart and regarded as unblemished (Eph. 5:27; Col. 1:22). Sacrifices in the Old Testament were regarded as acceptable when they were without defect (Exod. 29:1). We are morally cleansed by Jesus' work; this is about the result of Jesus' work for us and the surety of our position before God. Best correctly speaks of the cultic sense of these terms.[7] Some debate whether 'in Christ' points to the sphere into which we are elected (in Christ) or the means by which we get there (by means of Christ). In one sense, both are implied, but here God is praised for the benefits we receive, while verses 7–11 will tell how we get them, so sphere is probably better in the light of the book as a whole since our position in Christ is the point of the letter.[8] The position implies a moral call to be what God has given to us.[9]

So we stand before God (*before him*) in *love*. It was out of love that God chose us and brought us into the blessing that leaves us *holy and blameless* in Christ. Love is the sphere that emerges from God's act of election, and it is not a mere emotional response but a moving towards another with his or her best interests in mind. It may be misleading to ask if this is God's love or ours as it may be that the expression speaks of both, but the stress is on God's initiative. Most assume that we are speaking of human love by linking this expression to *holy and blameless*. Others argue that it

---

6. Schnackenburg, p. 53.

7. Best, p. 122.

8. Hoehner, p. 177, opts for an instrumental use, arguing that is reinforced in vv. 7–11.

9. Schnackenburg, p. 54.

refers to God's love if we attach it to either the concept of 'chose' in verse 4 or 'predestined' in verse 5, something that is discussed as to which is the better point of connection. Philippians 1:9–10 and 1 Thessalonians 3:12–13 exhort believers to love in the context of their being called holy. That call points to human love, just as most other uses of 'love' in Ephesians point to human love (4:2, 16; 5:2). The point of being a child of God is to reflect his character and attributes through the Spirit he gives us. The result is to model that love as a reflection of God's own love and enablement by the Spirit. God becomes the initiator of everything in this praise context. So love works in the same way as God's forgiveness and mercy; it mirrors his attributes (Luke 6:36: be merciful as he is merciful; 11:4: forgive because we are forgiven; Gal. 5:22: love as a fruit of the Spirit; Rom. 5:8; Eph. 3:17 speak of being rooted and grounded in love, which probably is not a reference to human love[10]). The position we have is a result of love, and the way we are to respond is rooted in our loving. As 1 John 4:19 says, 'We love, because he first loved us.' As was just noted, there is a debate whether the phrase *in love* belongs in verse 4 or verse 5. The phrase could perhaps be connected to the opening phrase *he chose us* in verse 4, but that is too distant to be the likely referent. The interpretation, however, whereby the results of election, holiness and blamelessness are seen to take place in a context of God's love is little different from the option in which love is seen as broad. One could also argue that the phrase goes with 'predestining' in verse 5, introducing the next participle. That is unlikely structurally, as the other participles in the praise string have no modifiers before them. A foreordination taking place in love as the subtheme of an election leading to holiness and blamelessness in love also says something little different, so in one sense these are options of interpretation that make little difference. Paul's point is that we, as the product of God's choice from long ago, are morally cleansed and bathed in love from start to finish, from God's love to our loving. Appreciation and love are to be the products of receiving God's love. In other words, the placement of 'love' in the Greek at the end of verse 4

---

10. Best, p. 343, on Eph. 3:17.

serves as a bridge and should be seen as intentionally broad in
scope.

5. Within God's election was his foreordination into adoption
through Jesus into him – that is, into his body, the community that
is Christ's. The dependent participle, *predestining*, elaborates the way
in which, or the ground on which, election took place, as well as
giving a result. So either God elected by means of foreordaining
(looking back) or he foreordained us into adoption (looking
forward). It is hard to know which exact nuance is intended here.
Either way, God is responsible for the execution of his plan.
Foreordination points to deciding beforehand or predetermining.
That divine decision is rooted in the mystery of his character and
knowledge which was always with him. God has directed that we be
adopted as *sons*, as God's children, *according to the pleasure of his will*.
Everything about this psalm of praise extols God's activity and
plan. This makes the unit a eulogy. To speak of foreordination at
the start and his will at the end of this verse does the same thing.
The term 'foreordained' or 'predestined' is rare in the New Testament, used only five other times (Acts 4:28; Rom. 8:29–30; 1 Cor.
2:7; Eph. 1:11).

Adoption into sonship means we have become something we
were not before and have become part of a new family. Adoption
is another rare term (Rom. 8:15, 23; 9:4; Gal. 4:5). There is likely
Roman background to the choice of this term, given that the Old
Testament does not discuss adoption directly as levirate marriage is
a distinct practice, although Romans 9:4 speaks of Israel as an
adopted son probably also on the basis of the Roman example.[11]
The Roman practice was for a natural father to release his son to
the adopting father three times. After the third time the adoption
was complete. Adoption meant a new life and family, a new
opportunity.[12] It was done for that purpose and usually provided the
adopting father with more heirs. Adoption was quite common in
the ancient world. From the perspective of the child, it was an act
of pure grace because he or she did nothing to receive the new

---

11. Hoehner, pp. 195–197.
12. Best, p. 125.

status given by the new family. In the case of the adopting adult, it was the granting of a new improved status for the child and a benefit to the family that was the result. So as a new heir, the adoptee receives much.[13] God acts positively here to rescue. As the letter will argue in 2:2–3, believers have gone from being sons of disobedience to being sons of God, a promotion directed by God's activity, to their great benefit (Gal. 3:26 – 4:5). God has done well in all of this. In fact, he has made us into something we could not be without him, a solid reason to praise him.

All of this takes place *through Jesus Christ*. Paul acknowledges Christ's work here. He spends a little time on this in 2:11–22 but his fuller development is in Romans 3:19–26. That saving work places us in the family of God the Father. God brings us to himself through Jesus. This is yet another indication of God's grace as we are mere recipients of these benefits by God's actions through Christ. When this note of praise points to actions by his good pleasure, it is the Father's actions that are meant (1:4, 5, 6, 7, 9, 11, 12). So the focus of the praise is reinforced by saying all this took place *according to the pleasure of his will*.[14] It pleased God to act with such initiative and kindness. The direction of God in his character drives the programme and is the reason to praise God. Often election is portrayed as capricious, but it is rooted in the character of a good God. What we describe as a process simply was an act emerging from his person and who he is. For those who appreciate God's goodness, this is not a frightening teaching. For those distant from God, that distance contributes to the discomfort with the teaching. The openness of the gospel to any who will hear invites people into that goodness and grace of God. Another thought is important here: we tend to discuss all of this as an issue of sequence, but in God, before time, this programme simply resides

---

13. Schnackenburg, p. 53: 'Reflections on the "rejected" are totally lacking in Ephesians.' So the remark is positive only.

14. Qumran also highlights the elect nature of their community with a reference to good pleasure or purpose (1QS 8:6; 1QH 4:32–33; 11:9; CD 3:13–16). Where Qumran stressed the keeping of the law, Paul speaks of grace in Christ; see Arnold, p. 83.

in his person and character. Our limited understanding of it has to rest there, in who God is. There is no coincidence in a person being in the family of God. It is a work of God, rooted in his goodwill and the opportunity he provides for rescue and redemption. It results in the praise of his glory, which is where Paul goes next.

6. The psalm of praise now points to God's glory and the amazing praiseworthy nature of grace. Everything that has been said about God's activity lifts us up to this place, to glorify and give honour to God for his work. The refrain *to the praise of the glory of his grace* is focused on how all of this honours God. The term *glory* in Greek refers to the idea of reputation, while the Hebrew term behind it refers to something that has weight, a picture that is easily turned into the idea of merit.[15] We might say God in his actions has a 'gravitas' that deserves honour (Phil. 1:11; 1 Pet. 1:7), because it is God in his character and acts who is praised. This stands in contrast to an alternative rendering where it is only his glorious grace that is praised ('his glorious grace', NRSV). In these refrains Paul is lifting up the persons of the Godhead, not just an attribute of God's acts. These acts of grace point to praiseworthy character. This remark about the praise of God's glory will be repeated twice more in the passage, also showing that the person of God is the point, though a reference to grace is absent in those later references, perhaps because it is assumed in what is being described (vv. 12, 14). The second and third refrains look in sequence at the work of Jesus and the Spirit. There is a Trinitarian substructure to these notes of praise. There are also several dimensions to God's acts: they are for adoption, they bring us to him, and they result in the praise of his glory of grace (vv. 5–6).

The topic that elevates God's glory is his *grace*. This will be a theme of the letter, especially in Ephesians 2:8–10. It is emphatic here as Paul speaks about the grace with which he 'graced' us. Grace involves the unmerited gifts God gives to those he saves. That grace is *freely bestowed . . . in the Beloved*, a reference to the work of grace through Jesus that Paul will cover next. *Freely bestowed* translates the verb 'graced', a verb that we do not express this way in English but

---

15. BDB, pp. 458–459; *HALOT* II, pp. 457–458.

is the point, as it is the act of grace in Christ (v. 3) that is in view (also 'in him', v. 4; 'through Jesus Christ', v. 5).[16] To refer to Jesus as the *Beloved* signifies the close relationship Christ Jesus has with God (Matt. 3:17 = Mark 1:11 = Luke 3:22; Col. 1:13). It echoes texts where others are chosen for a special relationship (Isaac, Gen. 22:2; Israel, Deut. 33:12; the Servant, Isa. 42:1). Jesus is the mediator and context of all spiritual blessing.

7. So what is it we are praising that involves Jesus? That is the theme of verses 7–12. It is redemption through his death, forgiveness and the riches of grace. *In him we have redemption through his blood.* Technically, 'in him' is 'in whom', which refers back to the Beloved One (v. 6) – that is, 'in Christ'. Jesus' death is what the reference to the blood points to: an act that has brought a rescue (Matt. 26:28; Rom. 3:25; 5:9; 1 Cor. 10:16; 11:25, 27; Heb. 9:11–12). Redemption points to the payment of a price that leads to something (often the freeing of a slave: Exod. 21:8; Lev. 25:48; *Letter of Aristeas* 12.33; Philo, *Good Person* 114). Here it is Jesus' sacrificial death that pays the moral penalty of the debt sin creates (Rom. 3:24; Heb. 9:15).[17] Ransom is a common idea in the New Testament (Mark 10:45; 1 Pet. 1:18–19; Heb. 9:12; Rev. 1:5; 5:9). The image of Jesus as a lamb of sacrifice underscores this picture (1 Cor. 5:7; Rev. 5:9–12; 6:1). It is him for us. The New Testament is not concerned with to whom this debt is paid, but focuses instead on the fact that it is paid, with the gift of the indwelling Spirit delivering spiritual capability and freedom to walk with God as a result. The expression pictures deliverance (Exod. 6:6) and the resultant position in which we now exist. The verb *we have* is present tense, so it looks at where we are now in the light of what we were given by grace. Redemption includes the *forgiveness of our trespasses* (cf. Col. 1:14; Titus 2:14). None of this is deserved; it is *according to the riches of [God's] grace.* Later Paul will pray that the Ephesians might appreciate the riches of the inheritance we have in Christ, another allusion to verse 6. This redemption and forgiveness through Jesus' sacrificial death is a key part of that treasure.

---

16. Thielman, p. 53.
17. Hoehner, p. 206.

8. This grace from God through Christ has been lavishly poured out to us: *that he lavished on us*. It is a gracious plan worked out in *wisdom and insight*. This grace is portrayed as having been poured out liberally on us, given to us in abundance (Rom. 5:20). The relative pronoun 'that' here is attracted back to the antecedent 'grace' to underscore the connection. Riches of grace in abundance are ours through what Jesus has done. The context of the provision is divine *wisdom*: God's programme rests in the unique skill God provides which is rooted in his own wisdom. Paul says something similar in 1 Corinthians 1:25–31. It is a wisdom from above given to us. The second term, *insight* or 'understanding', often overlaps with wisdom. The pairing is common in the Old Testament (Prov. 1:2; of God: 3:19; usually of wisdom given to people: 8:1; 10:23; of God in creation: Jer. 10:12; comes from God to people: Dan. 2:21 – the point also here in Eph.). We either have a double reference for emphasis or a reference to the practical application of the wisdom God supplies. If the terms do not simply overlap for emphasis, wisdom applied with discretion is the point. Either way, the point is that the riches we have in Christ are applied with the full application of divine insight. Add *all* to both terms in this description and the abundance is fully applied in every kind of way. This wisdom and insight is supplied to the believer as verse 9 speaks of the secret of his will being revealed to us. This is reinforced in the prayer of Ephesians 1:15–19, with its emphasis on divine enablement that comes with his power (Col. 1:9).[18] So not only have we received the position and benefit of redemption; we have also been given the equipment to live well in that space.

Some apply the phrase to the way God's mystery is revealed in verse 9, looking forward ('he lavished on us in all wisdom and insight'), and make it apply to God's wisdom.[19] However, modifiers in the passage normally follow their main idea. So Paul develops the connection of the bestowal by proceeding next to how it works to our benefit (so 'he lavished on us' his grace). The passage sets up what follows in the letter, and it does so here.

---

18. Schnackenburg, pp. 56–57.
19. Best, pp. 132–133; Arnold, p. 86.

9. At the centre of God's programme is the disclosure of the mystery contained in the plan: *he revealed to us the secret of his will.* This verse explains how grace abounded to us through the revelation of the mystery. That mystery, as Ephesians 3 will show, allows Gentiles and Jews to share equally in the divine benefits that Christ provides, part of what leads to the summing up of all things in Christ (1:10). Paul will elaborate on this theme in Ephesians 3:1–13. Paul's praise for every spiritual blessing is wrapped up in the three participles noted thus far: God blessed (v. 3), he foreordained (v. 5) and he revealed the mystery (v. 9). These three participles are a key to the sequence of the praise. It was *his [God's] good pleasure that he set forth in Christ* that set up the plan and executed it. *Mystery* is a Jewish apocalyptic term and refers to the revelation of something previously undisclosed or something now given detail that was previously lacking it (Rom. 16:25; 1 Cor. 2:7; Eph. 3:9; Col. 1:26–27). God makes the mystery known, as it cannot be figured out by human deduction. It is like the *rāz* of Daniel 2:18–19, 27–30, 47. The idea that the world would be blessed through God's work in Israel was something that Genesis 12:3 promised. Now that promise is seen and realized in what Christ has done (Gal. 3). For God's programme, all things resolve in Christ.

10. The programme is aimed at a cosmic goal, the *fullness of the times* and *to sum up all things in Christ* (author's translation). By *all things* is meant *things in heaven and things on earth.* Nothing escapes the touch of Jesus the Messiah. The key term here is the Greek word *oikonomia,* which refers to administering something. The plan is aimed at administering the restoration of creation, stewarding the creation back into alignment with God, a realignment in the light of the fall. The act of divine stewarding is aimed at moving into the *fullness of the times,* or the consummation of promise. The 'summing up' of all things in Christ looks to creation, heaven and earth, 'coming together' into a harmonized whole.[20] By God's design, Jesus is the ultimate reference point for making sense of the creation (Col. 1:20; Eph. 2:16). To be in Christ is 'to be caught up in God's gracious purpose for a universe centered and united in

---

20. BDAG, pp. 55–56.

Christ'.[21] Even though we are looking at consummation, the note of praise here stresses that the corner on the path to this goal has already been turned by what Christ has done and is doing (Eph. 1:22–23). Galatians 4:4 shows that the fullness of time started for Paul with the birth of Jesus, even though its completion will come later (Eph. 1:14; Rom. 8:19–23).

11. In Christ, the calling of believers involves being claimed as a possession of God. This is a result of the programme God is working out according to his will. Believers have been allotted a place with God. We become *God's own possession, predestined* as part of the *purpose of him who accomplishes all things according to the counsel of his will.* The key verb in this part of the praise is *klēroō.* It refers to something received or appointed by lot (1 Sam. 14:41).[22] This term appears only here in the New Testament. Here the picture is of an inheritance or a group God has taken possession of as his own. It has fallen to us to be his. Colossians 1:12 is similar in force, looking to the believer's allotment with the saints. Ephesians 1:18 points to the riches of God's inheritance.[23] In making us his own, God has also given us benefits. What exactly does inheritance mean? Do we *have* an inheritance, with the stress being on what we have received, or *are* we the inheritance, something God possesses of which we are a part? The stress in the note of praise is on how we are related to God and his actions. This fits the idea that we are a people for God's possession, something that makes us precious not just because of what we have but because of who God has made us. Either way, this act and our secure place before God was and is intentional. Just as Israel was called to be God's special people, so are those who are in Christ (Deut. 32:9). The predestination of this according to the purpose of the counsel of God's will is an idea repeated from verses 4–5, making it almost a refrain in the passage. Our experience of grace is no accident. It is a key part of all the things God sought to accomplish in Christ.

---

21. Lincoln, p. 34.
22. BDAG, p. 548, meaning 2.
23. Bruce, p. 263.

12. All God has done in Christ makes the believers in Ephesus among the *first to set our hope on Christ*. It also results in *the praise of his glory*, another repetition of a refrain, looking back to verse 6. There is a discussion about what the *first to set our hope on Christ* means. Is a distinction between Jews and Gentiles intended at this point?[24] Or is this simply a way to argue that Paul is discussing the first generation of those in Christ? Up to this point in the praise for what 'we' have experienced, no ethical distinction has been made. So only a refractory kind of reading would raise the issue of ethnic distinction at this point.[25] The word for *first to set our hope* (*proelpizō*) is another term used only here in the New Testament. Those called to offer praise for the acts and character of God are the first in line together for what God has done.

13. What placed the Ephesians in line for blessing was their response to the *word of truth*, when they *believed in Christ*, the *gospel of [their] salvation*.[26] The beginning of verse 13 about hearing and believing is linked with the verb 'to be sealed' later in the verse: 'so you Ephesian Gentiles were sealed when you heard and believed'. That response marked them *with the seal of the promised Holy Spirit*. So this verse focuses on the message of salvation and the response to it, with its consequent eternal result.

That message, tied to Christ, is a reflection of truth about life (Eph. 4:21; Col. 1:5; Rom. 10:14) and constitutes good news for their deliverance. Their response involved belief (1 Thess. 2:13). This is more than intellectual assent; it is trust, a continuing dependent orientation to Jesus. The result is a sealing by God's Spirit (Eph. 4:30), a down payment that ties them to the promise

---

24. Bruce, p. 264; Foulkes, pp. 62–63.

25. So Hoehner, p. 231, on v. 12 makes a point I accept. He goes on to argue that this distinction remains throughout this passage on praise, a position I shall question.

26. Lincoln, p. 38, shows the range of how the gospel is described by Paul: 'In Paul the gospel can also be called "word of the Lord" (1 Thess 1:8; 2 Thess 3:1), "word of God" (1 Thess 2:13; 1 Cor 14:36), "word of Christ" (Col 3:16), "word of life" (Phil 2:16), or "word of reconciliation" (2 Cor 5:19).'

until all of it is completed. The seal in that culture was a stamp that identified someone or authenticated something. The Spirit is a promised benefit of the hope of deliverance (Joel 2:28–29; Jer. 31:31–35; Ezek. 36:24–28; Luke 3:16; 24:49; John 14:16–17; 15:26; Acts 2:30–36). So this provision is called *the promised Holy Spirit*. His indwelling presence means he brings with him hope that will end in total deliverance (Eph. 1:18). This description is not a reference to baptism as the benefit is said to come with the moment of belief, but it is what baptism pictures as it portrays the cleansing that comes with the faith that delivers (Rom. 6:2–4).

There is an interesting shift in verse 13 from 'we' and 'us' to 'you'. This appears to introduce a theme developed later, that Gentiles are now included in God's plan (Eph. 2:11 – 3:13). So Paul is specifically highlighting the inclusion of Gentiles in the divine plan originally set forth for Israel. Another reading of this shift distinguishes Paul's group from the Ephesians, looking merely to their response. However, this is of less cosmic significance in the divine programme and undervalues the passage as an introduction to the book, in which the Jew–Gentile contrast becomes a key to the reconciliation the book describes as a goal of the plan (Eph. 2:11 – 3:13; 4:17–32). The idea of their response bringing them into God's family as Gentiles now in Christ is part of the larger frame that points to cosmic reconciliation. It is possible that Paul does introduce the distinction at this point only to return to the union with 'we' in verse 14 with reference to our inheritance, showing the uniting of the two into one. So a decision to see unity emphasized until verse 12 does not preclude noting an ethical distinction present in verse 13. Nor does it require seeing 'first to hope in Christ' (ESV) in verse 12 as only referring to Jewish believers. That may be making this move too early in the argument. That Gentiles should share in the promise, including the gift of the indwelling Spirit, was at the core of Paul's ministry and perhaps a shock given the past history between Jews and Gentiles (1 Macc. 1 – 2; Eph. 3:1–13; Col. 1:25–27). Lincoln's claim in rejecting this distinction, arguing that it does not appear in the prayer that follows, is not correct as the prayer's content extends into Ephesians 2:1–10 where the idea of being raised together out of a cultural separation from God is part of the point to be appreciated.[27] Ephesians 2:1–3 is a précis of what Paul says in more detail in Romans 1 – 3, where the Gentile and Jewish contexts are very much in the background and juxtaposed. The corporate and ethnic togetherness is also clearly the point in Ephesians 2:11–22, a text elaborating on 2:1–10.

14. The Spirit is called a *down payment*, having been associated with a seal in verse 13. The down payment is a pledge (2 Cor. 1:21–22). In everyday life, a pledge is a token given as a guarantee until a promise is completely fulfilled (see Gen. 38:17–18). The indwelling Spirit is a guarantee that God will keep his commitment in Christ. So, besides being an enabler for the life God gives to those he renews, the Spirit identifies us as belonging to God.[28] The Spirit is busy working within believers until all is done. In Romans 8:23, the Spirit is called the first fruits to make the same point.

What God has given in his grace is called *our inheritance*, something we receive as God redeems his *own possession* on a day to come (Exod. 19:5; Isa. 43:21; Mal. 3:17; Acts 20:28; 1 Pet. 2:9). The reference to *possession* alludes to an idea already expressed in verse 11 in different terms tied to the idea of being an inheritance for God. Redemption is a second part of God's deliverance, as earlier in verse 7 redemption tied to the already present forgiveness of sins was noted. Here we speak of where that forgiveness and redemption will ultimately take us (Eph. 4:30: the day of redemption).

There is discussion over the exact force of the ambiguous phrase *redemption of the possession* (author's translation). Is the Spirit a seal of the redemption we receive ('until we acquire possession of it', RSV) or does he point to a redemption of God's own possession ('until the redemption of God's own possession', NET)? The decision is finely balanced. In one sense, both are the case. The issue is where Paul seeks to go with the point. Salvation brings us into a secure, unending relationship with God. It makes us his in a way not true of those who do not participate in the blessings of salvation that

---

27. Lincoln, p. 38.

28. For an argument that sealing by the Spirit operates by analogy with circumcision, appealing to parallels in Jewish literature for circumcision being called a seal, see Ferda, 'Sealed with the Holy Spirit', pp. 557–579.

come through faith in Christ. In the end, it is the latter – that we become his – that makes the inheritance we have precious. As the entire passage sets its focus on God, a key part of the point becomes this idea that we are his possession by his design and action. That truth will feed into our identity, which is the topic of Ephesians 2.[29]

All of this results in the *praise of his glory*, the third such refrain in the passage (vv. 6, 12). For Paul, there is much to praise God for in the grace he brings in Christ and in his gifting those who respond in faith with the indwelling Spirit. The Father plans and elects, the Son redeems and the Spirit seals and guarantees.[30] Salvation allows us to know God truly and be with him for ever. This is the gospel of truth Paul extols by focusing praise on the God who designed and executed these benefits on our behalf, forever changing the people who appreciate what it is God has done.

Theology

The theology of the unit is one of praise tied to an awareness of all God has done for believing sinners from eternity past into the present and looking ahead to consummation. These believers have received from God everything they need for a fruitful spiritual life. They can bless God for all he has done on their behalf because they are rooted in his choice of them in eternity past, tied to the work of Christ, and are living in a context of the forgiveness of sins, redemption and the provision of the Spirit as a down payment and seal of what is to come. We are part of a larger drama in which God is summing up all things in Christ to the praise of the glory of his grace. This awareness of and gratitude for what God has done is

---

29. Schnackenburg, p. 68, opts for the alternative reference to our inheritance, arguing that the idea of God's people is nowhere expressed in Ephesians. But the 'one new man' of Eph. 2:15 is such a reference, the creation of an entity that makes believers distinct from the world. Lincoln, p. 41, notes that redemption is always an act of God. For God to make redemption for possession of that which is his is the point, even though we are clearly beneficiaries of being tied to him.

30. Hoehner, p. 243.

fuel for the direction and stability of the Christian life. When we realize how much God has done for us, the sense of gratitude that emerges leads to responsiveness for the challenges of living the new life we have received from God. The sovereignty of God leads into grace and mercy from God. These divine acts planned long ago mean that the promises and the acts he performs on our behalf have a future destination that will lead to full redemption.

C. Prayer for understanding of God's power (1:15 – 2:22)

From a note of great praise to God, Paul turns to a prayer of thanksgiving. The prayer is focused on gratitude for his believing audience as well as a request to God that they gain a greater understanding of the riches, hope and power in which they share. It is especially the power he wants them to appreciate. The chapter break at this point gets in the way of the argument and the length of the prayer. Once Paul mentions power in 1:19, he stays on that theme even into 2:1–10. It is the power of God to raise us up spiritually and give us new capabilities that is the highlight of his description of God's grace in the illustrative and concluding part of the passage. Even the discussion of how Gentiles have been moved to become a part of the one new man in 2:11–22 is about God's power as shown in grace and the positioning we now have as those seated together in Christ. Paul's implied point is that no power in the world and no force that stands against God is greater than what we receive from God in salvation, a point that sets up where the letter will conclude when he notes that our battle is not against flesh and blood but against spiritual forces that require the armour of God if we are to stand on the ground we have gained (6:10–18). This awareness also will fuel the capability to do what Paul exhorts them to do in 4:1 – 6:9. So Paul is not merely laying out the identity of Christian believers in his doctrinal section of the letter; he is also laying out the capability to live the renewed life. Identity is the starting point, while drawing on divinely provided resources allows us to get there. Ephesians 2:10 may, therefore, be the theme verse for the book.

This unit proceeds in three parts. There is a request that the believers might be able to understand the hope of their calling, the riches of their inheritance and the power they have access to, a power like that which was demonstrated in Jesus' resurrection–ascension. Then we have the example of the application of that power to the new life that the Ephesians, and other believers like them, have received. This available power has already made an impact on their lives. Finally, we have all of this explained in more detail at its corporate level: how God brought Gentiles and Jews into a new entity and the fresh sacred space he has created in the one new man.

i. Prayer for understanding of their hope, riches and especially power (1:15–23)

Context

This prayer combines thanksgiving with a request that results from the appreciation Paul has for them, something Paul does frequently in his letters (Rom. 1:8–10; Col. 1:3; 1 Thess. 1:3; Phlm. 4). Ephesians 1:15–23 is one long Greek sentence, just as 1:3–14 was one long sentence of praise. Their faith and love motivate Paul to pray for them to have a deeper appreciation of all they have received from God. The report of their continuing faith and love inspires Paul to remember them to God and ask him to give them this deeper understanding of all that God has done for them. Paul pairs faith and love elsewhere in his writings (Gal. 5:6).

Comment

15. Paul turns to prayer full of thanksgiving because of all that God has done for them, so the unit begins with a look back at what was just said in praise: *For this reason.* God's praiseworthy act on their behalf is the initial reason why Paul prays. There is a second reason that also fuels his prayer and thanksgiving: *I have heard of your faith in the Lord Jesus and your love for all the saints . . .*[31] Paul links the two ideas

---

31. There is a text-critical issue here about whether a reference to love for the saints was in the original letter, since some key manuscripts omit it. However, the more likely explanation is a simple error of sight whereby the dual use of *tēn* in the verse led to a phrase being skipped over: Metzger, *Textual Commentary*, p. 533. The inclusion fits an emphasis in the letter as a whole on love for each other (4:2, 15, 16; 5:2, 25, 28, 33).

of faith and love in a classic connection to Christ. On the one hand, there is faith, and on the other hand, there is love, so that faith's contribution in relating to others well is seen in the love it produces. Their faith in Jesus as Lord over salvation and the benefits Paul has just so richly described has led them to love all those set apart to God, all the saints. The three-way chain will be an emphasis in chapters 2–3. In noting this reason for his prayer, Paul is also commending the living, vibrant faith the Ephesians possess.

The remark about the report has led some to argue Paul cannot be the letter's author as he spent time in Ephesus and knew the congregation first-hand.[32] However, he has been away from them for some time – he left Ephesus in AD 55 and probably wrote Ephesians during his imprisonment in Rome in AD 60–62. So he reacts to the report impressed with their continuing faith, something a leader, once he or she leaves a group, is pleased to hear. To the extent that this letter is more of a circular address to congregations in the region, it may be the case that the report he has heard is about the region as a whole, including some congregations he did not know personally.

16. Paul notes that he prays for them constantly with thanksgiving, writing that *I do not cease to give thanks for you* when he remembers them in his prayers (cf. Rom. 1:9; 1 Cor. 1:4; Phil. 1:4; Col. 1:3; 1 Thess. 1:2; 2 Thess. 1:3; 2:13; Phlm. 4). The remark is rhetorical and speaks to a consistency of prayer for them. His mention of them in his prayers yields thanksgiving because they live out what they believe with concrete expressions of love. The report Paul has heard about them shows they are a community that live out what they believe. That is a cause of thanksgiving for Paul as such authenticity brings honour to God, so he issues a prayer that this tendency might deepen even more. What the Ephesians do well, he wants to see with even more depth, as there is always room to grow.

17. In this verse we get to Paul's request to God for them. God is described as *the God of our Lord Jesus Christ, the Father of glory.* In describing God as *the God of our Lord,* Paul is making a Christian claim, much as the phrase 'the God of Abraham, Isaac and Jacob'

32. So Best, pp. 158–159.

would invoke Jewish expectations of promise. God has glorified
Jesus by what he has accomplished in salvation. Paul is interceding
for God to act on behalf of the Ephesians. The Father directs his
plan as the praise in verses 3–14 has made clear. He is a God worthy
of honour and *glory* as the earlier note of praise also showed (see
also 2 Cor. 4:4–6). He possesses splendour as well as the power to
make what Paul requests happen.[33] It is the God who radiates knowledge and light who is in view. It is with an awareness of God having
this wonderful character that Paul makes what would be a reason-
able request.

He asks that God might give them *a spirit of wisdom and of revelation*
in the full *knowledge of him*. The full phrase is ambiguous and is
rendered as such above. There are two options for the meaning of
spirit here: (1) a human spirit of wisdom and revelation; or (2) the
Holy Spirit who gives wisdom and revelation. So some translations
speak of the Holy Spirit here (ESV, NIV). The argument for this
rendering is that human beings do not possess a spirit of wisdom
and revelation that comes from God, so the Holy Spirit must be
meant. In favour of this rendering is that the expression 'a spirit of
revelation' does not signify a human quality. However, there is a
response to this objection, namely, that believers have received the
Spirit already, as verses 13–14 declared. If the Spirit is intended,[34]
then a special work of disclosure to know God by the Spirit must
be in view. Yet this alternative also has problems. The verb *give* looks
like a request for God to send something that is not already present,
making this less than likely to be the sense, given that the already
present indwelling of the Spirit has this impartation of wisdom in
response to revelation as part of the goal of indwelling. So most
translations opt for 'a spirit of wisdom and revelation' (NASB, NLT,
NET, RSV), which would mean our human spirit influenced by or
with reference to wisdom and revelation from God. The picture is
of a spiritual maturity rooted in a proper perception of the way

---

33. Best, p. 162.
34. So Best, p. 163; Fowl, p. 56; Schnackenburg, pp. 73–74; Hoehner, p. 256;
    Thielman, p. 96. Lincoln, p. 57, also correctly notes that the decision is
    a finely balanced one.

things are in terms of knowing God. The Holy Spirit is still in view here, but in a more indirect way. This view renders the verse *a spirit of wisdom and of revelation in the knowledge of him*.[35] The NET renders this *give you spiritual wisdom and revelation in your growing knowledge of him*. Colossians 1:9 seems to go in a similar direction with the stress being on what we are able to receive from God. The declaration that follows in Ephesians helps us see what is being said, namely, the eyes of their hearts have been enlightened already. So the work of the Spirit is an assumption of the request which moves to the next point in the sequence about what they are now able to understand as a result of this enlightenment. Such openness to God from within us also has an impact in deepening our awareness of God, as the next two verses will make clear. It is not an understanding that comes naturally, nor is it a function of mere human wisdom (1 Cor. 2:6–16), but it takes an openness to God's presence and direction to get there. The knowledge and wisdom combination tells us that we are not just talking about mere facts here, but about the application of truth to life, a practical understanding of how to live life.

18–19. Before Paul continues the request, he notes how the eyes of the Ephesians' hearts *have been enlightened*. The reference to *heart* speaks of the seat of understanding, 'the centre of personality'[36] (Deut. 28:28; Job 34:10; Dan. 2:30). This mention of their access to the light is an allusion to the impact of the Spirit's presence in them (2 Cor. 4:6; Eph. 1:13–14). It confirms that the Spirit is already active and that the request grows out of what they already have. In fact, the participle 'enlightened' functions as a cause that allows the request to be made with the hope that it will be achieved. That

---

35. Foulkes, p. 68; Bruce, p. 269. Interestingly, Gnilka, p. 90, does not choose, saying both impulses are in view, but notes that the landing point is how we respond to what God does as the prayer does not assume human passivity. In this light, the prayer is that God will give us a disposition that opens us up to his Spirit's work. All interpreters see this as the ultimate goal of the prayer regardless of how one views the Spirit/spirit issue.

36. Best, p. 165.

participle simply underscores the provision God has given them that is still present and active in them. It is the 'illumination of conversion'.[37] It is not only an act of God, but also a resulting status.[38] In other words, it is an 'illumination capability growing out of conversion'. So they can have hope of this deeper insight because their hearts have already been enlightened to go there.

The request is that they may know three things: (1) *the hope of his calling*; (2) *the wealth of his glorious inheritance in the saints*; and (3) *the incomparable greatness of his power toward us who believe.* When Paul gets to *power*, he will focus on it because the other two topics depend on what God by his power is able to do through and for us. There is a rich hope that we need to appreciate, a trajectory of the faith walk that enables a richness of life. There is also a treasure trove we have received by grace that is to motivate that calling and walk. It is all driven by the power we have access to in Christ so that success is not only possible, but eventually guaranteed when God finishes what he will accomplish through the Messiah.

The *hope of his calling* looks to the time when God will fully redeem us. At that time, peace with God among peoples and the creation will be fully restored and all will be reconciled (Rom. 5:2–5; 8:17–30; 12:12; 15:13; 2 Cor. 5:17–21; Gal. 5:5; Col. 1:5; Titus 1:2). This alludes back to the summing up of all things in Christ in verse 10. Our calling has a landing place that is hope. That hope is both individual, in terms of my walk with God, and corporate, in terms of people able to walk together without hostility. It is a certain hope that awaits us, so it calls for an attitude of hope now. It takes us in this optimistic direction. Paul wants the Ephesians to appreciate this as it frames what they are going through in life now (Rom. 5:4–5; 2 Pet. 1:4–8). By knowing where we are certainly headed, we can face the difficulties of this life without being overwhelmed. The goal also gives us a glimpse of where we should be headed now. This looks back to verse 12 and anticipates 4:1, 4.

The *wealth of his glorious inheritance* is much of what the rest of the letter is about. Grace gives believers many blessings and forms our

37. Lincoln, p. 58.
38. Barth I, p. 149.

identity. This is seen as a rich treasure of benefits. It is about more than simply getting to heaven; it is about what we have and will have as a result: the walk with God, the fellowship of the saints and the reconciliation and peace that come with consummation. This inheritance is his and yet its benefits for us come graciously from him as we share in it. The verse alludes to having awareness of this whole package. This is God's inheritance because his people are his possession and they are the beneficiaries of that relationship. It is an honour to belong to God and to receive what he gives as a result. This is where the core of a stable personal identity in Christ comes from: we belong to the Creator God and are precious to him. This idea is applied to Gentiles in 2:11–22 and looks back to a degree to verse 7.

The focus on power is underscored by the fact that four different terms denoting power are present in verse 19: *power, working, strength* and *might* (author's translation). The full expression is *the incomparable greatness of his power toward us who believe, as displayed in the exercise of the might of his strength* (author's translation). It is hard to determine any distinction between the terms so that the effect is rhetorical: any way you can think about or express power is what you have access to as a believer.[39] Colossians 1:11 is similar in stacking up power terms. If there is any distinction, then *dynamis*[40] is potential power and *energeia*[41] is realized or active power,[42] while the last two terms are basically synonyms for the capability God possesses to act: *kratos* is used to affirm God's attribute of power in exclamations like 'power be to God' (1 Tim. 6:16; 1 Pet. 4:11; Jude 25; Rev. 1:6; 5:13), and *ischys* refers to God's might or strength (Eph. 6:10; 1 Pet. 4:11). God grants this superabundant enablement and its benefits to those who believe. Without this power, no part of the calling or hope would be possible. This focus on power in the prayer shows that it is what the Ephesians should especially grasp, appreciate and utilize. In the

---

39. Fowl, p. 59, opts for a rhetorical approach to these four terms.
40. BDAG, p. 262.
41. BDAG, p. 335; Eph. 3:7; 4:16; Phil. 3:21; Col. 1:29.
42. Aristotle, *Metaphysica*, 9.5.1 §1047b.31; 8.5 §1049b.24; 9.1; Hoehner, p. 269.

face of other powers to be mentioned in verse 21 and in 6:12, it is important to know that access to and drawing upon God's power is what enables believers to overcome whatever opposes us.[43] Such overcoming power is the point of the use of the term *incomparable* or 'surpassing' (*megethos*) elsewhere (Exod. 15:16; 2 Macc. 15:24).[44] For Paul, there is no doubt that God can supply what has been requested. It is visible, effective power that he is discussing, not any kind of abstract idea of perceived power. He wants the Ephesians to pursue such depth of enablement. The pronoun switch in the verse from the previous use of 'you' to 'us' shows Paul including himself and all believers in this awareness and in the hope of the prayer. Although the request in the prayer ends here, the prayer continues in an extended set of illustrations, reaching all the way to 2:22, of the kind of power God has shown to us already.

20. The power we have access to is like that which *raised [Jesus] from the dead and seated him at [God's] right hand*. Schnackenburg calls this combination of ideas 'the fundamental sermon on Christ'.[45] The repetition of the word for power expressed (*enērgēsen*) links the verse back to verse 19 (*energeia*). God demonstrated what he can do for us (1 Cor. 6:14; Phil. 3:10) when he raised Jesus from the dead and gave him a seat that showed that Jesus shares in the execution of salvation in the world (Matt. 28:18). The resurrection is a key New Testament theme (Rom. 4:24; 6:4; 10:9; 1 Cor. 15:4; 1 Thess. 1:10; 1 Pet. 1:21).

The phrase *seated . . . at his right hand* alludes to Psalm 110:1 (cf. Rom. 8:34; 1 Cor. 15:25; Col. 3:1; other key NT texts are Matt. 22:44; 26:64; Mark 14:62; Luke 22:69; Acts 2:30–38; Heb. 1:13; 8:1). The *right hand* represents a place of power and victory (Exod. 15:6; Ps. 89:13; Isa. 41:10; 48:13). In a context of monotheistic Judaism, this is a key text. It shows Jesus seated in heaven with God, sharing honour and glory with him. The key point is the elaboration of the power we have access to in Christ. It is life-giving power that is in view.

---

43. Barth I, p. 152.
44. Thielman, p. 100.
45. Schnackenburg, p. 76.

The syntax of the verse is importantly governed by a verb followed by two participles. God worked out his power when he raised and seated Jesus. In one sense he has also done the same for us already, as 2:5–6 will argue (cf. Col. 2:12). Even with that initial resurrection, there is still more to come (1 Cor. 15; Phil. 3:20–21). The position of Christ in God's programme secures the position of believers and the church. To be in Christ is to be networked for eternity. There is no higher power to be connected to than God. That connection makes us secure to face whatever may come our way. Two more verbs will follow in verse 22 in wrapping up the argument: God (1) has subjected all things under Christ's feet and (2) gave Jesus as head over the church.

21. The heavenly seating of Jesus shows that he is above all kinds of powers. Paul again stacks up related words to make the point that Jesus is above every power. He is seated above *all rule, authority, power* and *dominion* (Col. 1:16; 1 Pet. 3:22).[46] *Rule* and *authority* are often paired in Paul (Eph. 3:10; 6:12; Col. 1:16; 2:10, 15). The same term for *power* is used in Romans 8:38; 1 Corinthians 15:24; and 1 Peter 3:22. *Dominion* appears in Paul only in Colossians 1:16 and here. There is no point trying to distinguish between the terms; it is Paul's way of saying 'in every conceivable category'. These categories represent a development from the time of the Hebrew Scriptures as angels and demons were seen to have orders and various roles to which they belonged. Reading the early chapters of a Jewish work like *1 Enoch*, as well as *2 Enoch* 20 – 22, shows the conception behind such categories. For Paul, this authority is not one into which Jesus entered as a result of his death and resurrection, but a position he reclaimed in a way that made it evident to all (Rom. 1:2–4; Phil. 2:6–11).

In fact, this authority is complete in all directions. It is over *every name that is named* (cf. Phil. 2:9). There is power in the naming of a known name. The book of Acts speaks regularly of healing in the name of Jesus Christ (see Acts 3:16). Given how important magic was in Ephesus where Diana was worshipped, the remark is

---

46. On these terms see Arnold, pp. 112–114. He covers this in even more detail in *Ephesians: Power and Magic*.

contextually important as well (cf. Acts 19, esp. v. 13). It was common in magical contexts to utter a name to try to gain control of the forces being confronted.

The statement is comprehensive in three ways: (1) all categories of power are named; (2) the use of space shows Jesus' superiority in being seated above; (3) the rule has no limit in time. So the ideas of *all* and *every* underscore Christ's position. It makes no difference whether the authority in question is visible or invisible: Christ is above it (Col. 2:10, 15). Neither the authority of Rome nor that of hostile spiritual forces can stop what God is doing in Christ. In a context where Rome claimed such total power or shared the state's power with provincial cities, the remark is important.[47] No nation is more important than the people God forms in Christ. This is part of the reason why Paul notes in verse 20 that the source of power is in the heavenlies. There is a distinction in these categories between visible and invisible rule, but they are not to be separated entirely as one influences the other (Eph. 2:1–3). Human institutions that go awry are seen as influenced by transcendent evil forces. This is not a common approach in many modern views of reality, but for Scripture it is a most important observation.

The extension of the reference to heaven also makes it likely that evil spiritual forces are primarily in view. The angels were seen as cooperating with God, unlike hostile forces. In Ephesians 6, there will be a reference to the battle. There the spiritual conflict is between evil spiritual opposition and merely flesh and blood (also Eph. 2:2). That reference likely looks back to this passage in chapter 1.

The duration of Christ's position also matters: it is *not only in this age but also in the one to come.* This is a way of saying that the rule remains for ever by appealing to the common Jewish view that there is this age and an age to come (*4 Ezra* 6:9; 7:12–13; 8:1; *2 Apoc. Bar.* 48:50; *m. Peah* 1:1; Matt. 12:32; Mark 10:30; Rom. 8:38). The connections believers have in Christ equip them to face anything any

---

47. Thielman, p. 109, cites a graffito in Ephesus that declared Rome's power would never die. Baugh, p. 128, notes Polybius's claim that Rome had subjected the entire earth (*Histories* 3.3.9).

opposition can throw at them at any time. The resurrection–ascension is a permanent vindication of Jesus (Rom. 1:2–4; 1 Cor. 15:20–28). It also made an eternal provision for the saints.

22. There are two more consequences to the resurrection–ascension. Paul has already mentioned the acts of God for Jesus in his raising Jesus and seating him at his right hand. He now develops the core effects of those acts.

First, God *put all things under his [Jesus'] feet*, an allusion to the initial role of humanity in the creation (Gen. 1:26–28) as well as to the divine authority Jesus possesses as part of the shared rule over creation (1 Cor. 15:20–28). Psalm 8:6 is cited here, a text with roots in the central Genesis 1:26–28 passage that mentions the creation of humanity and the call to rule or manage the creation well. Jesus is the second Adam and more (see Rom. 5:12–21, where the topic is justification and Jesus' representation of the human race). This citation is not merely an appeal to the human Jesus. The authority Jesus has over creation is styled as that of the firstborn of creation in Colossians 1:15–20, where 'firstborn' also speaks of rank and is not a description of origin. In that text Jesus creates, placing him on the Creator side of the Creator–creature divide. The move is significant, given that in Judaism this role for Adam had been transferred to Israel (*4 Ezra* 6:38–59; 1QS 4:23).[48] The real transfer of representation resides in one greater than even a great nation. God's rule is mediated to the world through the comprehensive authority of Jesus. Though that accountability has yet to show itself completely, it is there. The future day of redemption will bring its full display (Rom. 8:18–39; 1 Cor. 15:24; Eph. 1:10).

Second, God also gave Jesus *to the church as head over all things*. The text does not here say that Jesus is head of the church but that as head of the universe he is given to the church. There is debate about the meaning of the term translated *head (kephalē)*. Is it a term denoting rank or does it mean source? In this context, with the issue of authority so dominant, rank is much more likely (so also Col. 1:18). The image of head is often seen in terms of that which commands the direction of the body (Galen, *De usu partium*

---

48. Arnold, p. 115.

1.454.1–14). All things are submitted to Jesus and he, as head over all, is given to the church. The victory achieved at the cross has resulted in an exalted Jesus (Col. 2:10–15), and the church is a special beneficiary of all of this. So Jesus is connected to the larger world and to his own people. In both he has authority. Those of faith recognize it; for others, it is present whether they recognize it or not. The one with whom the church is intimately related has authority over the whole of the creation. The 'cosmic Lord has been given to the church'.[49] 'God has given Christ to the church in Christ's capacity as head over all things.'[50] The ultimate gift of grace is the powerful Christ himself. It is this network that allows those who trust Christ to rest in their identity in him, for the one who leads them also has authority over the creation. The idea of Jesus being head of the church is stated more directly in Ephesians 5:22–33.

The term *church* simply means 'assembly' (Deut. 23:2 LXX), but in this case we have the special assembly of the people of God seen in its wholeness (1 Cor. 10:32; Gal. 1:13; Col. 1:18, 24) rather than just a reference to a local congregation. Christ sits over all who gather in his name.

23. Numerous issues greet us in this verse. How does *plērōma* (*fullness*) link verses 22 and 23? What is its meaning? What about the idea of being filled (*plēroumenou*)? The image of the church as a functioning person has Jesus as the head and the church as *his body* (Rom. 12:4–8; 1 Cor. 12:12–31; Eph. 2:16; 4:4, 12, 16; 5:30; Col. 1:24; 2:19). In a sense, the church as Christ's body is the visible manifestation of Jesus' presence in the light of his heavenly seating (Eph. 5:22–33). The image of the body and head makes the point that this is one entity with the same life flowing through the whole.[51]

The description of the body follows, if we see the 'fullness' clause as in apposition to the 'body'. So the body of Christ is seen where Christ is expressing himself and pouring out his fullness. A connection to verse 22 is too remote. Paul describes that presence

---

49. Lincoln, p. 67.

50. Thielman, p. 111.

51. Foulkes, p. 73.

tied to God's work in Christ and in the body as a *fullness of the one being filled with all things with respect to all* (author's translation). Christ is the one filled by God and who in turn fills the church. The church is to be the expression of the divine presence that comes from Christ, who himself expresses the presence of God (Eph. 3:19; Col. 1:19; 2:9–10). The term *plēroumenou* is passive: 'that which is filled'; the same is true of *plērōma* ('a fullness supplied'). The idea is not that the church fills or completes Christ (which would require taking *plēroumenou* as middle, with active force), as that is the reverse of the relationship the New Testament describes. The idea expresses a variation of the movement in the earlier word of praise that saw the summing up of all things in Christ (1:10). Christ shows himself in the world through his church, into which he pours himself – by which is meant his character and grace. In turn, that filling is a complete one, touching everything. Various pictures of filling from God are used elsewhere in Ephesians (4:10, 13; 5:18). Through Christ the church has everything it needs from God to be what it is called to be. Victory over these hostile forces will not only come one day; it is possible now, whatever they throw the church's way, provided the church draws on the enablement Christ gives.

Theology

This prayer is about believers understanding how much they have because they are in Christ. It is especially God's power exercised on their behalf that they are to appreciate. They have riches and a great hope fuelled by the capability the connection to Christ brings. They have access to the one whose power brings life and whose authority is comprehensive and lasting for all time. That power is most strongly signified by what God did in raising Jesus and giving him a seat above all authority for all time. The Ephesians have connections to such power. Nothing can oppose them that has access to a greater power. Secure in that recognition and reality, the church can be all it is called to be in the world. Paul has not finished illustrating the point; the next passage actually continues the picture. In fact, all of chapter 2 portrays the exercise of Christ's restoring power on behalf of the church. The chapter break here can mislead us into thinking that Paul's prayer is finished, but it actually is extended into a theological illustration that continues through Ephesians 2.

The power they have access to has already been at work among
them in Christ. It is to this deepening of the point that Paul now
turns as he looks directly at their salvation experience.

ii. Power for new life by grace (2:1–10)

Context

Paul has just considered what God has done for the church in
Christ by looking at what God has done for Jesus and the equipping
God has given the church as a result. Ephesians 2:1–10 presents a
new angle on the topic of the prayer in chapter 1. Paul turns his
attention to what God has done directly to and for believers in the
provision of salvation by grace. He describes an exercise of power
on their behalf that brought them out of spiritual death into life.
He also describes how this act has bonded them together as
co-participants in God's grace. The rationale for the prayer and the
focus on power continue as Paul wants them to appreciate what
they have already received. Such a review gives them confidence
about what is available to access now. Past benefits can become a
basis for current appropriation of what God has made available.

Comment

1. Paul looks back to the previous spiritual condition of his
audience. He opens with another long single sentence that runs
through to verse 7. His readers were *dead in your transgressions and sins*.
The use of the second person looks to the situation of the
Ephesians in a largely Gentile context. The shift to first person
plural in verse 3 will consider things from a Jewish angle, meaning
that no-one escapes the need for Christ. In that form of argument,
we return to the way Paul proceeded in Romans 1:18 – 3:31. All
have sinned and fall short of the glory of God (Rom. 3:23), with
Romans 1:18–32 covering Gentiles, 2:1 – 3:18 picking up the Jewish
need, 3:19–20 summarizing the charge and 3:21–31 giving the
solution in the light of the charge. In Ephesians 2, Paul starts his
thought here in verse 1 and digresses in verses 2–3. However, verses
1–3 discuss the people's bondage and resultant need of the grace
of God described in verses 4–10. He will pick up the idea in verses
4–5, with the wording in verse 5 almost matching that of this
verse.

This verse considers their past spiritual condition as one absent of spiritual life (Eph. 2:12; 4:18). The picture is of people who, although they are physically alive, are spiritually dead, useless, detached from a functioning relationship with God. They are in need of the grace God provides through Jesus. Their trespasses and sins placed them in such continuing peril (Rom. 6:23; Col. 2:13). It is tragic to be alive and yet dead (Gen. 2:16–17). They were spiritually powerless. Earlier Paul noted how our transgressions are forgiven in Christ (1:7), and in other texts the New Testament speaks of how Jesus meets this need (John 3:3; 5:24; Rom. 6:23). The combination *transgressions* and *sins* is a hendiadys, another example of Paul working with a stack of synonyms. No distinction in meaning should be sought between the terms.

2. The former lost state of his readers is where Paul turns in a digression of sorts to set up the display of God's power in Christ that follows in verse 4. It was in trespasses and sins that the Ephesians *formerly lived*. The figure of the walk is translated in terms of a former way of life. This introduces a 'then but now' contrast that is common in Paul (Rom. 11:30; Eph. 5:8; Col. 3:7). That walk and its choices in life were directed by forces outside of themselves which they followed: *following the course of this world, following the prince of the power of the air, the spirit that is now at work in the sons of disobedience.* The 'walk' further refers to the ethical dimensions of a person's life (Eph. 2:10; 4:1; 5:2, 8, 15), and it was dipped deep in sin. In fact, the Jewish term for reflection on moral conduct was *halakah*, which means 'walking'.[52]

There is shared responsibility among three agents for this spiritual death: the world, Satan and the guiding environment. These create a climate leading one into sin and death. There are negative spiritual forces at work in the world, and when one follows them, disobedience is the tragic and damaging result. So this world, apart from God, is a dangerous place, as it has been since the fall in Genesis 3. It is teeming with hostile powers and choices about values that take people in destructive directions, whether they recognize it or not. Left to its own devices, it yields destruction as

---

52. Foulkes, p. 77.

a fallen world in need of redemption. This is why, if we are left to our instincts, the results are often poor. But how we respond to this environment is our responsibility. Paul has no interest in deflecting blame, even though spiritual forces are at work. There is no suggestion that we are victims. We act as responsible agents and are accountable for the poor or wrong choices we make.

The roots of this environment are complex. There is the fallen nature of what surrounds them now, which contrasts with the environment and culture to come in the 'coming ages' spoken of in verse 7. The present evil age will be reversed by a better age to come. The Spirit that we received with faith (Eph. 1:13–14) enables us not to be trapped in this old environment. Ephesians 4 – 6 will make the point that we are to preview what is to come by the way we are now enabled to live.

The mention of the *prince of . . . the air* is a reference to Satan. It is why Paul describes the ultimate battle believers have as not against people but as a spiritual battle (Eph. 6:11–12). The term *the spirit* that follows is slightly more likely to refer back to the impact of the authority at work in the air than to refer directly to the ruler. That authority, coming from Satan, is an influence on our spirits that guides us in our disobedience; we are the target of hostile acts.[53] Paul paints a picture of a guiding atmosphere in the world for which Satan is responsible; people imbibe it, and it is full of death and danger. It is an unseen influence that still carries much weight. So there are two powers at work in the world: one divine (1:20) and another destructive (2:2). Everyone aligns with one or the other. As sons of disobedience in the past, we were misaligned (5:6).

The Ephesians, by grace, have switched sides in this battle, as 2:4–10 will show (also Col. 1:13). This Ephesian epistle is the outworking of what that shift of allegiance means. Paul is saying, 'Pay attention to what I am saying.' Despite all that Christ has accomplished, evil has not yet been eradicated. That part of the programme comes later, so the Ephesians must battle in this age to be faithful in the midst of this tension until the age to come arrives. Living 'between the times' requires consciously walking in grace.

---

53. Hoehner, pp. 314–315.

God has given the capability to accomplish a walk of grace. That is what Paul wants the Ephesians to grasp about the power he has prayed about in 1:19. He wants them to draw on that power and succeed in resisting evil.

3. Paul notes that the behaviour of Jews and the religious circle he emerged from was also caught up in this web at one time: *Among these we all once lived in the passions of our flesh, following the desires of body and mind, and so we were by nature children of wrath, like the rest of mankind.* In turning to the use of the first person, Paul adds Jews to the aggregate of people who were in need, much as he did in making the more detailed argument for the gospel and salvation in Romans 1 − 3.[54] Though some see Paul making the contrast between the Ephesians and his apostolic entourage, it is better to see the Jew–Gentile contrast here setting up what he explores in detail in 2:11–22. The argument that the use of *all* in this verse precludes that view misses the point that what Paul is doing here is adding his group to those in need in a way that includes them in the dilemma all find themselves in, adding them to the mix by turning the spotlight his way. Everyone was in the same boat of need, whether Jews or Gentiles, Ephesians or those among Paul's entourage. Things were dire until God stepped in.

All lived in the same way, even though it manifested itself in distinct ways. The desires of the *flesh* and *mind* directed them in self-serving ways. This self-focus and the pursuit of our own passions often leads into sin. It resulted in the status of *children of wrath*. Even though the environment was threatening and tempting, it was their personal responsibility and choice − their very own activity and nature − that led to this result. The phrase *by nature children of wrath* describes what human beings are by nature; *body* and *mind* show a person's desires and thoughts acting in concert with the whole person. The mind of the flesh is a consistently negative image in

---

54. With Bruce, p. 283; Witherington, pp. 253–254; Barth I, p. 216; against many who prefer a reference to all Christians in the shift to the first person. Regardless of the view taken here, it is the aggregate that is the ultimate point. All of us share the same need because we all share the same problem. No ethnicity is immune.

Paul (Rom. 1:21; 8:5, 7; Col. 2:18). The term translated *body* is actually 'flesh' and emphasizes the physicality of our destructive acts. We are not disembodied spirits; we think and then act it out physically. Whatever tendencies have been inherited from previous generations – and we did inherit them – we are who we are by nature and act accordingly (Rom. 5:12; *4 Ezra* 7:62–69, 116–118).[55] Our actions show us to be directly responsible. Paul speaks of our doing with our bodies what we think.

Our actions are deeply rooted in who we are apart from God. We are like those who came before us and yet we are responsible for those actions. We are fully corrupt. Theologians use the term 'depravity' to describe our need apart from divine renewal. That depravity is pervasive, present in all of us, rather than being total in the sense that we are as bad as we could be or worthless in our being.[56] God still cares about us in our lost state, as verses 4–10 will show. It is not the outside forces that drive us; ultimately when we act, we own those actions with the internal endorsement we give to them. That makes us responsible for our own acts and choices. It makes us subject to God's *wrath* (Rom. 1:18–32; 3:9–20). Our condition is such that there is no excuse for being in need – and there is no-one to blame for our plight but ourselves. It is a grim corporate résumé, the *imago dei* gone astray – that is, the image of God in deep need of reformation.

4. Paul now turns to the reversal grace brings and how God's power has already been exercised on behalf of believers. As dire as things were, God acted to overcome and reverse the condition people were in, and used his power to do so. The contrast is introduced with the phrase *But God, being rich in mercy.* The cause was *because of his great love with which he loved us.* God saw the mess we were in and reached down to pull us out of it, not because we deserved rescue, but because he loved us enough to act on our behalf.

Two attributes of God were at work in his move to rescue people from their plight: mercy and love. *Mercy* shows that God was kind in acting on our behalf. He did not have to do it. There was no

---

55. Thielman, p. 127.

56. Snodgrass, p. 99.

entitlement that required it. We did not deserve it. He simply took the initiative to save us. Mercy is a core attribute of God by which he shows an intense faithfulness and loyalty towards people; it is tied to the Old Testament term *ḥesed* (Exod. 34:6–7; Deut. 7:7–9; Ps. 145:8; Jer. 31:3; Mic. 7:18; cf. Luke 1:68–79; Rom. 11:30–32). Mercy is linked with forgiveness (Eph. 1:7; Titus 3:5; 1 Pet. 1:3; 2:10). Such mercy was a characteristic of Jesus' ministry (Matt. 9:27; 15:22; 17:15; Mark 5:19). This mercy comes in richness to the believer. There is an abundance tied to it, because of the depths out of which it brings us. *Love* was also a motivation for God's action (John 3:16; Rom. 5:5, 8; 8:39; 1 John 4:10).

5. To remind us of the context of God's action, Paul repeats the idea that we were dead when God acted for us: *when we were dead through our trespasses* (cf. 2:1). What God did when we were in the midst of that condition follows, as Paul arrives at the point he was driving at when he first mentioned our condition in verse 1: God *made us alive together with Christ* (cf. John 5:21; 6:63; Rom. 8:11; 2 Cor. 3:6). The verb translated *made . . . alive together* is used only here and in Colossians 2:13. God moved us from death in the depths to the heights of heaven (Rom. 6:1–11). The idea of *together* is important, as the Greek prefix *syn-* is present in all three verbs in verses 5–6. God has made his people alive by connecting them all to Christ so that they share the same blessings. Our union with Christ is another major Pauline theme as it supports our personal identity (Rom. 6 – 8; Col. 2:6 – 3:17). Paul will develop the corporate bond that is a result of this in verses 11–22. The verb minus the prefix appears in John 5:21; 6:63; and 1 Peter 3:18.

By grace you are being saved (author's translation). To be *saved* is to be delivered (Rom. 10:9, 13). Ephesians 1:6–7 already described this *grace*. Paul is so captivated by this idea of grace that he cannot wait until he gets to its development later in the passage, so he makes an aside here. This aside is at the core of the passage, with the reference to grace being placed first for emphasis in the Greek parenthesis that completes the verse. Paul repeats the idea in verse 8. The grace and power of God gave life out of mercy and love. Grace is undeserved favour, and the verses here explain why it is grace. God is the one who, out of his own initiative, made us alive when we were powerless to do anything. The result was new life, or what other texts call 'being born again' (John 3:3–5; 1 Pet. 1:3) or 'new creation' (2 Cor. 5:17). It is faith in Jesus the Messiah that triggers these benefits (Eph. 2:8). The shift back to the second person (*you*) is to remind his readers of the grace they are experiencing. The perfect participle (*sesōsmenoi*) looks at something done in the past whose effect continues. In other words, the new life was established in the past but now continues. The emphasis in Ephesians on the present nature of faith and deliverance also appears elsewhere in Paul (1 Cor. 1:18; 2 Cor. 2:15; Phil. 2:12).

6. Paul continues to discuss what God did for us in bringing us out of death by adding two more actions beyond making us alive: *He raised us together and seated us together with Christ in the heavenlies* (author's translation). Being *raised together* describes a shift in status (Col. 2:12; 3:1). This is a very realized eschatology, a spiritual resurrection that has taken place already, meaning that some of the promised hope of the end has already begun to be fulfilled. Elsewhere Paul normally looks at the resurrection as a future event, even to the point of critiquing those who speak of a resurrection now (1 Cor. 4:8; 2 Tim. 2:18). However, there the criticism is of the suggestion that everything that will take place with the resurrection has been completed in the present. Here he highlights a current change of status that takes place on account of faith in Jesus, with more to come (Rom. 6; 1 Cor. 15:49; Gal. 4:26; Phil. 1:6). It is important to be aware of what we have now and where it is taking us. Still, not everything tied to salvation has come to us now. There is more to come, namely, a physical resurrection and full restoration, as noted elsewhere in Ephesians (1:10, 14, 21; 2:7; 4:30). Our citizenship has changed, as has our capability for how we are to live as a result (Rom. 7:4; Gal. 2:20; Phil. 3:20–21; Col. 1:13–14). Paul wants his readers to realize that that same power is available to them now, even as they await the rest of what salvation will bring.

God gave us a seat in heaven above all the forces that could oppose us when he seated us with Christ. Our union with Christ extends to a connection with him in terms of access to his position and authority. The believer has exceptional connections. The remark about our being seated with Christ refers back to the very important point Paul made in 1:19–21, when he says that Jesus was seated above all authority for all time. This is an authority that will be concretely expressed in the future (Matt. 19:28; 1 Cor. 6:2–3; 2 Tim. 2:12; Rev. 3:21; 20:4; 22:5). So not only do we have a new life; we have a new status and a new community to which our allegiance belongs. This sets the context for the current walk of believers in the midst of spiritual and moral conflict (Eph. 2:10; 4:1, 17; 6:12).

7. This drama of grace is going to play itself out in a display in the future. In fact, that is one of God's goals for salvation. God has made us alive and raised and seated us together with Christ in order *that in the coming ages he might show the immeasurable riches of his grace in kindness toward us in Christ Jesus.* Grace ends up testifying to the glory of God through the kind exercise of his grace. The character of God ends up on display as a result. People will see how salvation is abundantly good. Grace is 'a masterpiece of goodness'.[57] The Ephesians participate in that abundance now. The array of positive descriptions piled onto each other echoes the kind of thing said about Augustus in the Graeco-Roman world.[58] However, it is not Roman emperors who give such gifts, but God. The society around them has nothing on what God has given his people. This display will continue as it relates to the *coming ages*, a way of saying 'the future in all of its forms' (Matt. 12:32; Mark 10:30; Luke 18:30; Eph. 3:9–11 [without the phrase]; Phil. 1:6). Of course, as salvation reaches its full realization that demonstration will be complete. Salvation in the present has a trajectory for this display into the future. From age to age, grace paints a picture of God. The *riches of his grace* repeats the idea from 1:7 as well as 1:18. The unmerited favour we receive has a depth to it that dips deep into the *kindness of God toward us in Christ Jesus* (Titus 3:4).

8. Paul summarizes his point with an explanation introduced by the word 'for': *For by grace you are saved through faith.* The perfect participle (*sesōsmenoi*) could stress their having been saved or the present

---

57. Bruce, p. 288. He adds, 'When he brings into being the reconciled universe of the future, the church will provide the pattern after which it will be modeled.' Schnackenburg, p. 96, speaks of 'philanthropic goodness', that is, something given as a pure gift from God, not earned nor a product of our entitlement, but a reflection of his amazing grace.

58. Thielman, p. 138; Harrison, *Paul's Language of Grace*, p. 231, n. 73.

result, in terms of 'you are saved'.[59] It may well be that we should see the latter here. They stand in a position of 'having been saved' by God's grace, a status rooted in a past response to what God has generously provided. The reference to *grace* is thrown forward in the verse for emphasis. It repeats the aside of 2:5, showing that this is where Paul has been going all along. Two more things are said beyond what was stated in 2:5. First, it is *that* grace, a detail shown by the added article, looking back to verses 5 and 7. Second, the access to grace comes 'by' or 'through' *faith*. The gift is not automatic but is found in a response to what God has done, a trust that embraces and receives the gift (cf. Rom. 3:25–28; 5:1, 15, 17; Gal. 3:2–5, 8–9; Eph. 1:13, 19; 1 Pet. 1:5). The declaration stands in contrast to the culture, given that figures like Julius Caesar and Augustus were both declared to be saviour of the world in inscriptions like one found in Ephesus.[60]

This *faith* or trust is continuing. It is more than an intellectual recognition of what God did; it is a belief personally embraced and applied, so it is received (see John 1:12). It recognizes that what God has done in Christ applies to my situation and need, and sees that Jesus is Lord over the salvation God has provided (Acts 2:30–38; Rom. 10:9). It recognizes that if I am to be made alive, God must provide the new life, and has done so in Christ. So I become aligned in faith to God's work in Christ and see it as what I need in order to function. That is what makes the response one of faith, because faith is trust, not just a decision. 'Faith involves the abandonment of any attempt to justify oneself and an openness to God which is willing to accept what he has done in Christ.'[61]

This is not from yourselves – in other words, you do not produce your own salvation. There is much discussion about the antecedent

---

59. Hoehner, p. 341.

60. Baugh, '"Savior of All People"', pp. 331–340. Here is the inscription about Julius Caesar as translated by Baugh: 'The cities of Asia, along with the [citizen-bodies] and the nations, (honor) C. Julius C. f. Caesar, the high priest, *imperator*, and twice consul, the manifest God (sprung) from Ares and Aphrodite, and universal savior of human life' (p. 336).

61. Lincoln, p. 111.

to the word *this*. What does it refer back to in the context? Is it faith, or salvation as a whole? The neuter demonstrative is normally used for a broad reference to the topic of the context, so salvation as a whole is in view. If Paul had wished to single out 'faith', to make that clear the gender would have been feminine to match the gender of the Greek word for 'faith' (*pistis*). Also, it makes more sense to say that salvation is not from works than to say that faith is not from works, which is tautologous. Note the plural 'works' in verse 9 (*ergōn*), which means we are not discussing one thing but a series of actions. That additional affirmation clarifies the context. The earlier context also supports this broader reference, given that verse 1 talks about when they 'were dead' and so unable to do anything to spiritually better themselves, pointing to an inability to access salvation as a whole. This salvation is a *gift* sourced 'from' *God*, which is the force of the phrase *of God* in translations (cf. Rom. 3:24, where the topic is justification; and Rom. 5:15, 17; 2 Cor. 9:15, using the related term *dōrea*). The Greek word here is *dōron*,[62] the only time Paul uses this term. In the Greek sentence, God is placed first for emphasis. Literally, the phrase reads, 'God's is the gift.' Grace is of God through and through. Our part is to receive it in faith, but the act of power that brings new life comes from God. Two of the Reformation's five *sola*s came from this verse: *sola fide* and *sola gratia* ('by faith alone' and 'by grace alone').

9. To keep the emphasis that salvation is all from God, Paul states the point negatively: this salvation is *not from works, so that no one can boast*. It was noted above that the term for *works* here is plural. No product of our lives saves us (Rom. 3:28; 4:4–5; 9:32–33; 11:6; Gal. 2:16; 3:2–5, 7, 9; 2 Tim. 1:9; Titus 3:5). Salvation is not a reward; it is a gift. No-one is in a position to say, 'I gained salvation by my labour.' The 'works' here are not just works of the law; Paul refers to any labour we think commends us to God or demands that he save us. The reference to a scope broader than the law fits the larger Hellenistic context of the letter.

---

62. BDAG, p. 267; it can highlight the idea of a gift as opposed to a mere privilege.

Boasting is excluded, because grace is something we did not earn. Paul often speaks of this impossibility of boasting (Rom. 3:27; 1 Cor. 1:29; 3:21). The only boast that counts is about God or the work tied to Christ (Rom. 5:2, 11; 1 Cor. 1:31; 2 Cor. 10:17; Gal. 6:14; Phil. 1:26; 3:3).

10. So what was God's purpose in saving us? Paul explains, using the word *for* to introduce the goal of what God has done. What is grace for? We have been made into God's *workmanship*. The emphasis in the Greek word order at the start of the verse is literally, '*His creation* we are.' 'His creation' is thrown forward to highlight that we are God's work. In fact, believers are a creative product of the power of God. The term used, *poiēma*, often refers to God's act in creating (Pss 64:9; 92:4; Rom. 1:20). There is often a note about something satisfying about what has been made, or something that should be appreciated about it. Paul elsewhere speaks of our being a 'new creation' (2 Cor. 5:17; Gal. 6:15; 'new man' in Eph. 4:24; Col. 3:10, translated as 'new self' in NIV, NRSV and ESV). This is another way to say we are born again; we have a spiritually infused life that has a capability it previously lacked.

There also is a goal in making us this way: we have *been created . . . for good works*. Titus 2:14 makes the same point. The verb translated *created* is also often tied to creation (Matt. 19:4; Col. 1:16). There is a positive role for works, not as a cause of salvation, but as a product of it (Acts 9:36; Col. 1:10; 1 Tim. 2:10; 5:10; 6:18; Titus 2:7, 14; Heb. 10:24; 1 Pet. 2:12). In fact, this is a major goal of salvation. God delivers us and gives us the gift so we can live in ways that honour him. The capability and empowerment God gives to us in the Spirit set us up for these works, which *God prepared beforehand, that we should walk in them*. We are not saved by works, but saved for works! We are now able to live in the ways God designed (Gal. 5:22–23). This will become the point in Ephesians 4 – 6 and it is rooted in what was extolled about God in 1:4. Note the difference in the walking we do now compared with the way we walked before God's gift in 2:1–2. God's grace and power through the Messiah and in the Spirit have made that possible. We are still in the shadow of the prayer request of 1:19. Look at what God's power has done for us! God designed a path that he now equips us to follow (Rom. 6:4). The idea of the walk of life is frequent in the letter (Eph. 2:2; 4:1, 17; 5:2, 8, 15).

Theology

This unit gives an overview of many core themes tied to salvation. It makes clear that a person's condition outside of Christ involves a need for God's work. Whether Jew or Gentile, we are dead in our trespasses and sins. The resultant position is that we are children of wrath (vv. 1–3). The movement to new life is completely rooted in God's work. He is the one who makes us alive, raises us and seats us in heavenly places. This gives us a new citizenship and identity in Christ (vv. 4–6). This act of God comes out of his mercy and love. The result is a demonstration of the depth of God's grace both now and in the future (v. 7). All of this shows that salvation is by grace through faith. None of it is our own doing; it is a gift from God. It has nothing to do with works and there is no reason for any boasting in what we have done (vv. 8–9). The result is that we are a product of God's creative work and power. We have been made alive in Christ for good works. That path was already designed for us to walk in the capability we now have to live in a way that reflects what God desires from our lives (v. 10).

Paul desires that we appreciate the privilege of this new life and the power God has already extended to us. The remarks also underscore the prayer request of 1:19 that we might come to understand the immeasurable greatness of God's power extended towards us. This rooting of our identity in Christ and in what God has done means that our connection to him is worth more than anything else in life. It is also designed to create a sense of gratitude that fuels a life lived worthy of what God has done, growing out of the note of praise that extends as far back as 1:3–14.

iii. A new life of reconciliation of Jew and Gentile (2:11–22)
Context

Paul turns now to thinking more corporately about what God has done for the community. He takes the reality of the hostile and formerly separate Gentiles and discusses their relationship to Jews both before and after their connection to Christ. Paul is forging a new identity for them, or better, is asking them to recall God forging such a new identity for them. Jesus has brought together those who had been hopelessly at odds with one another and with God. This unit shows how Christ has become our peace, drawing together and reconciling that which had been estranged. In that act of peace tied to the cross, Jesus has made a new entity, the one new man, which now needs to grow into fullness. This corporate overview shows how salvation is about more than the saving of individuals;[63] it is about a restoration of the creation at all levels. This makes possible a different kind of relating in the world that is a goal of salvation and which can also attract others to God. The power of reconciliation is something the church needs to appreciate as it is one of the most concrete ways to display that God is at work. Here is yet another aspect of God's working of power that the church is to appreciate (1:19). The doctrinal comment serves to underscore the prayer request.

There is another important point in this section. This unit is the ground for the good work of evidencing reconciliation that the church is supposed to carry out in the world. God has done a work of reconciliation between people, and not just between the individual and God. This reconciliation is the first work that is an illustration of where God is taking us as a community. In other words, 2:11–22 develops 2:10 as an example by reviewing the start of the journey. The work of our unity together and of reconciliation with people is rooted in what God has done for us.

Comment

11. Paul now turns his attention to who the bulk of the Ephesians were as Gentiles before they entered into the promise by faith. What has been said of individual salvation also has a corporate application, so Paul opens this paragraph with *therefore*. How God saves the individual leads into what that means for a larger circle of relationships. One flows inevitably into the other. This is part of the summing up of all things in Christ (1:10). *Remember that formerly you, the Gentiles in the flesh* . . . Remembrance is important as it reminds us where we started. It is all too easy to forget what God has done for us and where we once were after having been in a different place for a long time. Paul does not want them to forget how indebted

---

63. This idea, and the importance of a corporate perspective on salvation, is nicely discussed in Darko, 'What Does It Mean to Be Saved?', pp. 44–56.

they are to God so the present imperative (*mnēmoneuete*) calls them to continue to recall these realities. The phrase *in the flesh* followed later in the verse by the reference to circumcision by hands looks at one level of identity – that initial, physical level of self-understanding for Gentiles and Jews respectively. In the flesh, before God acted, the Gentiles were far from God. This was *formerly*, the way things were before God acted to change them, as verse 13 will show. The 'formerly but now' approach mirrors the way Paul reviewed the salvation of the individual in 2:1–3 by starting with where they were before God acted. The theme of an important recollection, an *anamnesis*, forms the genre of the unit (cf. Exod. 13:3).[64] Doctrinal recollection is what Paul sets forth here.

Here also is the basis for the you–us contrast we have argued was previewed earlier. Jews and Gentiles were, at one time, quite separated from each other. A separation from God because of sin had left them also estranged from each other. One led into the other. These Gentiles were outside of blessing, *called 'uncircumcision' by the so-called 'circumcision' that is performed . . . by . . . hands*. Ezekiel 44:7, 9 shows this situation, something God was going to work to reverse, while access to blessing had also been part of the initial calling of the nation of Israel to be a blessing for the nations (Gen. 12:3; Isa. 42:1, 6; 49:6). To leave people where they are, outside of God, is not the kind of community Paul sees the gospel envisioning.

Paul signals a problem with mere physical circumcision by his labelling of it as a circumcision *by human hands*. References to things done by hands are always negative in the New Testament (Mark 14:58; Acts 7:48; 17:24; Col. 2:11; Heb. 9:11, 24; in the OT LXX, Isa. 2:18; 10:11). This is Paul's first hint that Jews also needed what God would provide in Christ.[65] There is a circumcision of the heart that Paul regards positively (Rom. 2:28–29). There is the rite, the circumcision made by hands without the heart, and then there is having the heart behind the rite (Lev. 26:41; Deut. 10:16; Jer. 4:4; Phil. 3:3). Paul is saying that without the heart, the act is irrelevant (Rom. 2:29;

---

64. Schnackenburg, pp. 102–103.

65. Best, p. 239, is probably wrong to see nothing negative here given the use of it being performed by hands. Still, it is a subtle criticism.

1 Cor. 7:19; Gal. 5:6; Phil. 3:2; Col. 2:11), even though the rite was commanded in Genesis 17:10–14. Still Gentiles, as reported by Jews, saw this rite as odd and ridiculed it (Josephus, *Ant.* 2.137; Philo, *Special Laws* 1.2).

Yet the Gentiles were also on the outside looking in. They did not even have the rite. From a Jewish perspective, Gentiles lacked the sign of covenant relationship with God (Ps. 147:20: no other nation knew his ordinances).[66] The hostility between the two groups could be intense, as a book like 1 Maccabees shows during the Maccabean War. This event and others like it show that many Jews saw Gentiles as a threat to the practices of their faith. The estrangement was at two levels – from God and from each other – and it could be deep.

12. Paul now gives a résumé of the spiritual qualifications the Gentiles lacked before God acted: *in the former time you were without Christ, alienated from the citizenship of Israel and strangers from the covenants of promise, not having hope and godless in the world* (author's translation). The Gentiles lacked serious spiritual credentials in five areas. The last point in the list, that they were without hope and godless in the world, shows how dire their corporate situation was. The listing is the reverse of what Paul says about Jews in Romans 9:3–5 (also Rom. 3:1–2).

They were without a *Christ*. There was no expectation of a deliverer sent from God, a promise Jews had from long before (Gen. 49:10; Pss 2:1–7; 110:1–4; Isa. 9:1–7; Dan. 7:13–14; Mic. 5:1–4). Best notes that a Jewish list might not start here because of the importance of the law and temple.[67] So starting here is a Christian perspective on the hope of the nation: they were looking for a Messiah.

The Gentiles did not have *citizenship* with the people of *Israel*, a chosen people of hope (Deut. 7:6–8). They stood *alienated* from Israel. The perfect tense (*apēllotriōmenoi*) points to a continuing status. This is a reference not so much to a nation, since Rome occupied and controlled the territory of Israel, as to a recognized

---

66. Bruce, p. 292.

67. Best, pp. 240–241, 244.

people: a community organized around the one true God. Not only were Gentiles alienated from that group, but there had also been a long history of conflict and tension between them.

The result was that they were also *strangers* to the *covenants*, the line of promises tied to Abraham (Gen. 12:1–3; 15:8–18; 17:1–14), Moses (Exod. 24:1–8), David (2 Sam. 7:12–17; Pss 89:3–4, 26–37; 132:11–12) and the nation at large (Jer. 31:31–34; 32:38–40; Ezek. 36:23–36). There is some discussion about whether the Mosaic covenant is included in this as it is characterized by Paul as coming after *promise* in Galatians 3. Whether it is part of the promise or not depends on whether the Mosaic covenant is seen as tied to its stipulations or as a direction in which God is taking his people. In the former, it is not a covenant of promise. Ephesians 2:15 says as much at this level (also Gal. 4:24). In the latter sense, it is a covenant of promise because it pointed to the hope (Luke 24:44–47; Rom. 4). Wrapped up in this hope was the expectation of deliverance into a new unending life, the hope of resurrection (Acts 24:15; 26:6–8; 28:20; Rom. 8:30–38; 15:13). Note how the covenants have a promise. The hope is tied to all that comes with Christ, as the rest of the passage will show.

There are two outcomes noted at the end: they had *no hope* (1 Thess. 4:13) and were *godless* (1 Cor. 8:5; Gal. 4:8; 1 Thess. 4:5). Without a messianic hope and without a covenant connection to God with its hope of deliverance and life, Gentiles were on the outside looking in as far as Paul is concerned. There is irony here, because Gentiles followed many gods and considered monotheists like Christians and Jews as atheists for not having their array of gods. Ephesus was no exception as the city thrived because of its relationship to Artemis. The issue from Paul's perspective was the lack of promise tied to those connections and the lack of real divine presence. The gods they had were 'gods in name only'.[68]

13. *But now* things had all changed. Paul introduces what God had done in Christ: *in Christ Jesus you who used to be far away have been brought near by the blood of Christ.* The phrase *in Christ* is thrown forward for emphasis. This is where the revolutionary alteration of

---

68. So Foulkes, p. 88.

relationship took place. The reference to nearness does not mean proximity but entrance, as verses 18–22 make clear (cf. Acts 2:39). The argument is like that of Isaiah 57:19, although there it is likely about Jews whether near or in diaspora (cf. Acts 22:21) and it might include nations alluded to in Isaiah 55:5 and 56:6–8.[69] The idea of being near also came to be used of proselyte discussion in Judaism (*Mekilta* on Exod. 18:5).[70] Paul is saying that alienation and estrangement are gone – not only between God and these groups, but between these peoples as well. What Christ did changed the Gentiles' contact with God and also their relationship to Jews. The passive verb speaks of God bringing them near, so they did not have anything to do with this move; it was God's act that did it. It was the sacrificial death of Christ that made it all possible (Rom. 5:9; Eph. 1:7; Col. 1:20). God forms a triangle by what he does in Christ; reconciliation pulls people together before God. Paul now shows exactly how because Gentiles are not the only ones who have been moved into this position.

14. Paul provides an explanation of how the Gentiles were brought near as this verse begins with the linking word *for*. The explanation begins with the note that Jesus *is our peace*. That explanation is set out in more detail in verses 14–18. This is not just about peace between people and God, but peace between peoples, thus *our* peace. The allusion to peace may evoke the messianic hope of Isaiah 9:6 and 52:7, where the gospel is associated with peace and the Prince of Peace. The latter passage connects to the idea of the near and far in Isaiah 57:19. This is what Jesus' death accomplished. Caesar may be exalted in society as responsible for Rome's peace, the Pax Romana, but Jesus is responsible for the peace of humanity.

He is the one *who has made us both one*. Jesus has brought the estranged together. He is the one who has *destroyed the middle wall of partition, the hostility*. The phrases *made* and *destroyed* are the first two of three uses of a participle in verses 14–15 to describe what Jesus has done. With that barrier removed, unity is possible. In fact, that is the point. The peace that has been made has reconstituted how

---

69. Thielman, p. 158.
70. Lincoln, p. 139.

Gentiles and Jews should see themselves in relationship to each other. They share a place in the body of Christ.

Believing Gentiles and Jews are one in Christ (Rom. 12:5; 1 Cor. 1:13; 12:12–13, 27). Jesus took the two groups and made them a part of each other as they were connected to him. He took what separated them and destroyed it. The term *middle wall* (*mesotoichon*) can refer to an outside wall or to a division in a house or temple (1 Kgs 6:16–17), while *partition* (*phagmos*) is often a reference to a fence that hedges one in (Isa. 5:2; Matt. 21:33; Mark 12:1).

It is much discussed what this division was and what produced the *hostility*, or enmity. There are three views. First, some interpret it in terms of the 4 ft-plus wall that separated the outer area of the temple from the inner area (Josephus, *Ant.* 15.417). This marked the limit to Gentile access to the temple area, marked by signs designating it as such: 'No foreigner is to enter within the balustrade and forecourt around the sacred precinct. Whoever is caught will himself be responsible for (his) consequent death.'[71] Paul was arrested on the false charge of having violated this custom by allegedly bringing a Gentile into the temple area (Acts 21:29–30). The problem with this view is that it is hard to know if Gentiles far removed from Jerusalem and the temple would have understood the allusion. It might well be a picture of what is in view here, but the wall itself is not the point; rather, it is what it might symbolize. The picture of a renewed temple at the end of this passage in verses 21–22 might favour this option.[72] Against it is that the terminology for that wall does not match the term Paul uses here.

A second view suggests that Paul understood a separation of heaven from earth as rooted in Gnostic cosmology, such that Israel was protected from the errors of idolatry. The fullness of the phrase *middle wall of partition* and the reference to the law as an obstacle in verse 15 argue against this view, as it is not clear that partition points to heaven when the law is contextually in view.

---

71. Foulkes, p. 89; the citation is from the *Corpus Inscriptionum Iudaeae/Palaestinae*, vol. I.1, edited by H. M. Cotton et al. (Berlin: De Gruyter, 2010), no. 2.

72. So Arnold, pp. 159–160.

A third, more general view is that the reference is a metaphor for the social and cultural separation of the two groups.[73] It is likely that this is what is meant, although the temple wall image might also be in play. Jews in Ephesus were known for keeping the law (Josephus, *Ant.* 14.228, 234, 240), so it is likely that the social distance the law created is in view. The law was seen as a fence in Judaism (*m. 'Abot* 1.1; *Letter of Aristeas* 139–142; *1 Enoch* 93:6). That enmity was destroyed by the death of Jesus, *in his flesh*, as we connect that phrase with the previous one rather than with what follows. Its placement between the two descriptions of activity in verses 14–15 has made its reference disputed, but its connection with the previous idea is more likely because of proximity. This placement is distinct from that of many translations, including the RSV and NET which tie 'in his flesh' to nullifying the law of commandments. The difference is not great as it is Jesus' death that accomplishes this, but the question is whether Paul is focused on the point of origin or the result. Regardless of the view taken, the expression's central location underscores how Jesus' death is in the middle of all that has been accomplished. Jesus' death brought peace, not so much by removing the enmity of the law itself, which was from God for a time (Gal. 3), as by addressing the attitude of distinction and pride that the law could produce, as well as the conditions of separation and condemnation it brought (Col. 2:14). Verse 16 has the phrase 'bringing the hostility to an end' to reinforce the idea here. What also opens up the opportunity for Jews and Gentiles to function together in peace is the shift in the role of the law. Jesus' death deals with the law's penalty, disposing of it. One consequence is that the law's ascetic practices are no longer in play. Importantly, Paul highlights the

---

73. So Lincoln, p. 141, though his idea of seeing an adaptation of a cosmic Gnostic reference is unlikely. It is not attested early enough to be in view; see Bruce, p. 296, who sees the temple barrier as possibly in view as part of a larger metaphor. The whole problem of views and the syntax is fully discussed in Best, pp. 253–258, who opts for the simple metaphor of view 3 and takes the syntax as we do, with 'in his flesh' looking back. Hoehner, pp. 371–373, opts to take the 'in his flesh' phrase with what follows.

practices that are no longer obstacles because Paul's view of the law focuses on the promise realized. So the law is still effectively present in the fact that the promise stands realized, so that other legal stipulations setting up that promise are no longer in force. Galatians 3 says this in a distinct way with a focus on circumcision. Those stipulations now put aside are in view here. It is the wall that Jesus destroys by what he did with the law in his flesh – not the law itself, as aspects of it still have value, but the attitudes and conditions of separation that the law produced. In the new temple (vv. 21–22; 1 Cor. 3:16–17) that Jesus creates, all the nations can share equally in access to and in the worship of God (see v. 18; Isa. 2:1–4).

15. The third participle of the sequence in verses 14–15 appears here: *when he nullified the law of the commandments in decrees* (author's translation). So Jesus (1) made the two one, (2) removed the barrier that produced enmity and (3) nullified the law of the commandments in decrees. Jesus' death took care of the law and its penalties. This third point gives us more details on the second point: it tells us how the barrier was removed. Jesus did what others could not do by bearing the law's penalty and thus opening the door for a different kind of access to God (Rom. 3:19–31; 7:6). The impact was a shift in how God administers salvation: where the law was a primary guide before, now it is the Spirit in Christ (Rom. 7:1–6; 10:4; Gal. 2:19; 3:1 – 4:6; Eph. 2:18). The role of the law in 'regulating the covenant relationship' between God and people has passed.[74] The reference implies the new covenant (2 Cor. 3:1–6), a covenant that is not like the one made at Sinai (thus Jer. 31:32). So the nullification in view is this switch in the administration of God's programme, which the Hebrew Scriptures had anticipated in the announcement of a new covenant. The reference to *commandments in decrees* tells us that it is the law as stipulations that is in view here. There are no distinctions here between ceremonial and moral portions of the law; all the stipulations are in view, and it is the penalties tied to that law that is the point of focus. Colossians 2:14 gives us even more detail, saying it was our indebtedness that Jesus dealt with on the cross (Gal. 3:13). The law as promise with its direction of pleasing God is realized in

---

74. So Arnold, p. 162.

Jesus and continues its life through the means the deliverer provides. Ephesians emphasizes the result, while Colossians tells us how that result came about. The pedagogue role of the law is gone (Gal. 3:25). It is in this sense that Jesus fulfils the law (Matt. 5:17–48; Gal. 5:2–15; 6:2). His provision enables us to do what the law pushed for in its stipulations: to love God and others (Rom. 13:8–10).

The results of Jesus' death on the cross changed the world and the potential relationships between people: *that he might create in himself one new man*[75] *in place of the two, so making peace.* This is the first of two purposes Paul notes for Jesus' work. Jesus has formed a new community. Just as if one is in Christ, one is a new creation (2 Cor. 5:17), so with Jesus' work there is a new community in the world. The new *man* is humanity reformed, no longer tied to Adam but now in Christ, incorporated into the new people God is forming from him. Colossians 3:10 also uses this image, and in that context we are told that in the 'new man' there are no distinguished groups of people but all share an identity focused on Christ. This is part of the workmanship God created us to be (Eph. 2:10; the Greek verb *ktizō*, to create, is used in both verses). Both Jews and Gentiles who believe and benefit from what Christ has done are moved into this new entity. The picture is not of Gentiles becoming Jews or simply moving into their space. Those who were near and those who were far are both now brought into something new, which is why Paul calls it the *one new man*. We see the reconciliation in that we know they are Jew and Gentile, but now Christ unites them. The result is the 'peace' that Paul affirmed as tied to Christ in verse 14. This will be called 'one body' in verse 16. It is a new race in which the weaving together of that which had been separate is clear.

This has been called the 'third' race, neither Jew nor Gentile,[76] though we are to retain the understanding that God has woven these two together in a way that allows us to see the two made one. There is no segregation in Christ, even in the midst of recognizing

---

75. This expression is translated as 'new humanity' (NIV, NRSV) or 'new people' (NLT) to show its corporate thrust.

76. Lincoln, p. 144. See Clement of Alexandria, *Stromateis* 6.5.41; *Diognetus* 1 – 'new race' and not Jew or Gentile; Tertullian, *Scorpiace* 10.

a distinction in where each group came from before being united, for reconciliation is only clear when the former estrangement is appreciated. In practice, this will allow each group some measure of distinction, as opposed to homogeneity (Rom. 14 – 15). Gentiles are not made into Jews or vice versa.[77] They are who they are and yet they now function side by side and together, with Christ uniting them rather than the law dividing them. Their bond of oneness transcends the distinctions they also might have in some everyday practices. This reconciliation is available only to those who embrace what God has offered, for this deliverance into reconciliation comes by faith (vv. 8–10). There is no idea in Paul of a dual covenant whereby Jews and Gentiles are saved by distinct paths to God. All roads come in and through Christ.

16. There is a second purpose to Christ's becoming our peace. Beyond the creation of the 'new man', Jesus' work also brings reconciliation of the two groups to God. So Jesus is our peace (v. 14) that he *might reconcile us both to God in one body through the cross* (Rom. 5:10; 2 Cor. 5:19; Col. 1:20, 22; 2:14–15). The term for *reconcile* (*apokatallassō*) has a prefix tied to it and is the first attested use we have of the term, along with Colossians 1:20 and 22. It makes the reference to reconciliation emphatic. The one 'new man' is now equated with the church, with the reconciliation going in three ways: reconciliation of Jews to God, reconciliation of Gentiles to God, and reconciliation of Jews and Gentiles to each other as a result. It is important to note that all are reconciled to God. Here is an indication that Jews needed the reconciliation as much as Gentiles. Unlike other restorations, there is no idea that the text is describing the restoration of a previously lost unity, as the separation had existed between these groups ever since the formation of the people of Israel. What has been regained is the purpose for which people were created – that is, to relate positively to the living God in a restored image of God. In other words, this is a core corporate goal of the

---

77. Fowl, p. 95, says it this way: 'For now let it suffice to say that the new person created in Christ brings Jews and Gentiles together into one body without requiring them to submit to a homogenizing erasure of their identity as Jews and Gentiles.'

entire exercise of salvation, and the church has an obligation to witness to this result of the gospel to show salvation's scope. In fact, doing so testifies to the character of the gospel in restoring broken relationships, even at a corporate and social level. These social implications of the gospel have often been undervalued in the church, which has often been slow to see the corporate reach of the gospel, preferring instead to focus on how salvation affects the individual. Yet both individual and corporate dimensions are present in this text.

Through that reconciliation, Christ finds himself *thereby bringing the hostility to an end*. The untranslated 'in it' that concludes verse 16 probably refers to the cross, not to Jesus; but the two are, of course, intertwined. If Christ were meant, we would expect a reflexive here, since Jesus is already in view as the actor in the sentence. The alternative reflexive does appear in a variant reading that is not as well attested. In addition, the enmity being removed does not involve any enmity tied to Christ himself, but a reference to him might suggest that is the case.[78] The act of Christ in his death removes the barrier and clears the shared path to God for both groups (Gal. 6:14). That one act was like a bulldozer clearing the way for access. The enmity here is different from the enmity in verse 14. There it was between the groups, while here it is between them and God, so the loop is now closed. Normally it is God who reconciles, but here it is the Christ. The divine act tied to salvation reveals the exalted status of Jesus.

17. Christ's work has led to a message for the world. He came and *preached peace to you who were far off and peace to those who were near*. This is a reference to the goal of Jesus' life and coming and what has happened as a result of that, since in his ministry Jesus focused on preaching in Israel (Matt. 10:5–6; 15:24–27). The apostles, through the Spirit, preached that message, the roots of which are in what he came to do and be (Eph. 3:5, 8). The apostles are seen as representatives of Christ. Jesus' ultimate goal was wider than just Israel. So Paul talks of *you* and addresses the Gentile readers directly yet again, as he did at the start of this unit. The reconciliation

---

78. So correctly argued by Best, p. 266.

resulting from Jesus' life and death was for all the creation and those in it (Rom. 8:18–39).

The terms *far* and *near* repeat the contrast between Gentiles and Jews that has been evident in the entire passage. Peace was offered to both, and both received it in relationship to each other and to God. This looks back to verses 12–13, where this unit started. Those who were far away are now near. The language of Isaiah 57:19 is in the background.[79] The only difference with Isaiah 57 is that there the referents were Jews in exile; here it is all who are far away and can be brought near. The principle of that passage now applies to a broader group. The idea of evangelizing in the verse takes language from Isaiah 52:7. The preaching of *peace* represents an alternative to 'the hostile name-calling mentioned in 2:11' that is the result of Christ's work;[80] the injection of his presence changes everything. Paul ties the note of peace to Christ and not to the Pax Romana. That would be a counter-cultural note. The way to bring people together was not through the structures of the surrounding society but through what Christ has done.[81]

Ephesians 2:17 also looks back to verse 15, where believing Jews are also incorporated in the one 'new man'. The reference to peace fits with verses 14 and 16. So we have a verse that summarizes much of the unit. Paul says in verse 14 that Jesus is our peace, and in the current verse that peace is preached as a result of Jesus' coming (Acts 10:36; Rom. 10:14–17; Eph. 6:15). To get to peace, one must respond to the offer.

18. Paul now shares what results from that peace: *through him we both have access in one Spirit to the Father*. Everything Gentiles were separated from in verse 12 has now been reversed. They have a

---

79. For the idea that Ezek. 37 is also in the background, forming a framework for the unit, see Suh, 'Use of Ezekiel 37', pp. 715–733.

80. As eloquently put by Barth I, p. 266.

81. This theme as it is manifested in Africa, but could be applied elsewhere, is shown in Yorke, 'Hearing the Politics of Peace', pp. 113–127. For how this reconciliation fits with other Pauline letters and how uniquely its cosmic scope is presented in Ephesians, see Turner, 'Human Reconciliation', pp. 37–47.

Messiah, they have a connection with Israel, they participate in the covenants and they possess hope in a relationship with God. Paul has extolled and recalled to memory the distance amazing grace has covered through Christ. Separation has been dealt with and distance no longer exists. In a Trinitarian take on the results of the proclamation, both groups possess the Spirit and have access to the Father because of the work of Christ (cf. 1 Pet. 3:18). The point is not to refer to a cause but to the results of the response to the proclamation, because, as Hoehner says, 'to say that Christ preached peace to Jews and Gentiles because we have access does not make good sense'.[82] To see cause here puts the cart before the horse. This is only the cause *if* one has responded. The Trinitarian theme is also in 1:4–14; 3:14–17; 4:4–6; and 5:18–20.

The key word is *access* (*prosagōgē*).[83] The picture is of access to the family and people of God, since it is *to the Father* they have access. Access that also gives the secure status of God's family members is the point (Rom. 5:2). There is more than the idea of introduction here; it involves participation, so the term is intransitive in force. Whether one thinks of access in the temple because one is qualified to be there by the presentation of a sacrifice (Lev. 1:2–3, 10), or of an audience with a king (Xenophon, *Cyropaedia* 7.5.46–47), the point is the freedom to be present (1 Kgs 8:41–43; Isa. 56:6–8; Zech. 8:20–23). Christ's death makes that possible both now and in the age to come. The book of Hebrews makes a similar point in speaking of our drawing near, which is a response to the access we now possess as believers (Heb. 4:16; 7:19; 10:19–22).[84]

The distance they have come since what is described in 2:1–3, 11–12 is amazing: from death, wrath and separation to entry and welcome. The two groups share the possession of the same Spirit, linking them to God and to one another, the sign of the new covenant (1 Cor. 12:13; 2 Cor. 3). There is no longer a distinction in terms of their access (Rom. 3:21–24; 10:12; Col. 3:11; Titus 2:14; 1 Pet. 2:4–10; Rev. 5:9; 7:9). The remark shows how important the

---

82. Hoehner, p. 388.

83. BDAG, p. 876.

84. Bruce, p. 301.

Spirit is to the gospel (Rom. 8:14–16; Gal. 3:14; 4:6). The gospel
gives us not only salvation and eternal life, but also a way to relate
to God during all that time. The presence of the Spirit makes them
holy, a sacred space that Paul will develop into a picture of a temple
in verses 19–22 (1 Cor. 3:16; 6:19).

19. The access they have and the removal of the barrier means
that reconciliation has produced a revolutionary result. The point is
noted emphatically with the use of two Greek terms for 'therefore'
or *so then* (Greek *ara oun*). Gentiles are *no longer foreigners and noncitizens,
but you are fellow citizens with the saints and members of God's household.*
The repetition of the *syn-* prefix from 2:5–6 underscores the unity
that emerges when Jews and Gentiles are seen as *fellow* (or co-)
citizens. The picture of being *members* in the *household of God* also
underscores the entrance into the family of God and the new social
community he has formed in Christ. Welcome to the family as a full
member is the point.

The verse is first negative, in explaining what they no longer are,
and then moves on positively to say who they are. They are *no longer
foreigners.* This is a reversal of a status noted in verse 12. The second
term, *paroikos*, anticipates the term to come in the verse, *oikeioi*: they
were outside of the house looking in, *noncitizens* or 'aliens', but
they are no longer such aliens; now they are in. Paul turns positive.
The Gentile believers now share citizenship (*sympolitai*) with the
saints and are full household members. This term of citizenship
also links back to verse 12 (*politeia*). The picture is of full kinship
with others. The family of God is made whole when Jews and
Gentiles are united in faith in Christ (Gal. 6:10; Heb. 11:13; 13:14).
There are no levels of citizenship in Christ; all share in the family.
That family is made up of the saved of all ages, but what Paul is
referring to here are those who are a part of this new house, the
new man (vv. 15–16).[85] When all is summed up in Christ (1:10), he
is the reason why we have what we have from God – not our
ethnicity or anything else we might bring (Heb. 3:2, 5–6; 12:22–24);
and what God has done in Christ is a turning point in that work.
This is a heavenly citizenship (Gal. 3:26; Phil. 3:20). The term *saints*

---

85. Arnold, p. 168.

refers to all those set apart to God in Christ as those who have responded in faith to the gospel. They do not earn that saintly status; it is a gift that comes with being the recipients of God's grace. This will mean there is no preference for the Jew or Gentile, something Paul addresses more fully in Romans 11. God is building a new sacred space on earth in the midst of a creation needing redemption. So the picture of a temple will follow.

The church is a community whose corporate, multi-ethnic identity is central to its self-understanding and witness.[86] Their sense of community is tied explicitly to their being connected to God and his functioning presence, something that makes them as a whole a temple of the presence of God, both as individuals, as 1 Corinthians 6:12–20 teaches, and as a group, no matter their locale, as Ephesians 2:19–22 will affirm. The correlating responsibility is to show who we are in our relationships and in our vocations, something the household codes of 5:22 – 6:9 will develop along with the entire application section of the letter in chapters 4–6. This involves a push for a multi-ethnic presence, sensitivity and awareness across the church. Such awareness serves as a godly example of relationships within that community, before the world and in interaction with the world. It makes a people out of those who were not a people and transcends national or ethnic identities for those in Christ, yet in a way that honours each group that makes up the whole.

20. This new temple (v. 21) is built on a solid foundation, as Paul switches to an architectural image: it is a *foundation of the apostles and prophets, Christ Jesus himself being the cornerstone*. Since this is a new work (vv. 15–16) and the apostles are mentioned first, it is apostles and prophets of the new era that are in view, not Old Testament prophets. They are also seen as a unit because the two terms are tied together by one article. From these the building is being built. *Apostles* includes people like Barnabas, not just the Twelve (Acts 14:1, 4, 14; 1 Cor. 9:5–6). New Testament *prophets* spoke into the situation of the churches (Acts 11:28; 13:1–3; 21:9–10; 1 Cor. 14:4,

---

86. The idea expressed in this paragraph is developed with a nice treatment in Pereira, 'Ephesians', pp. 1–12.

6, 30–31). Paul will come back to mention this group as he discusses the 'mystery' in 3:5–6. He covers both groups in 4:11.

The essential building block is *Jesus* himself, referred to as a *cornerstone*, likely an allusion to Isaiah 28:16 LXX (cf. 1 Pet. 2:6). There is discussion as to whether the term *akrogōniaios* refers to a corner-stone or a capstone. However, the context here is clear: we are dealing with the building from the ground up without having reached the end of it yet. So a foundational cornerstone is probably meant, as also in 1 Corinthians 3:10–17.[87] In singling out Jesus, it is also clear that his position is distinct from and crucial to the building, as is indicated by everything else the letter has said about him.

The metaphor works with others in the letter about Jesus. Elsewhere, when the body is meant, Jesus is seen as the guiding head at the top of things (1:22), but that is a distinct image. The two images work together to describe who Jesus is, but they are not similar images. They go side by side to make distinct points.

21. It is in Christ that the building also grows: *in him the whole building, being joined together, grows into a holy temple in the Lord.* This new entity is a sacred space in the midst of a common world. The church is dynamic as it is growing (cf. 1 Pet. 2:5). The joining together of the pieces of the temple allows it to grow. Another *syn-* prefix of the participle *being joined* [or 'fitted'] *together* (*synarmologoumenē*) points to the repeated emphasis on God bringing Jew and Gentile together. The present tense sees this as currently taking place. This exact term will appear again in 4:16. The growth pictures the reality that more people are coming into the church, and may suggest that maturity is being added to the church all the time. The emphasis here is on the adding of people as the church grows, but their maturity is where the discussion is headed later. People are fitted into and are transformed in the church (2 Cor. 3:18; Phil. 3:21). In Colossians 2:19, a metaphor using the body makes a similar point.

God is responsible for this fitting together, so it is something the parts of the temple should recognize. They are designed to function

---

87. Hoehner, pp. 406–407, gives a detailed defence of 'cornerstone'. Opting for 'capstone' is Lincoln, pp. 154–156. He sees it as fitting the idea of Jesus exalted as head.

together. God also has given them all that is necessary to make that design work. The image is important as it takes a great deal of work to smooth the edges of stones so that they fit together to form a building. The fit is snug.[88] The term *the whole building* refers to the singularity of the church in all its locales. Grammatically, Paul could be referring to each church, but the image in the background is of the one foundation and the one building that is the temple. So the unity of the design is another key point; God has brought them together to function together.

The term for *temple* (*naos*) is important. It refers to the most sacred part of the temple, the holy place and holy of holies (Matt. 27:51; Mark 15:38; Luke 23:45). This is the place where God was said to dwell. The point is that the church is God's inner sanctum, the place of God's presence, in the world. We have truly been brought near. This temple is holy, set apart to God, and is that which represents him in the world. For a city that had its own magnificent temple to Artemis, the image is a powerful one. The real transcendent presence resides in the church, not with the goddess. The church's presence points to God's presence. In another series of texts, Paul makes it clear that we are accountable for how we function in this sacred space (1 Cor. 3:10–17; 2 Cor. 6:16; 1 Tim. 3:15).

22. Paul now focuses on the Ephesians in particular. In Christ as well (v. 20) they *also are being built together into a dwelling place of God in the Spirit*. Once again the *syn-* prefix on *oikodomeisthe* expresses that they are *being built together* into this dwelling place of God. As in the previous verse, the present tense points to a current activity. The term for *dwelling place* is *katoikētērion*. It is a rarely used term in the LXX referring to God's dwelling place whether in heaven or in Zion (Exod. 15:17; 1 Kgs 8:13, 39, 43, 49; 2 Chr. 30:27). Paul says that the Spirit activates and energizes the community. So, in Christ, a sacred dwelling of God exists empowered by God's Spirit. The Trinitarian activity is highlighted at the end of the unit.[89] God is in the midst of his people, and that includes the Gentile believers.

---

88. Thielman, p. 184.
89. Snodgrass, p. 139.

These closing verses make it clear that to be brought near (v. 13) is to be brought in.

Theology

The dominant idea of this unit is the reconciliation and unity God has brought across racial lines in the work of Christ for those in the church.[90] The constant refrain of 'together', repeated three times in the closing verses, makes clear this emphasis on appreciating reconciliation as a goal of the gospel. The powerful bringing together of Jew and Gentile into a new sacred work of God in the world is the point. That idea of appreciating the power of God takes us back to the prayer request of 1:19. This appreciation is not just for individuals, but is a corporate idea to be shared across the church. Gentiles and Jews are to appreciate that all are full members of the household of God. Their shared identity does not obliterate who they were but accentuates the fact that it is God who has brought them together, giving them a new relationship and network, making them true spiritual kin. The passage calls them to recall these truths and then to act on them. The attitude runs counter to the normal ethnic focus people have. The point is not that people should not see race, but that they should live with an appreciation that races were designed by God in Christ to function together. As absent as that reality often is in the world, it should look different in the church. At the centre of it all is the work of Christ and the reception of it by those who are his.

---

90. For how this reconciliation ties together many scriptural themes in Jesus' ministry, Paul and Revelation, see Keener, 'One New Temple in Christ', pp. 75–92. Here is Keener's conclusion (p. 92): 'How central is our unity in Christ? It is central enough to transcend all other loyalties, so that loyalty to Christ entails loyalty to one another as God's family, above all ethnic, cultural and earthly kinship connections. It is central enough that Paul repeatedly emphasizes it as a necessary corollary of the gospel. It is central enough that the worship God desires is a united worship of believers from many peoples and languages. We are different, bringing diverse cultural gifts; but we are one, for God, the Lord whom we worship, is One.'

2. PAUL'S CALLING IN THE MYSTERY TO MINISTER TO THE GENTILES CULMINATES IN PRAYER FOR STRENGTH AND A BENEDICTION OF GOD'S CAPABILITY (3:1–21)

Paul now takes up his own role in all that he has described and prayed for in the praise of God's work on their behalf and in the prayer to appreciate God's power and life-giving work of grace. At the centre of that work is Paul's understanding of the mystery – how Gentiles have been incorporated into the people of God. It now stands revealed that Gentiles are full co-participants in the blessings that come in Christ Jesus. With their role in place, Paul prays that the Ephesians might be strengthened for the task of reflecting Christ and appreciating the boundless extent of God's activity for them and Christ's love to them, so that they can be filled with God's fullness. Paul closes the unit noting that God is able to do even more than we ask or think. What Paul asks of the Ephesians, God is more than able to do for them.

A. Paul's calling to minister the mystery for Gentiles (3:1–13)

Context

Paul moves to pray, only to get distracted by the nature of his own calling. This passage is a long parenthesis that also is full of theological content about God's plan. Within that plan lies what Paul calls a mystery now revealed. He flashes a spotlight on his role within this currently activated divine programme of bringing Jew and Gentile together. This mystery, of how Gentiles are full members of God's programme, is now more fully revealed. That plan reflects the wisdom of God now on display before the creation. Nothing that is currently taking place with Paul, including any persecution, should discourage them; he is getting on with the task of carrying out the assignment God has given him to make this mystery known. That plan reflects the riches of Christ in a programme God is executing. Paul presents it mostly in one long sentence, running from verses 2 to 13 and consisting of 189 words![1] In this section, Paul is presenting his right to write to them. It is an appropriate extension of his ministry on behalf of Gentiles, a ministry in which he claims to have special insight.

Comment

1. All that Paul has described leads him into what he will say next, so he says *For this reason* . . . The idea, however, breaks off into a long parenthesis, and only emerges as a prayer for them in verse 14. The repetition of 'For this reason' in verse 14 shows the resumption into prayer. What distracts Paul is his self-description as a *prisoner for Christ Jesus on behalf of you Gentiles.* In describing himself as a *prisoner* or one who is fettered, Paul is pointing to his persecution and suffering for the cause of Christ as his representative. The term *desmios* (*prisoner*) is not the normal term used by Paul, but he does use it elsewhere (4:1; Phlm. 1, 9). Later, he will use the alternative image of an ambassador in chains (6:20). This term notes his presence in prison (Phil. 1:12–26). Acts 22 – 28 describes how and why Paul was taken from Jerusalem to Rome as a prisoner.

---

1. Hoehner, p. 417.

The irony is that he was arrested on the false charge of having brought a Gentile into the temple area, although what Paul is referring to here is his ministry's focus on bringing the message about Gentile inclusion to the world (Acts 9:15; 22:21; 26:19–23; Gal. 1:16). There also is a double meaning here. Paul is a prisoner because of Christ and also because Christ has called him to serve the cause of God in the gospel. This special focus now gains Paul's attention as something to develop in his letter. It becomes clear that Paul does not want them to be overly concerned about his being in prison because suffering for the faith comes with his call (Eph. 3:13; Phil. 2:17; Col. 1:24; 2 Tim. 1:8).

2. Paul's digression begins by raising the possibility that they may have heard of his role in the programme of God: *if indeed you have heard of the stewardship of God's grace that was given to me for you*. Two key ideas dominate this verse: the idea of a stewardship Paul has, and the fact that it was given to him by God for them. Paul is likely assuming that they are aware of this, having *heard* of it before he wrote. The indirect manner in the way Paul says this is probably an indication of the intention to circulate this letter more widely than Ephesus and so not all might know about the special nature of Paul's commission.[2] There also is the factor that it has been years since Paul was with the Ephesians, so the remark is a kind of reminder. Paul expresses the idea in Greek as a first-class condition, which presents the premise as being the case. His expectation is that they do know this.

The term *oikonomia* speaks either of a plan, or of the exercise of a *stewardship* role of administration in the execution of that plan or mission. In 3:9, the term clearly refers to God's plan, as it did in 1:10. So it would make sense for that meaning to be here. God has a plan or programme which he is executing and in which Paul has been given a specific part that focuses on the Gentile community. If the alternative sense is taken, then Paul refers only to his role as a steward of a specific aspect of God's plan, with an enablement he calls *grace* given to him to execute it for the Ephesians. Paul's description of his task elsewhere can also go in either

---

2. Thielman, p. 192.

direction (as a steward: Paul is among the stewards of God's mystery in 1 Cor. 4:1; yet his commission according to the stewardship or management act from God is 'given to me' for the Gentiles, Col. 1:25). This is one of those places where it is hard to be sure of the exact nuance, but it makes little difference in the meaning as the ultimate point is the same: Paul has a commission he is exercising from God that has brought him into contact with Gentiles. This responsibility is part of the divine programme given to Paul, where grace or enablement is at work in his ministry. This all tends to favour the alternative reading where the stewardship is Paul's and *grace* is about the enablement God has given him to minister to Gentiles. This is what the Ephesians should have heard about. A reference to the grace of God in general would not be expressed with such indirectness. However, it is not a commission merely for Paul; it is for those to whom he is writing. Paul's role is one of service to others; it is a commission he has received from God to be exercised for them.

3. Part of the divine commission to Paul involves the direct knowledge he has received about the mystery: *by revelation the divine secret was made known to me, as I wrote before briefly.* In noting this, Paul is indicating the reason why he has the authority and capability to speak to these issues. He is a steward, not an inventor, of the precious message God has given to him.[3] God revealed this to Paul directly, so what he expresses is not the product of his own mind or initiative. The goals of grace and reconciliation are God's agenda. Paul cites *revelation* as the basis for his work and understanding, particularly in settings where there is sensitivity about the topic being covered (Gal. 1:12, 16, probably alluding to the experience of Acts 9 and developed in Acts 22 and 26, esp. 9:15; 22:15; 26:16–18). The mystery Paul preaches is now fully disclosed: God made it known to him. This knowledge, then, is not only given for Paul to teach others, but came from God directly. His insight here serves the church because God called him to reveal it.

Secret, or 'mystery', is a common theme in Paul's writing (Rom. 16:25–26; Eph. 1:9; 3:4–5, 9–10; 6:19; Col. 1:27). The term 'mystery'

---

3. Fowl, p. 107.

is tied to the Old Testament term *rāz* (Dan. 2:18–19, 27–30, 47). It refers to something not previously disclosed but now revealed (Eph. 3:4–5; Col. 1:26; 2:2–3 [revealing what is hidden in Christ]). That mystery can attach to something that has already been revealed and can fill out that previously known thing. That is the case here. As early as Genesis 12:3 there was the idea that the programme of God would bless the world, as in choosing to form Israel God was also seeking to bless the world. The mystery that Paul was preaching about how Christ had brought Gentiles into blessing filled out that initial promise. When Paul explains the content of the mystery in verse 6 as reflecting the fact that Gentiles are full beneficiaries of the promise of God, he summarizes and repeats what he already argued in 2:11–22. In Colossians 1:27, the mystery is Christ in the Gentiles, the hope of glory, but in Ephesians the emphasis is on the corporate oneness of Jew and Gentile and the share the Gentiles have in blessing. This disclosure of the mystery is for all people, making it stand in contrast to mysteries in other Graeco-Roman religions, which were only for initiates to understand.

Paul says he wrote beforehand to them about this. The expression could mean 'wrote in brief'. So when exactly did he do this? It seems most likely that he is referring to what he has just said, especially in 2:11–22. The remark, then, is reflective and in part a recognition of his digression before he goes on to pray. Paul is saying, 'See above for my insight on this', and that insight is what is about to cause him to pray.

4. Paul invites them to reflect on what he called them to remember in 2:11–22. He has put them in a position where the Ephesians are able to *perceive my insight into the mystery of Christ*. His hope is that they will see that what he has told them has the mark of God speaking through a witness who knows what the call of God is. The perceiving spoken of here is public reading, the hearing of the message in the community. In the ancient world, many people could not read and written materials of any sort were relatively rare. Paul's letter would have been sent to the community and read in front of them.

Why would he make such a claim about his understanding? It is likely because a move to unify Jew and Gentile is socially revolutionary for Jews. It is swimming uphill. Paul's claim is that this is not his idea, but one from God. This is not him boasting so much as explaining the role God has assigned to him (2 Cor. 11:6). He is a 'mediator of spiritual insight'.[4] His insight involves the *mystery* of *Christ* – either the mystery that is Christ and his work, or the mystery about him. Paul is speaking specifically about the impact of Christ's work, as the next few verses make clear. The remark looks back to the understanding called for in the prayer of 1:17–19. Part of knowing God and the riches God has provided in Christ is restored relationships.

The mystery of Christ is multifaceted: in Colossians 1:27 it is described as 'Christ in you, the hope of glory'. Paul is not one-dimensional in his thinking, nor is the gospel he preaches one-dimensional.[5] Christ has an impact on the individual and on the community. His impact can and must be considered from either angle.

5. Paul elaborates on how the revelation of the mystery has worked. The mystery *was not made known to the sons of men in other generations as it has now been revealed to his holy apostles and prophets by the Spirit.* There is a double contrast in terms of when this understanding became available and in who got initial access to it. It was not known to people before, but now it has been revealed by God to the apostles and prophets who operate with the presence of the Spirit of God. It is for all who will receive it, but the revelation came through those called to receive it. Even today this is so, as our understanding of the faith is mediated through the scriptural record of what the apostles and prophets of old received. This revelation then was 'hidden' (v. 9) at one time, but not any more (Rom. 16:26; Col. 1:26). Its disclosure represents a major development in the programme of God.

---

4. Lincoln, p. 176, but his take that such boasting in a non-hostile context shows that a pseudonym is at work ignores the mediatorial emphasis Paul sees in a world that thinks otherwise. The issue that introduces tension here is not the hostility of others in the church, but the counter-cultural nature of the calling. Ephesians is very much about the church's place in the world and how to live in the context of that conflict (Eph. 6:12).

5. Foulkes, p. 100.

It is important to be clear about what was hidden and what was not. The Old Testament always had the blessing of the world in mind (Gen. 12:3; 22:18; 26:4; 28:14). It also pointed to a comprehensive deliverance one day (Ps. 89:20–29; Isa. 2:1–4; 11:10; 49:6; 55 – 56). What is new is the idea of the Messiah sending the Spirit to indwell Gentiles and their resultant coequal status in one body tied to Christ. There is continuity and discontinuity in the content of what God is doing in Christ. An implication in all of this is how the role of the law shifted as a result (Gal. 3:1 – 4:6; Eph. 2:13–18). The reference to *apostles and prophets* refers to people in the new era, not the old, as 2:20–22 showed. The *Spirit* is the one in whom this revelation took place. The Spirit is at work in the activity described in this letter (2:18, 22). The apostles and prophets do not speak on their own accord but with a revelation from God. One final point is that Paul is not saying he alone is the source of this message and insight; it is shared with other apostles and prophets. All of this shows that the era of the new covenant did bring new structures in the administration of God's plan, opening up a new era. How this all unfolded for Gentiles is seen in Acts 9 – 20, with Paul having a major role.

6. Paul describes the content of the mystery. It is *that the Gentiles are co-heirs, co-body members and co-sharers of the promise in Christ Jesus through the gospel* (author's translation). As earlier in 2:5–6, 21–22, the *syn-* prefix reappears, indicating the equal status Gentile believers possess. This complete equality changes the way believers are to relate to each other when it comes to race. In fact, that is part and parcel of the gospel message. In Christ, God has brought peoples together. Paul underscores the point by stating the equality three ways: with regard to *heir*-ship (1:11, 14, 18; Rom. 8:17 – children and heirs; Heb. 11:9; 1 Pet. 3:7), membership in the *body* (2:16; 4:4; also 1:23; 4:12, 16; 5:23, 29–30) and connection to the *promise* (Gal. 3:6–29). This promise Paul states in other contexts. It has to do with receiving the Spirit of God, an allusion to new covenant blessing (1:13; Rom. 4:13; 2 Cor. 3; Gal. 3:8, 14). However, to speak of being *co-heirs* suggests there is more to the promise than what has now been inaugurated. All will share in what is to come.

All these benefits come in *Christ Jesus* through *the gospel*, the good news. Paul notes Jesus' work in 2:13–18. Since they have responded to preaching with faith, they participate in this grace (2:8–9). The access to blessing is total. It may well include the idea that Christ's coming reign on earth is something all who are his will share in, including possibly the land promises that also offer Israel peace (Isa. 2:1–4). All share in the comprehensive peace Jesus brings. These acts of God also reverse the curse of 2:12, part of the summing up of all things in Christ (1:10).[6] So we invoke the full list of what they were excluded from in 2:12. As much as the Old Testament promised land and *shalom* to Israel, the remarks here suggest that the blessing on the world will include this for all who share in the Messiah, who is the medium for all these blessings, as in the era to come all people will be at peace and any national borders will mean far less, even as those promises are also realized in the comprehensive peace to come. It is not a problem for the list to the original recipients to be expanded in this way, as the original recipients still receive their promised blessing, while God's word is upheld and shown to be faithful.

7–8. Paul ministers this mystery as a steward empowered by God: *Of this gospel I was made a minister according to the gift of God's grace which was given me by the working of his power.* He is a steward of many mysteries according to 1 Corinthians 4:1. This was a ministry of which he was not worthy, being *the least of all the saints.* Yet God gave him *this grace.* The word for 'steward' is *diakonos*, referring to a servant (6:21), but this servant has been given a grace, a gift that is an ability that equips him for this role and which is called *grace* because it was undeserved. Paul is describing a calling here. In 1 Corinthians 12:4, the array of spiritual gifts are called *charismata.* These are divine enablements tied to roles in which we serve God. That is why these enablements are associated with God's *power*, yet another allusion back to 1:19. This is another dimension of God's power that the Ephesians are to appreciate.

Paul's utter lack of qualification for this role is underscored by his self-description as the *least of all the saints.* This grace, this enabled calling, was given to him despite his unworthiness. He rhetorically exaggerates his lack of rank by literally calling himself the 'leastest'

---

6. Arnold, p. 192.

(*elachistoterō*) of the saints, a superlative that can be rendered 'the least of the least' (cf. 1 Cor. 15:9). Paul's humility stands out. In all likelihood he is thinking of his past as a persecutor of the church (1 Tim. 1:15). In bringing all of this up he is not boasting. He presents where God has placed him and how he has equipped him (1 Cor. 3:10), in a stunning reversal of fortune. Paul points out the responsibility of being such a servant in 2 Corinthians 6:3–8 (cf. Rom. 15:16; Phil. 2:17). Given how we normally think about power and authority, it is interesting that Paul chose to highlight this picture of the servant as opposed to his role as an apostle.

Paul specifies his call as *to preach to the Gentiles the unsearchable riches of Christ*. This is but one aspect of what Paul's ministry is to highlight, with the second aspect described in verse 9. The theme of the riches that come from Christ appears again (1:18; also 1:7; 2:7). Paul is saying to his audience, 'Look at all you came into when you came to Christ and believed in him; to make that clear to Gentiles is what God has called me to do' (see Acts 9:15; 22:21; Rom. 11:13; Gal. 1:16; 2:8–9; 1 Tim. 2:7). The term *unsearchable* also points to the idea of these riches being unfathomable, without limits (Rom. 11:33). Everywhere you turn, the wealth of who Jesus is and what he has done is there to be noted. For Paul, it is a privilege to preach the wonder of God, a deep reservoir of blessing.[7]

9. Paul has a second goal as a part of his call. It is *to enlighten all regarding what is the administration of the mystery which had been hidden from the ages in God, the one who created all things* (author's translation). Paul is committed to making *all* aware of God's programme and how it is unfolding. It is a divine programme rooted in the Creator. Not only is it a divine plan, it is a plan that comes from the Creator, the one to whom all are accountable and who has designed it to be so. In Romans 9 – 11 Paul also speaks of the mystery and of how the current lack of response by many in Israel will be reversed by a major response from them.[8] This he also calls 'unfathomable'. The fact that all of this comes from the Creator God means it will be executed.

---

7. Foulkes, p. 103.

8. Thielman, p. 213.

Paul repeats the idea that the mystery of Gentile equality was *hidden* (cf. v. 5). He intensifies that description by noting that this hiddenness was *from the ages* (Rom. 16:25; 1 Cor. 2:7; Col. 1:26). This is a theme tied to the kind of revelation this is about God's programme both in the Old Testament and in Second Temple Judaism (Dan. 2:2, 47; *1 Enoch* 103:2–6; 106:19; *2 Esdras* 14:5; 1QH 7:26).[9] Some want this to refer to the aeons, which in the ancient world can refer to spiritual forces, but that is unlikely given Paul's usage elsewhere (Col. 1:26 speaks of 'generations'). These forces are mentioned in the next verse, not here. The Christian distinctive is that such revelation focuses not so much on disclosing events as on the work of a central figure, Jesus. Paul is suggesting here that the progression and timing of the revelation is something God has directed.

Paul's call is to shine a light on all of this and help people appreciate the *administration* by which this is coming to pass. The note about stewardship looks back to verse 2, where Paul's role in the programme is the subject. Here it is his understanding of what the Creator God is administering that is the point. Bruce speaks of two stewardships in the section: one involving God's grace (v. 2) and one involving the hidden mystery (v. 9).[10] Of course, they are tied to each other. The image of enlightening looks back to the prayer request of 1:18. The Ephesians are a subset of a larger audience Paul serves.

10. Paul sets out an ultimate purpose for all of this activity: *that through the church the multifaceted wisdom of God should now be disclosed to the rulers and the authorities in the heavenly realms.* God's disclosure and Paul's role in it is for the sake of the heavenly realms. The verse goes back to the statement in verse 8 about Paul being given 'this grace'. The reference to heavenly forces is probably a way of saying that it is for the recognition of all parts of the creation. The gospel speaks to the entire cosmos.

It is the *wisdom of God* found in the programme that is being disclosed. The phrase about wisdom trails at the end of the verse

---

9. Schnackenburg, p. 137.

10. Bruce, p. 319.

in the Greek for a touch of emphasis, almost as if it is disclosed at the end of the idea, much as the mystery worked. The repetition of the idea of the mystery being disclosed *now* also marks out this time as special (another related 'now' is in 2:13). What was hidden (v. 9) is now revealed. The extolling of divine wisdom has a rich tradition in the Hebrew Scriptures (Prov. 8) and in Second Temple Judaism (Wis. 7:22–23).

The revelation is to cosmic forces. As the battle is a spiritual one (Eph. 6:12), this is appropriate and also is emphasized, since this expression is thrown forward in the Greek. No power will be unaware of what God is doing and the authority to save that he possesses. They all see what is happening and will come to understand what is taking place. The message is for all in the heavens; the angels share in its joy already (Luke 15:7, 10), but it is the evil forces that need it the most. The idea is not that Paul is preaching to them, but that they observe what God is doing. John 17:21 shares the same idea expressed in a prayer of Jesus.[11]

This cosmic display is seen *through the church* and what it does. The creation is to see and appreciate what the church does, so the church should be careful about what it shows. The church is seen as a painting of grace, with God at work on the canvas. It is significant that it is the church as a whole, not just its leaders, that is a part of the display. Paul is urging the whole church to be what it ought to be so that what God has done can be transparently evident. When true reconciliation takes place, it paints a powerful portrait. To see God bring formerly separated people together is something to marvel at. It shows the multisided wisdom of God. Reconciliation has many angles, and God is working them all. This is another way of speaking of how the unfathomable riches of Christ are displayed (v. 8). Those riches are best displayed in the restored and reconciled relationships the Spirit of God brings.[12] The reversal of personal divisions in God is a defeat for the divisive forces in the world. In all of this the special place of the church, and its being what it is designed to be, is made clear.

---

11. Best, p. 325.

12. Fowl, pp. 112–113.

What is fascinating is that the church makes known its call by living it out.

11. This cosmic plan also has an eternal purpose, as the standard by which all of this is done is *according to the eternal purpose that [God] accomplished in Christ Jesus our Lord.* Cosmic reconciliation takes place in Christ, as does the manner of its disclosure. That work has an *eternal* goal – that is, this programme is part of the most central and lasting thing God is doing in his creation. The expression translated *eternal* means literally 'of the ages', and the idea of something being *accomplished* speaks of a divine goal realized. We had hints of this earlier in the letter in 1:4–5, 9–10. The mention of Jesus' Lordship is no accident here. He is in charge of the programme's execution and is at the centre of it. It was the call of Jesus that set Paul off on his part of the task (Acts 9), and it is Jesus' work that has brought about the unity.

12. In Christ comes blessing: *in whom we have boldness and confidence of access through our faith in him.* What all gain in their faith is confident access to God, a reconnection to the reason why they were created in God's image. In Christ we gain a reconnection to the living God. Three key terms describe this connection.

The first term, *parrēsia*, means *boldness*. It appears in Acts 4:13, 29 and 31 to describe how Peter and John, before the Jewish leadership, declared without hesitation who Jesus is. The description means that believers approach God openly and address him as family members. They have every right to be there because of what Jesus has done. Hebrews 4:16 and 10:19 make a similar point. We can enter God's presence and approach the throne of grace because of what Jesus' death has accomplished. The same point is made in 1 Peter 3:18 by focusing on how Jesus' death as the just for the unjust brings believers to God. There is an absence of shame because of what Christ has given.[13]

The second term is *prosagōgē*, which refers to *access*, an open door. Paul already made this point in 2:18. Romans 5:2 also refers to the access we have by faith. God is approachable because of what has been done in Christ.

---

13. Foulkes, p. 106.

The third term, *pepoithēsis*, speaks of *confidence*. It reinforces the other two descriptions in that it describes the context for boldness and access. We speak and enter confidently because of what has been done in Christ. The picture is of an open door for a family member, a citizen with full rights to know and approach God. This confidence we have as participants in the new covenant is spoken of in 2 Corinthians 3:4. The double use of ideas tied to confidence makes the point with emphasis.

The catalyst for these benefits of access is *faith of/in him*. I have rendered this ambiguously on purpose. Is this our faith in him or Christ's faithfulness? The phrase can be taken either way. Christ, in his faithfulness to the task of God, provides this, but we must entrust ourselves to him and what he provides. This reinforces what was said in 2:8–9, as well as in 2:13–18. It is not our work that delivers, but Christ's provision on our behalf in the context of grace. The choice may be a false one, as one is what generates the other. We do not get the access without either. These benefits are rooted in faith from start to finish. Yet the cycle gets completed with our trust, so any leaning in the passage goes in this direction of response. It anticipates 3:17. As long as one recognizes that the faith is in what Jesus has done, the role of the Christ in this expression is also not far away from its force, as 2:13–18 showed. Our faith and the work that emerges from it is an expression of response to and gratitude for what Jesus has done (2:10). The entire second half of the letter will address this response in far more detail.

13. Paul now applies the point of the digression: *So I ask you not to lose heart over what I am suffering for you, which is your glory.* Paul understands that this calling faces opposition, but he is willing to face it. These labours are in the interests of the Ephesians, so they should not lose heart or be discouraged because Paul is in jail.

He asks the Ephesians *not to lose heart*. The infinitive *egkakein* refers to fear or discouragement (Luke 18:1; 2 Cor. 4:1, 16). Paul's attitude is seen in 2 Timothy 2:10, where he speaks of enduring everything for the sake of the elect, and also in Colossians 1:24, where he says he rejoices in his suffering. Philippians 1:18–26 also has Paul rejoicing that through his ministry the name of Jesus is lifted up. The suffering Paul experienced was no surprise. The entire second half of Jesus' ministry sought to prepare his disciples for the rejection that was coming. Paul does not whine or complain. He carries out his stewardship with faithfulness. In Acts 14:22, he says that it is through many tribulations that one enters the kingdom, and in Acts 5:41 the leaders rejoice at being considered worthy of suffering dishonour for the name of Christ. They do not look for or seek out trouble, but if it comes while they are faithful, they are not discouraged. The early church had a similar attitude. In Acts 4:23–31, they pray for boldness in the midst of the challenge of arrest and rejection.

Thus Paul's suffering is for their benefit, their *glory*. Their presence and ministry brings God honour and will one day shame those opposed to God's plan. Paul's role in making that happen is to their benefit, even though he is imprisoned for that ministry.[14] Colossians 1:24 also made this point. There Paul spoke of filling up what was lacking in Christ's death, meaning that the apostle took on the same path of faithfulness that Jesus undertook, meeting rejection as the Saviour had done, and continuing on the path Jesus' death had opened up. Paul's path had been full of this pressure (2 Cor. 4:7–12; 1 Thess. 2:2, 9). There is growth under such pressure (Rom. 5:3; 2 Cor. 1:6; 1 Pet. 1:3–9). So the result will be good in the long run. The remark as a whole anticipates the request for strengthening of the inner man in 3:16.

Theology

This digression has several elements. Some look back to what Paul has said in Ephesians 2, while others look forward to the prayer that comes at the end of this chapter. God has a programme and Paul is a steward in that programme. He carries out faithfully the assignment God has given him: to make known that in Christ God has designed a way for Gentiles to become co-heirs with Jews – a programme of reconciliation (2:11–22; 2 Cor. 5:18–21). The equality is something that has recently been revealed, a part of the mystery of the programme of God that is revealed as a result of Jesus' work. This work of reconciliation is challenging, just like the message of Jesus about sin and forgiveness. Paul may be in

14. Sherwood, 'Paul's Imprisonment', pp. 97–112.

jail, but he is there because of faithfulness in ministry. Suffering leads us into glory. So Paul does not want the Ephesians to lose heart.

What we see is a theology of the plan and programme of God, centred in Christ, that takes us to deliverance but not without suffering. The lessons of suffering are important to learn in a hostile world. Paul is not anxious about his situation because he trusts God and understands the tension that comes with the assignment. He preaches without fear this hope of reconciliation that is a key product of salvation. He wants the Ephesians not to be overly concerned either, but to live out their faith in a way that points to the contrast with how the world functions, including in reflecting this reconciliation. It is sometimes suggested that reconciliation points to a social gospel and not the real gospel. Nothing could be further from the truth. The gospel drives towards peace with God and within God's creation, a work of restoration. Part of what makes that possible is the reconciliation that comes when people share a deep focus on Christ and what he has done. The gospel saves because it also points to this work of restoration. Part of the point of forgiveness is to form a new people who show that God has done a marvellous work in bringing together what was previously separated, not just in individual restoration but also across nations and ethnicities. After his prayer for them, Paul will develop this part of his reason for writing this letter, urging them to live out a unity that this goal reflects.

B. Paul's prayer for strengthening (3:14–19)

Context

Paul has presented the rich blessing the Ephesians have in Christ. The combination of riches, hope and power has been expounded as a reminder of how grace has brought Jew and Gentile together by faith in all Christ has done. Paul's own ministry reflects this calling, with insight into how God has performed this work of reconciliation. A second prayer follows for these truths to sink in so deeply that they will have an impact on how the Ephesians live in a world that lives differently. The power they have access to in the Spirit makes this kind of distinct way of life possible. Paul prays for

God to do this work in them. Ephesians 3:14–19 is another long sentence from Paul, like many others in the letter.

Comment

14. The prayer Paul started to communicate in 3:1 is now presented: *For this reason I kneel before the Father.* The phrase *For this reason* picks up how 3:1 started (*toutou charin*). Bowing the knee is a sign not only of prayer but also of reverence (bowing is used negatively in Rom. 11:4, in the context of bowing to idols). Often Jews prayed standing (Matt. 6:5; Mark 11:25; Luke 18:11, 13), so the bowing is an extra act of regard for God.[15] There are other examples of kneeling to pray in the New Testament (Acts 7:60; 9:40; 20:36), as well as some in the Old Testament (1 Kgs 8:54; Dan. 6:10–11 LXX Theodotion). In 1 Chronicles 29:20 and Psalm 95:6 kneeling is seen as part of the worship of God to honour him. One day, every knee will bow before God (Rom. 14:11, citing Isa. 45:23) and before Christ (Phil. 2:10–11).

It is the hope of reconciliation along with the programme it represents that moves Paul to intercessory prayer. But this reverence takes place in the context of acceptance and family, so the appeal is to *the Father.* Paul has just spent the better part of two chapters justifying this kind of approach to God (esp. 3:12). Here it is also because God is Creator, as verse 15 shows. It is a great and powerful God to whom we pray – an important point, as provision is the point of this prayer. Still, if anyone can approach God as Father, it is especially those who have gained access to his redeeming blessings. We pray to the Father through the Son.

15. Paul highlights that God is Father of all life by stating *from whom every family in heaven and on earth is named.* Salvation and life are ultimately and intimately connected, since deliverance leads to new life. All people are accountable to the Creator. In addition, he has the power to design that creation and its purposes. To be connected to this God is an honour, and to ask him for spiritual resources points to something he alone can provide. This is part of the point in speaking of *every family,* including those *in heaven.* Paul is speaking

---

15. Best, pp. 336–337.

of a spiritual battle in which powerful forces oppose the believer. Yet the power the believer has access to is greater than the opposition in the spiritual battle (6:12; cf. Phil. 4:13; 1 John 4:4). These angels and demons had rankings in ancient thinking, something the early chapters of *1 Enoch* show. In addition, to *name* someone was to show status in relationship to the one named (cf. Gen. 2:19–20, where Adam's naming shows his assignment to steward the creation well; for God naming, see Ps. 147:4; Isa. 40:26). God is the one responsible for the creation. He has named and is over every conceivable family. So the authority of God is being invoked by this description. Paul is illustrating the confident access he described in verse 12.

16. Paul now makes his request: *that according to the riches of his glory he may grant you to be strengthened with might through his Spirit in the inner man.* The prayer has three uses of *hina* ('in order that') that tie the whole request together. In this verse *hina* gives the content of the prayer. The other two uses, in verses 18 and 19b, give the goals of this strengthening in a kind of cascading sequence, with one goal feeding the other.

Paul is praying for them to be enabled and strengthened to face what is in the world. This power comes through the Spirit working deep inside the person. The enablement directs the steps of the believer. It is the *riches* of his honourable person that give us this rich enablement, an allusion back to 1:18.[16] This is a deep reservoir to draw from for the challenge of living in the world. Paul loves mentioning riches in this letter (1:7; 2:7; 3:8). With such access, there is no need to get discouraged.

Just as riches were noted in the earlier prayer, so was *might*, or 'power' (1:19). Divine strengthening is at the core of the request, as the idea will resurface in verse 18 (Ezra 7:28 LXX; Ps. 105:4; 1 Cor. 16:13).[17] This is about God giving enablement that otherwise would not exist. That is why the means of this enablement is the *Spirit* of God. They already possess the Spirit, who sealed their salvation (Eph. 1:13–14). So the request is about drawing on what God has

---

16. Hoehner, p. 477.

17. Arnold, p. 209.

already provided (Phil. 4:19; Col. 1:11). This Spirit and the indwelling that is a part of his presence is a core benefit of the new era Jesus brought (Ezek. 36:26–27; John 14 – 16; Acts 2). Spirit and power often go together, with the emphasis being on this extraordinary enablement (Luke 24:49; Acts 1:4–8; Rom. 15:13). This strengthening or fortification touches the core of the person, *the inner man* or inner person. This Spirit renews us spiritually from day to day, in contrast to the outer person, which is decaying (2 Cor. 4:16). The reference is to the core character of our whole person, what we might refer to as our heart or our spiritual side (1 Pet. 3:4). It is understanding now brought to action, setting the stage for the exhortation of the rest of the letter. Chapter 1 contained the prayer to grasp the power, while here we have the request to be able to apply it. The inner man is not merely a psychological description but a reference to all that makes us who we are to be in thought and action.[18] In Christ we are given the means and capability to be what we previously could not be.

17. This request for strengthening has a corollary request: *that Christ may dwell in your hearts through faith.* Paul desires that they might reflect the presence and character of Christ in their lives. Their faith will energize them to draw on the strength and mirror the character of God. The resource to get there is the strength God has given them in the Spirit. It is Christ dwelling in them, being at home in the person, that is another goal. Here Paul calls for his effective presence. The term for *dwell* (*katoikeō*) refers to a residing, a habitation, not a temporary stay.[19] This picture of dwelling is a variation of what was said about the community in 2:21–22. They are a dwelling place of God in the Spirit. They are in Christ and Christ is in them (Rom. 8:10; Gal. 2:20). His presence should influence their lives, and it is trust in him that brings that influence. So the *faith* here is not the initial faith alone, but also its continuing character. To trust Christ to save is to set the stage for trusting him in that subsequent walk of life. In that entire experience, they will come to know God intimately (Jer. 31:33–34; John 17:3). The reference to *hearts* is another way of discussing the 'inner man' of verse 16.

---

18. Best, p. 341.

19. BGAD, p. 534.

The context for this activity is *in love being rooted and grounded*. The word order of the Greek is reflected in my translation here to show that the emphasis is on love, as it comes at the start of the expression. The syntax of the phrase is ambiguous. The participles are grammatically unconnected by case in the phrase, pointing to a distinct point being made. Is it a result of the previous requests? Or is it a third request, or even an exhortation that is a key aside, which also might be making the point that when strength comes and Christ indwells, the love of God that drives the process is also realized and visibly established? It seems that the idea of either a third request or a side remark is best.[20] This is an idea not very far removed from a key theme of the entire letter of 1 John, as well as of Romans 5:5: that our love and response come out of an already established love God has for us. It also reflects John 15 and the call to abide in Christ because he abides in us. Paul is asking God that the Ephesians might come to appreciate and deepen these linkages. Our identity and security come from grasping the depth of God's love for us and drawing on it for spiritual solidity. As Fowl says, 'Being rooted in God's love provides a stability and security from which to grow.'[21] The perfect participles *rooted* and *grounded* look to the reverberating and lingering effect of a love rooted in the past. Colossians 2:7 has a related idea, seeing grounding in the context of this love and in the light of the presence of false teaching.

18. A result of all of this strengthening in understanding and action is *[that] you may be able to comprehend with all the saints what is the breadth and length and height and depth*. The Ephesians are to let pour over their souls the vastness of what God does. The verb *exischyō* means 'to be able to do something' and appears only here in the New Testament.[22] It is connected to the infinitive *katalabesthai*, which means 'to capture information', 'to comprehend something'.[23] The word pictures a process by which knowledge is gained.

---

20. It is unlikely that this phrase looks ahead to v. 18 given the intervening *hina*. So correctly Arnold, pp. 212–213.

21. Fowl, p. 121.

22. BDAG, p. 350.

23. BDAG, p. 520.

The odd part of the verse is that it looks incomplete: to comprehend the breadth, length, height and depth of what? There is no completion to the idea, and numerous single candidates abound. Is it love? Is it wisdom? Is it power?[24] Or is it just the raw vastness of it all? Most opt for the first, because of the previous mention of love. It certainly is included. However, it may be that making this choice gets too specific. One could rightfully suspect that the writer has written exactly what he intended here. It is the vastness of God's programme in all of its depth – the boundless vastness of salvation, pictured in many dimensions, and the things tied to it – that is being praised here.

Even though love abounds in the context, especially in verse 19, the ideas of strength, riches and even the unknowableness of God, understood as not attainable without revelation, are also present. Wisdom is attainable according to 3:10, even though the depth of the riches of Christ knows no limit according to 3:8. All of this suggests that we are talking about appreciating the limitlessness of all we have. That certainly includes knowing God's love in Christ, but other elements may also be in the mix. For example, wisdom is often portrayed in such ways (Job 11:5–9; Sir. 1:3; *1 Enoch* 93:11–14; Rom. 11:33–36).[25] Existing without any limits, these resources can be endlessly drawn upon, for they are always available. Paul wants all the saints to come to such an understanding and live accordingly.

19. An experiential goal concludes the prayer. The ultimate goal in all of this is that they might *know the love of Christ which surpasses knowledge, that you may be filled with all the fulness of God.* The reality of Christ's love is to so overwhelm them that it penetrates beyond understanding into life. This is a Pauline theme (1 Cor. 8:1; 13:2; Col. 3:12–14). Knowledge is supposed to take us beyond itself into this relational depth and action. When that expressed love is combined with God's enablement and strength, God expresses himself through the life and actions of the individual and the

---

24. Arnold, pp. 214–216. He notes seven options and opts for love and power, but wisdom is also in the context (3:10). The top three suggestions are those noted above.

25. See Lincoln, p. 211, on wisdom.

community. The prayer is that they all might be so *filled*, so the request is not for the individual but about what the community as a whole is called to become. God's presence and character have been revealed, and maturity is to be the result (4:13; cf. Col. 1:28 – note the presence of wisdom again there). That is what Paul's goal is in this prayer and, in many ways, in this letter: that God's love and wisdom and strength might so permeate them that they become mature as a people. Among the ways this will be seen is in their reconciliation (2:11–22) and in their living in ways distinct from the world (chs. 4–6).

Theology
Paul's prayer is for a vibrant spiritual life. This requires God's strength, an appreciation and embrace of God's wisdom, a living faith, resting in the security and stability that come from God's love, and an appreciation of the vastness and endless supply of all of these. God's Spirit supplies these things, and our faith opens the door to them. What is pictured is a vibrant relationship with God that takes knowledge and makes it real in the world. God's character is manifest so the community reflects in a visible way the depth and character of God. This prayer extends and applies the earlier prayer of 1:15 – 2:22. In appreciating and drawing on God's power, this spiritual life becomes not only possible but present in the whole of the community, as the riches of the hope begin to see the light of life each day.

C. Paul's benediction of God's capability (3:20–21)

Context
Paul has just spent much of the last three chapters expounding the idea that as God's people, believers have gained access to God's power and capability. In a final exclamation, he extols that capability to deliver the strength to the believer that he has described. We cannot even imagine, and nor should we limit considering, what God can do for us as he transforms us from sinners dead before God to children who live out his character. That God would have such a plan and give such a capability is worthy of praise and honour to the one who has so graciously given these blessings.

Comment

20. A doxology closes the doctrinal section of the letter. Such notes of praise are common in Paul (Rom. 11:36; 16:25–27; Gal. 1:5; Phil. 4:20; 1 Tim. 1:12; 2 Tim. 4:18). Paul ascribes honour to God especially because of his power: *Now to him who by the power that is working in us is able to do far beyond all that we ask or think.* The honour goes to the God whose power is present in us and is working through us. The point is made with the use of three words that point to power or enablement: *able* (*dynamai*), *power* (*dynamis*) and *working* (*energeō*). This looks back to 1:19–20 and 3:7–8, 16–19.

The *power* and *working* are from God for us. In fact, that power is at work in ways we cannot even conceive of as taking place. The key word here is *hyperekperissou*; this is an emphatic superlative meaning 'very much in excess of' or 'beyond all measure'.[26] It is beyond all we ask or can even think. So the ability here is comprehensive. In giving such praise, Paul is also reminding his audience that God can deliver on the hope being expressed here. In fact, he can do so in ways beyond what we think about or plan to do.

21. To this powerful one who is gracious with that power, Paul ascribes honour: *to him be the glory in the church and in Christ Jesus to all generations, forever and ever. Amen.* Such vast power and graciousness are worthy of endless, eternal praise. One supplies the verb in such outbursts of praise. So the idea is 'Let glory be to you, O God' (imperative) or 'Such glory is to you' (indicative) or 'May glory be to you' (optative). An optative idea may be too soft for the confidence of this affirmation. This is more than a wish: it is a declaration.[27] That *glory* is now and for ever in Christ and in the church. The term 'glory' (*doxa*) refers in non-technical contexts to something with splendour or something that is radiant.[28] So it is greatness or honour to be made manifest that is the point of the word, a visible prestige. This takes place when God is

---

26. BDAG, p. 1033.

27. Lincoln, p. 216.

28. BDAG, p. 257.

honoured and when his fullness is present among his people in the church.[29]

This is certainly to be the case in the *church*, as well as within the position of the church *in Christ Jesus*. All that happens in God's strength happens in Christ (1:22–23; 2:20–22; 4:15; 5:23). The church is where God is expressing himself most visibly in the world, which is why it is imperative that the church reflects the enablement Paul is asking for here. The church mediates the perception of God in the world. It is a mirror from God and for God to the world. This is why what Paul is about to exhort the church to in terms of practice is so important. Reflecting the character of God is central to how the church is to relate to a world that struggles in relationships. The chief end of man is to bring glory to God, but that is also the chief end of the church. The church is a unique place where this happens in and for the world, to the honour of God. This is why we invite people into it. It is also why its key calling is to witness to the world by the way it relates to those who are to be invited in.

The duration of this praise is also unending. That is expressed emphatically with the expressions *to all of the generations of the age of the ages* (author's translation). That means for ever. The closing expression of *amen* means 'so be it' or 'let it be so'. It represents an emphatic affirmation of what has just been said. We use the word so often today that it has lost some of its emphasis. A good paraphrase of it might be 'absolutely'. God's power is available to help us live as we should and, even beyond that, in ways we cannot imagine. The church is to believe so deeply in God that it lives in a

---

29. Although his argument is that glory is the point in 3:19, see Foster, 'Temple in the Lord', pp. 85–96; it is this verse that makes the point Foster is keen to have us see when he argues that glory is the point of 3:19 in terms of what we should be full of in the church. Showing forth God's glory is the result of people responding to God. It comes from God's glory, and the response results in it (3:16), but that response is rooted in reflecting the fullness of God's programme, character and presence. This is about more than love, glory or wisdom, but includes all of it.

way that honours God, empowered by him to love well with the strength and perseverance that enables them to live distinctly from the world with a humility that shows dependence on God. He is glorified – that is, lifted up – when we reflect him.

Theology

Our enablement, identity and security rest in the power of the God who works on our behalf. This final note of honour of God is both an expression of gratitude and a declaration of understanding about what believers have access to in Christ. This honouring of God or ascribing glory to him is not only to be a matter of words and the mind; it should have an impact on how we live (1 Pet. 4:11). So Paul will follow this doctrine with three chapters of exhortation about life and practice that grows from appreciating what he has said in the letter up to this point. Prayer and praise undergird it all by forming a heart that is dependent and responsive.

3. THE CHURCH IN THE WORLD (4:1 – 6:24)

The second half of Ephesians is all about application. The point of doctrine is always to have an impact on the way we see the world and to lead us into Christian living. So the bulk of this section is about the walk, the day-to-day life, of the believer. Paul starts with what we have, a unity in the faith through what we have received from Jesus. That leads into a call to live distinctly from the world, in holiness. It also means we should not expect the same thing of the world. Believers have an enablement to think and act that the world lacks. That difference feeds the church and its mission to show a different way to live. At the top of this distinctiveness is a love that is not threatened or afraid because it is secure in God and has his love as the model. That love is able to reflect the light of a different way of living and serves as an invitation to others who need it to leave the darkness. That love is a reflection of God's will and has the energizing work of the Spirit behind it. It is especially in the core household relationships in our world that we see this love: between spouses, between parents and children, and between masters and those who served them. This last application reflects realities of a first-century world that apply less directly today.

In the confrontation that comes from our presence in a world distant from God we see a call to take up arms – but not against people, for that is not the battle we face. This is a spiritual battle requiring spiritual resources against malevolent spiritual forces. Those resources are the elements of truth, faith and relating dependently to God that make a different kind of life possible. People outside the church are not the enemy but the goal. So Paul asks for prayer to share as he should with those who hold him in custody. Personal notes close the letter.

A. The walk (4:1 – 6:9)

Paul has just presented the core elements of the church's identity. It is richly blessed and has access to uniquely deep and unending power for the inner man and the community. So what should we do with such an array of resources? The call is to walk in a manner worthy of what has been received. The exposition is rather full, pointing to a series of life's spaces where it applies. It begins by establishing the unity we possess that is to be a source of orientation and strength as we face the challenge of life in the midst of a turbulent world. With this emphasis on enablement and unity in place, we can face the array of settings in which it needs to be applied.

i. Walk in unity (4:1–16)
Context
Paul points to unity by listing all the singular and unifying things we share (4:1–6). Then he speaks of how God gifts the church and what that provision of roles is designed to do (4:7–16). The church finds itself effective when each person who believes contributes with the gifts God has given him or her. The church is more of an organism than a hierarchy. Equipped for the task, the church can face the world when it draws on what God has provided.

Comment
    1. The core exhortation of the entire unit is here: *I therefore, a prisoner for the Lord, beg you to walk worthily of the calling with which you*

were called (author's translation). The *calling* has been spelled out in the previous chapters. They have access to enablement by faith that allows them to live as witnesses to being a reconciled people in the world. That power is rooted in an assignment to testify to God's gracious work, not just for individuals but also for groups of people. Paul has suffered imprisonment for bringing this message (3:1), but it is a calling in Christ that he shares with those in the church because the work of the church and the testimony to its unity is the work of all believers.

The imperative is for a worthy *walk*, a step-by-step life that honours the gospel (cf. Phil. 1:27; Col. 1:10; 1 Thess. 2:12). Translations speak of 'leading' or 'living a life' here, but that misses the 'one step at a time' picture of the verse. The walk dominates this final half of the letter (4:17; 5:2, 8, 15). This exhortation to a walk is like that in Romans 12:1–3, even down to the conjunction *therefore* that opens the verse (see also 1 Thess. 4:1). Paul's urging is an exhortation. The call looks back to 1:18: the 'hope of his calling' is this transformed way of life and the eternal walk with God that comes from salvation in Christ.

2. That worthy walk has certain core characteristics: *with all humility and gentleness, with patience, bearing with one another in love.* The tone of the Christian life matters. It is not bellicose, especially with one another. Being humble, gentle and patient, and giving each other the benefit of the doubt by bearing with each other, represent the key character elements of this walk of unity. Colossians says similar things in a longer section in Colossians 3:5–17, especially verse 12.

These virtues each have their own emphases. *Humility* (*tapeino-phrosynē*) refers to a lowliness of mind (Acts 20:19; Phil. 2:3; 1 Pet. 5:5).[1] This was not something the contemporary world regarded as a virtue, viewing it rather as weakness, although Judaism and the Old Testament did view it positively (Ps. 51:17; Isa. 66:2).[2] It is the opposite of arrogance, a trait Paul condemns elsewhere (Rom. 11:20; 12:16). The term *gentleness* (*praütēs*) often occurs in contexts of conflict (2 Cor. 10:1; Gal. 6:1; 2 Tim. 2:25; Titus 3:2). As a result,

---

1. BDAG, p. 989.
2. Thielman, p. 253.

it naturally leads into *patience* or forbearance (*makrothymia*). Gentleness is a fruit of the Spirit (Gal. 5:23), as is patience (Gal. 5:22). The term *gentleness* 'does not imply weakness, but self-control and a tempered spirit'.[3] Relationships can be challenging, but when we are patient and gentle, conflict need not destroy what is there in Christ (2 Cor. 6:6; Gal. 5:22; Col. 3:12–13; 2 Tim. 4:2). In fact, gentleness and patience are both key virtues when working through conflict (1 Thess. 5:14; 2 Tim. 3:10; 4:2). Humility and gentleness are a combination Jesus used to describe himself (Matt. 11:29), and they become an example to follow (Eph. 4:32). *Bearing with one another in love* allows one to negotiate the conflicts that inevitably emerge in relationships. It is enduring a behaviour and then working through it. Unity requires tolerance at a relational level without being indifferent to truth.

3. There is a goal in this effort. The application of the virtues of humility, gentleness, patience and forbearance means being *eager to maintain the unity of the Spirit in the bond of peace*. The goal is *unity*, and maintaining it takes work. That unity resides in the Spirit shared by the community (1 Cor. 12:13). The pursuit of unity works to maintain the linkage of *peace* among believers, a connection they have with each other as they share in the Spirit. This is not a peace to be gained, but one that is to be maintained. Just as the Spirit is a bonding agent, so is love in Colossians 3:14 (Rom. 8:6). Colossians 2:19 uses the related image of ligaments tying the body together. There should be a zeal to preserve this status Christ has achieved in the Spirit. Looking back to Ephesians 2, what has been achieved is a bonding between Jew and Gentile into one new entity designed for peace.

4. Paul drives home the unity Christ has produced with a list of things that involve unity as a result of salvation: *one body and one Spirit, just as you were called to the one hope that belongs to your call*. They were made for the unity they are called to maintain, being formed into a singular entity by God's presence as they represent him. And the hope that came with this entity was from being and continuing to be a place of peace and reconciliation, a witness to God's knitting people together through Christ. The theme of hope reaches back

---

3. Arnold, p. 230.

to 1:18 and the prayer for the realization of the hope of God's calling. So this call to maintain this peace in the body is part of what that hope involves as it is being realized. Division is an affront to that goal. The life to be lived is to drive towards remaining in this unity. Whether these verses are some kind of existing creed or a work of Paul is not clear, but there is a liturgical feel to them.

There are seven uses of the term *one* here and in the next two verses. The Trinity also emerges in these verses: *one Spirit*, 'one Lord' and 'one God and Father of all'. Even though there is no connective to introduce these verses, they surely give the basis for the call to oneness and unity. The *one body* has already been a theme of the letter (1:23; 2:16; 3:5–6) and will be a theme in the remainder of the letter (4:12, 16; 5:23, 30). This is the new man noted in 2:15 and the temple built by God in 2:20–22. This entity is energized and empowered by the *one Spirit*, as 2:16–22 also pointed out. The Spirit is the sign of the new era and the initial arrival of promise (Luke 24:49; Acts 1:6–8; 2:16–39). There also is *one hope* to the *call*, which is aimed at peace and a call to serve God as he makes this reconciliation take place, a theme of both chapters 2 and 3. All things will be unified, summed up, in Christ (1:10). The non-hope of 2:12 is now a full hope as a result of Christ's work detailed in 2:13–22. This hope is concrete, a certainty of the future, not a mere wish (1 Pet. 1:3–5). One day they will stand cleansed before God and at peace with each other (Rom. 5:2; Col. 1:27). They are called to preview that coming reality (Eph. 2:7; Col. 3:15). Unity matters to Paul as it did to Christ, being the topic of the prayer Jesus uttered before facing his own death (John 17). The believers' sealing in the Spirit guarantees that the realization of this hope is where they are headed (Eph. 1:13–14).

5. The listing continues: *one Lord, one faith, one baptism.* Just as the Spirit connects with the body, so the Lord connects with the faith as its object (3:12). A picture of what is included in the product of that faith is the rite of baptism, symbolizing the washing his work brought. They are baptized in him (Rom. 6:3; Gal. 3:27).[4] The church is connected to the one truth that in Christ the restoration to real life takes place (Eph. 2:1–10).

---

4. Bruce, p. 336.

The *one faith* is a reference to this faith in Christ, as there was no formal creed yet for this newly formed group so that the *faith* does not mean the full array of content about what we believe, although there is an impulse in this direction. What could be meant in terms of expression of doctrine appears in short statements such as we see in texts like Romans 1:3–4; 4:24–25; 1 Corinthians 15:3–5; 1 Thessalonians 1:9; and James 1:27.[5] There is a core faith that is in view here. It centres on Christ and his work that brings this deliverance and reconciliation.

The *baptism* involved is the combination of Spirit baptism and the water baptism that pictures it (1 Cor. 12:13; Col. 2:12). This is all connected to what Christ's work in death has achieved. Some readings of the verse ask us to choose between these elements, but they are all likely invoked in the reference. Christian baptism is distinct from John the Baptist's baptism, which said, 'I repent and am ready for salvation to come.' Christian baptism pictures that deliverance having arrived and the participation a believer has in it because of his or her trust in what God did in Christ. Christian baptism was seen as something distinct from the start (Acts 19:5).

It is only natural, then, that *one Lord* would head up this listing (Rom. 10:9; 1 Cor. 8:6; Phil. 2:11). Jesus is the one through whom all these benefits are filtered. It is no wonder he is also called the head of the church (1:22; 4:15–16). Elsewhere in the letter, Christ serves as the central figure in redemption (1:7), hope (1:12) and reconciliation (2:13–18). It is also significant that in a Jewish Greek-speaking context the confession of a person as *Lord* (*kyrios*) would point to the confession of God as one Lord from Deuteronomy 6:4, while for the Ephesians in particular the confession would exclude giving Artemis or any other god, not to mention any emperor, such a description.[6] Its placement next to the coming confession of the 'one God' shows the 'conceptual tensions' of Trinitarian logic.[7]

---

5. Best, p. 369.

6. Arnold, p. 234.

7. So Fowl, p. 134. He goes on to say, 'Paul's assertion about the one Lord includes Jesus within the identity of the God of Israel, apparently without compromising God's singularity.'

6. Ultimately the unity is based on the connection to God the Father: *one God and Father of all, who is over all and through all and in all.* Paul has been articulating God's plan since the very first word in the letter, as in 1:3 he praised God for giving believers every heavenly blessing in Christ. God's authority touches all, but in what sense is 'all' discussed? We shall see below. The confession of the uniqueness of God is something Paul articulated in 1 Corinthians 8:5–6.

An issue in the verse is whether the *all* here is masculine, referring to all believers, or is neuter, referring to all things. This decision is a close call. Usually when Paul refers to God as Father, he has familial relationships in mind (Rom. 8:15; Gal. 4:6; Col. 1:2; 2 Thess. 2:16; Phlm. 3). That favours a reference to believers.[8] In verse 7, Paul will be speaking of gifts given by grace to 'us', with only believers in view. Support for the term *all* meaning 'all things' throughout the verse comes from confessions like Romans 11:36 and Colossians 1:16–17 which hold to the sovereignty of God over all things and all being created for him and through him. 'All things' are said to hold together in him. 'All' is also a cosmic term elsewhere in Ephesians (1:10, 22–23; 3:9). The question seems to come down to whether the phrase 'he is in everything' (author's translation) applies to all people or only to believers. That point would appear to be unique to believers who have the gift of the Spirit. All things may be from God and through God; all things may hold together in him; but the presence of God is only in those who respond to him (1:22–23).[9] God has authority over all, but relationally he is closest as family to believers. The only way to read *in all* as applying to 'all' is to do so eschatologically in the suggestion that God will eventually express his presence and fullness in all the creation when he judges it. Ephesians 1:23 might go in this direction, and makes the choice a difficult one. The nearer context, however, indicates that the reference is to believers, as the emphasis is on what God

---

8. A text-critical issue appears here as some manuscripts have *hēmin* ('to us'), having believers in view. The manuscript support belongs primarily to Western and Byzantine texts and so is not original, but it may well reflect how the verse was read.

9. Bruce, p. 337.

has done for them in building unity. So God has authority *over* all in the church, and is present working *through* and *in* all of them. The confession culminates here as Paul has already mentioned the 'Spirit' and the 'Lord', and has now worked his way to the 'Father'.

7. Giftedness underscores the unity believers possess: *But to each one of us grace was given according to the measure of the gift of Christ.* This shows that one of the dimensions of preserving unity is for *each one* to live out the giftedness each has received. We are tied to each other in part through the gifts God gives us to make the body function effectively. The exercise of those gifts allows the church to be what God has designed it to be.

Here *grace* means a gift freely given, a short form of what Paul has noted in Romans 12:3–8 and 1 Corinthians 12:12–31 (esp. Rom. 12:6 and 1 Cor. 12:4 – introduced and called *charismatōn*; also 1 Pet. 4:10). There is no clergy–lay distinction in Paul; the *us* here is broad, as with 'we' in other verses in the letter (e.g. 1:12–13; 2:1–10). This also fits with Romans 12:6. *Grace* (*charis*) is equal to *gift* (*charisma*) in the parallels. All are gifted to serve the church in one way or another. These gifts have been measured out according to Christ's gifting. In Romans and 1 Corinthians, they are measured out by God and the Spirit as well (Rom. 12:3; 1 Cor. 12:4–11, 28–31). We are equipped to serve others. No-one is an island in the church. We need the giftedness others possess. Christ determines our roles, so as we serve we honour him.

8. Paul cites Scripture to make the point: *Therefore it is said, 'When he ascended on high he led a host of captives, and he gave gifts to men.'* Psalm 68:18 (68:19 MT; 67:19 LXX) is the passage quoted, probably used as a pattern or in a typological way. The psalm celebrates God's victory over his enemies and in Jewish tradition became tied to the victory of the exodus and the receiving of the law by Moses (*Tg. Pss* 68:11, 15, 19). Just as took place with God's victory through Moses, so now with Jesus. In Paul's quotation there is a shift from the 'receiving gifts' of the original psalm to 'giving' them that is the subject of much discussion. A second major shift is the move from the second person of the psalm to the third person. That move is more stylistic, in that Paul is taking the address of God's victory, possibly in pattern with Moses and now tied to Christ, and turning it into a more descriptive reading by shifting to the third person. Through these changes Paul is extending the direction of the passage. In the victory Christ brings, there are also benefits that come to us. The reference to *men* is generic, referring to men and women. The gifts Paul has in mind are given to all God's people.

The question of how Paul makes this move with the psalm is much discussed. It may well be that rather than citing the single verse, Paul is summarizing the larger psalm and using the language of the verse as a base, but with an appeal to the psalm as a whole.[10] The move allows him to save space in terms of the presentation of the argument. The fact that the Targum and Syriac Peshitta renderings of the verse refer to a similar reversal means that Paul's reading of the psalm is not unique. As the Targum has Moses receive the law to pass it on to the people of the nation, it reads, 'You ascended the firmament, Prophet Moses, you took captivity captive; you learned the words of the Law; you gave them as gifts to the sons of man.' The Peshitta reads, 'You have ascended on high; you have led captivity captive; you have given gifts to men.'[11] The point is not that Paul knew these Jewish texts, since they are late texts, but that a tradition that led to their reading might have been at work. The reading fits the ancient Jewish context. What was true of Moses is even truer of Christ.[12]

---

10. Arnold, pp. 247–250; also, in detail, Harris, *Descent of Christ*. Part of the issue here is whether the Jewish tradition of Moses receiving the law on the day of Pentecost goes back to the first century. Harris argues for this context and says the Spirit now replaces the law. Arnold does not accept Harris's approach, contending for a contrastive polemic to the tie to Moses and Pentecost, but Harris's monograph covers many details about the text and background. It is hard to see such a polemic in Acts 2. It has to be assumed to be in the background, which though possible is short of demonstrated, given that the dates for the Jewish linkage are late. More likely is a comparative link: just as God gave the law, so now God has given the Spirit and gifts to his people. See also Taylor, 'Use of Psalm 68:18', pp. 319–336; Lincoln, pp. 242–244.

11. Bruce, p. 342.

12. Thielman, pp. 264–268.

The picture of the verse is that on his ascension Christ won a victory, and the spoils, the gifts, went to those allied with him. Given the image of a spiritual battle that is in play in the book (6:12, with the earlier 1:20–21), the picture of a victory as a result of resurrection–ascension is not surprising. Paul's use points to the liberation of believers from the limits that sin had placed upon them, including death. Luke 24 and Acts 1 – 2 make the same point: Jesus' ascension points to a victory for believers, a triumph over death (John 7:39; Acts 2:33; also Col. 2:15). Another factor in the parallelism is that in Judaism, the psalm was later tied to the giving of the law to Moses, so the parallel is the giving of the Spirit and the accompanying gifts to believers. God's victory in the Old Testament is now tied to Christ.[13]

9. Paul moves to explain his reading of the passage. He does so in two steps, covering first *ascended* in verses 9–10 and then 'gave' in verses 11–13. The explanation is called a *pesher*, where a term in the passage is named and then explained. So the first explanation reads, *Now what is the meaning of 'he ascended,' except that he also descended to the lower regions, namely, the earth?*

Paul moves from ascent to a previous placement below, arguing that an ascent implies a previous descent. The reference to the *lower regions* and *the earth* is also variously read. There are four options: does Paul refer to Hades, to the earth in incarnation, to earth at Pentecost or to his death? In support of the earth in incarnation, see texts like John 3:13; 6:38, 41, 51, 58 and 62. Although a reference to a visit to Hades was a popular reading in the early church, with some appealing to 1 Peter 3:19, the view is not sustainable here as it is not clear how it leads to the giftedness of believers, the point of this text. Others contend for a reference to Jesus' death as that which provided the freeing, a point that is certainly theologically correct but is not so clear from the wording of this text. Why not simply speak of his death? It is better to see a reference to the incarnation that includes his mission to die for sin but not as the only thing in view (Phil. 2:6–11). An appeal to Pentecost here assumes

---

13. For a case combining the ideas of victory and provision, see Mouton, 'Ascended', pp. 1–9.

the Moses–Pentecost background noted and questioned above. It also ties the giftedness to descent, when it is normally tied to ascent (Acts 2).[14] So a reference to the incarnation seems most likely, inclusive of his death, and the ultimate stress is on the fact that the one who was incarnated also ascended and gave gifts to the church.[15]

10. Paul now moves to explain how the person who descended is the same one who ascended so he could fill all things. He says it this way: *The one who descended, this one also is the one who ascended above all the heavens, in order that he might fill all things* (author's translation). The impact of Jesus' work fills the cosmos. The order of the activity is descent followed by ascent, so the reference is to Jesus' work on earth followed by resurrection–ascension. The ascent put Jesus in a position *above all the heavens.* The allusion here is to 1:19–21. Location and authority are the point. The result is that he *fills all things*: his authority extends over the whole of the creation. The allusion here is to 1:10: all things will be summed up in Christ (cf. Col. 1:17; 2:9). Jesus has the authority over salvation to distribute the gifts of salvation, and the power to make that distribution more effective than anything that stands in opposition to him. That leads to an effective presence and filling in the church (1:22–23). These descriptions of Jesus present a view that does not leave him only as a prophet or messiah, but as one who has cosmic sovereignty, a description in a Jewish context reserved for deity (Jer. 23:24).[16] The Christ of glory fills the creation with his glory and gives gifts to his church to show himself at work.

11. Now Paul's exposition applies the cited text, turning to the theme of what Christ gave: *It was he who gave some as apostles, some as prophets, some as evangelists, and some as pastors and teachers.* This is the beginning of another long sentence that runs to verse 16. The

---

14. Foulkes, pp. 122–123.

15. Lincoln, pp. 244–248, discusses the three options of Hades, incarnation and Pentecost, opting for the last just ahead of incarnation. Arnold, pp. 252–254, opts for Hades. Hoehner, pp. 533–536, opts for death as the point of incarnation, which is quite possible.

16. Bruce, p. 345.

gifting involves leaders–teachers who guide the church as a catalyst to its internal growth and maturity. The list is clearly selective given other lists that include gifts of service, not just teaching and guiding (Rom. 12; 1 Cor. 12). Three of those named here parallel some in the list in 1 Corinthians 12:28: *apostles*, *prophets* and *teachers*. The order is similar, with *evangelists* and *pastors* added. God makes the church work in part by giving gifted people to it to equip the rest of the body for ministry. Where 1 Corinthians 12 and Romans 12 sought to identify the array of gifts, here Paul highlights the key role certain gifts have in moving the church to maturity.

Apostles and *prophets* were already noted in 2:20 as foundational gifts, as the base of the temple, that is, the church. They also had the mystery revealed to them (3:5). They planted churches and mediated revelation from God. *Apostles* means more than the Twelve (cf. Acts 14:14; 1 Cor. 9:1–6; Gal. 1:19; 1 Thess. 2:6–7). They are seen as specially commissioned for this task. The church still functions off of their work, as the New Testament is a product of those who functioned in such a role. How *prophets* work in a church service is discussed in 1 Corinthians 14. More than prediction is in view: prophets sometimes provide guidance and exhortation (cf. Acts 11:28; 13:1–3; 15:32; 21:10–11). *Evangelists* are only mentioned again in 2 Timothy 4:5, as a description of Timothy, and in Acts 21:8, about Philip. They are tasked with taking the gospel to the world. *Pastors* and *teachers* are tied together closely by one article. There is a question whether this is one office with two characteristics, or two very related offices. Ephesians 2:20 uses the same construction for two roles. Pastors, as shepherds, were to lead, teach and protect the flock (Acts 20:28; 1 Pet. 2:25; 5:1–4). In fact, pastors were expected to be teachers (1 Tim. 3:2; Titus 1:9). The Pastoral Epistles show what is involved in this role. 'Elder' and 'bishop' are related terms in the New Testament (Acts 20:17, 28; Phil. 1:1; 1 Tim. 5:17; 1 Pet. 5:1). These roles are catalysts that equip the rest of the body to do the work of the church. They are grouped together to make that point.

12. The role of these gifts is to equip the saints as a whole: *to equip the saints for the work of ministry, for building up the body of Christ.* The key to this verse comes in three distinct phrases: for equipping, for ministry and for edification. The distinction in prepositions (*pros*, *eis* twice) speaks against the three clauses all going back to the verb 'gave' in verse 11. One option is to place the last two in parallel, coming off of the first phrase. In that view, the equipping of the saints by the leaders has two goals: the equipping for ministry and the edification of the body. However, it seems best to see these phrases building on one another, so one leads into the other.[17] In other words, the saints as a whole are equipped for ministry, and the edification of the church results. Ministry was not designed for some and not others; nor is it done only by those who teach. Ephesians 4:16 makes the point that all participate in the edification ministry, supporting this reading. In addition, all are mature in verse 13 and walk in truth in verse 15, so the impact on all, including practical living, is in view. This reading still makes a point about the importance of teaching and leading in the church, but it also makes the point that the impact and ministry are picked up by all as a result.

The term *to equip* (*katartismos*) means to put things in order, like setting a bone.[18] So the saints are instructed to have their role in ministry. The *work[s] of ministry* is about works of service, which is the key idea in *diakonia*.[19] Edification speaks to the building up of the body. The picture looks back to 2:21–22. The move is to maturity as a community (v. 13).

13. Now Paul gives a core goal of this equipping: *until we all attain to the unity of the faith and of the knowledge of the Son of God, to mature manhood, to the measure of the stature of the fulness of Christ*. The goal is unity and maturity, a reflection of Christ's presence and character. Here the three prepositions match (*eis*, 'to') showing that the three goals merge into one grand target.

The expression *mature manhood* renders a Greek phrase that translates as 'perfect man', a complete person. Just as Paul compares

---

17. Schnackenburg, pp. 183–184, argues for the reading that stays focused on the leaders, not on stair steps. In that view the two final clauses are parallel and develop the idea of equipping that comes from these teachers. In this case a clergy–laity distinction exists. The view seems to bypass the point of v. 16, as well as the participation of all in v. 13.

18. BDAG, p. 526.

19. BDAG, p. 230.

the church to a head and a body in many texts (e.g. 1:19–23), so here he refers to a person who is fully grown to picture the entire community with the hope that it will be a mature community. *Mature* means it will be a community of good judgment, able to see clearly and respond accordingly. Two characteristics dominate such maturity: *unity of the faith* and *knowledge of the Son of God*. *Son of God* is the one reference to this title of Jesus here and in the Pastoral Epistles. Maturity is the result of a commitment to Jesus and all that he is. Knowing the Son means living out the truth in love (v. 15) and reflecting the way of life that mirrors his character (v. 21). The truth that Paul is going to emphasize is a lived truth, not just ideas. It is moral maturity that is tied to a proper understanding, as false ways are in the context (v. 14). At its base is apostolic teaching (Acts 2:42) and being formed into this new man (Eph. 2:15). Yet there is a product in terms of life's activity that is in view, so the expression looks forward to the development of the body into a place ready to face anything (Deut. 18:13; Matt. 5:48).[20] The 'already but not yet' tension here is common in New Testament hope. To pursue the Son is also to mirror the Father.

The statement about *faith* looks back to the unity of the 'one faith' in 4:5. The allusion to truth looks both forward to 4:15, 21 and back to 3:19, as well as to 1:4 with its goal of making us holy and blameless. It is Christ's *fulness* they are to emulate (cf. Col. 1:28, where the passage is about the individual, not corporate as here). Maturity is not a static state; the body needs constant growth and renewal to this maturity as new members come into the group and need instruction, and old members die. The teaching needs to be passed on from one generation to the next. This corporate maturity requires community participation and commitment. That is what Paul is exhorting the community to possess. The target is one that constantly lies before the church.

14. This maturity is necessary because of the threat that can hinder a mature life: *so that we may no longer be children, tossed to and fro and carried about with every wind of doctrine, by the cunning of men, by their craftiness in deceitful wiles.* Maturity fights the instability that comes

---

20. Arnold, p. 265.

with erroneous teaching about life, error that can deceive us. The exercise of these gifts will prevent believers from succumbing to such danger. This verse covers the risk that comes through not exercising these gifts, while verses 15–16 note the benefits of exercising them. So the purpose of these gifts is both negative and positive.

These gifts prevent the error of immaturity, so that we are no longer like *children* who are affected by the shifting forces of life, depicted as both waves and *wind[s]* (cf. Jude 12–13). Children lack the ability to discern and to exercise careful judgment about circumstances. They are like a boat at sea that is unable to deal with the elements. Maturity, however, can navigate its way through the turbulence. The remark is individualized here as infants in contrast to the singular mature person of the previous verse, for all need to apply themselves. To get to the collective, each person must engage in application. So the point is to be aware of what is going on around you and to exercise the discernment that good teaching produces. Good teaching produces a stability that enables one to weather the storm (Matt. 7:24–27; Luke 6:47–49).

The winds are driven by a *cunning* and *craftiness* that promises one thing and delivers another. This is why discernment is needed. The term *kybeia*, translated as *cunning*, sometimes refers to dice playing.[21] The false teaching takes chances with someone's choices, but because it is rooted in a cunning *craftiness* (*panourgia*) it is clear that the outcomes will be destructive (cf. 2 Cor. 4:2; 11:3–4, 13). Any doubt about the negative nature of the risk is sealed by the final phrase, *deceitful wiles*, or what is more literally 'toward the method of error'. The term for 'method' (*methodeia*) refers to a 'scheme' or strategy.[22] It is used only here and in 6:11. In this case it is a subversive goal that leads one astray. The idea of a scheme shows that there is a plan behind the luring. It alludes to the seductive schemes of the devil who works through people who lead others astray (2:2; 6:11). There is nothing accidental about the lure; it is designed to be destructive. Not all choices are neutral. Some choices

---

21. BDAG, p. 573.
22. BDAG, p. 625.

in life look good on the surface but actually take a person down a damaging path. These choices are constantly present, so life requires being well grounded. The maturity the teaching gifts produce prevents one from making the wrong choices. The mood of the text is like that in Paul's words to the Ephesian elders about their task (Acts 20:28–31).[23] Scripture is full of such warnings about deception (*planē*, 1 Thess. 2:3; 2 Thess. 2:11; 2 Pet. 3:17; 1 John 4:6; Jude 11).[24] The remarks are general, as Paul does not specify any particular concern. They are about the risks and choices inherent in life.

15. Paul turns to the positive, speaking about how an applied truth leads to the growth he has just described. The rendering *truthing* in my translation here is very literal, to show the force: *by truthing in love we will grow with respect to all things toward him, who is the head, Christ.* Context helps us to see what is going on. The picture involves truth applied or lived out in a context of love that draws on what God has provided and allows his work to grow the church. Doing truth is the idea, not merely speaking it. So renderings like 'telling the truth' or 'speaking the truth' do not say enough about what Paul means here. The idea does include true proclamation to counter the deceit, but it is more than that, as the exhortation fits into this entire exhortative part of the letter. He is discussing imaging or incarnating truth. The point is important, because many translations have 'speaking the truth in love', which is too narrow a rendering. The appeal to this more narrow meaning argues that the LXX uses the term this way (Gen. 20:16; 42:16; Prov. 21:3; Isa. 44:26), as does Paul (Gal. 4:16; Eph. 1:13: the 'word of truth'). However, the repetition of the term in 4:21 as truth being in Christ is looking to an incarnation of truth, not just ideas.[25] That and the entire applicational context favour a broader scope for the expression. The expression is combined with the idea of *love*, which also points to the concrete outworking of this truth. This is what good leading and teaching does; it protects, builds discernment and leads into maturity in actual choices. Understanding alone is not enough;

---

23. Schnackenburg, p. 187.

24. BDAG, p. 822.

25. With Hoehner, pp. 564–565.

application is real understanding. Such deep understanding including application is what Paul calls *truthing* here. Paul is saying that understanding is about more than merely knowing; it involves knowing what to do as a result and living authentically.

The growth is described as tied to the *Christ*. The maturity is to reflect him. It also draws from him, the *head* that guides the community (Col. 2:19).

16. Christ is the glue that holds the body together: *from whom the whole body, joined and knit together by every joint with which it is supplied, when each part is working properly, makes bodily growth and upbuilds itself in love*. Jesus is also the source of the body's growth. As love and gifts are applied with truth, the body grows.

The picture of being *joined . . . together* recalls how in the ancient world stones had to be smoothed by stonemasons in order that they might work together to form a building. The second picture, of being *knit together*, speaks of arguments being fitted together. There is an alignment of teaching that draws the body together (Col. 2:19). The emphasis on teaching has been consistent (4:4–6, 13, 15). The *syn-* prefix reappears for both terms (*synarmologoumenon, symbibazomenou*), as in 2:20–22 and 3:6. A corporate emphasis reappears as well, with the idea of all things working together. Putting this all together with the rest of the letter, the linkage involves people of various backgrounds and gifts of various types. As each part of the body effectively is in contact with the others, the body works together as it is designed to do. The emphasis on connection is obvious and purposeful. Believers are never meant to function as individualistic islands. The stress on the role of each within the corporate structure comes next, with the reference to each one *working properly*, or 'in measure'. It is this verse that undercuts a too excessive distinction between clergy and lay members. All are to contribute. Each member applies the measure he or she has been given by Christ to make the body work well and grow to a spiritual maturity rooted in love. Paul alternates between the metaphors of a building and a bodily organism because the church can be seen as both – a holy temple and a unified new man.

The emphasis on *love* is not accidental either. The goal of what God is doing in the world is primarily relational. Even the teaching serves this end. So how one lives is as important as what one believes. Love has dotted the last two verses of the section to drive home this point (see also 4:2). Sometimes the church's failure is not in what it believes but in how it carries it out. As 1 Corinthians 13 says, without love all you get is noise. Here we get a bonus. Not only is love applied as the body does its work, but love grows in the body as it works together.

Theology
This is a rich section; one of the most important tasks of theology is defining what the church is supposed to be. Using both building imagery that points to a holy temple and body imagery that points to a unified person, Paul exhorts the church to see and to hold on to its oneness. This is a unity to be maintained, as there is one God and one faith. It requires forbearance and love. Only a walk that promotes such unity is worthy of the calling that God has given to each believer. God has equipped the church to go there through a power and authority he possesses and has distributed through the Christ who has ascended over all. The gifts we have received are the spoils of a victory already achieved by his work on the cross. They are to be utilized in the battle that remains.

God has given leaders to guide the church in this endeavour, but their task is to equip others to play their part. All too often we leave the work of the church to its leaders, but here the body grows best when each member is equipped for works of service and for the edification of the body. Such equipping, rooted in solid teaching, allows for discernment when confronted with the disturbed waters of life and also makes one mature so that good judgment can follow. As all members play their part according to the gifts they have received and in line with the instruction they have embraced, the body grows, reflecting truth in love and mirroring the character of Christ. The growth that results leads into an even deeper capacity to love and walk with God, while being his witness to the world by living lives distinct from those around them. That is where Paul goes next.

ii. Walk unlike the Gentiles, in holiness (4:17–32)
Context
This subsection also divides neatly into two parts. First is a general exhortation to walk unlike their Gentile neighbours (vv. 17–24). The

call of Christ means a transformation of life and its goals, the way
of doing things. It means wearing the new man, displaying the
presence of Christ like one wears clothing. This is the new way of
life that is life in Christ. There follows a series of specific exhortations about different aspects of life, a listing of the kinds of things
Paul means: lying, anger, stealing, speech and a call to kindness
(vv. 25–32). The giftedness just discussed is supposed to take people
into such a way of living.

Comment

17. Paul now turns to specific application of what this
enablement means for the church. In many ways the remark goes
back to and picks up the points made in 2:1–3 and 4:1–3. One thing
is central to the Christian walk: to not walk as the Gentiles do: *Now
this I affirm and testify in the Lord, that you no longer walk as the Gentiles
do, in the futility of their thinking* (author's translation). The church
is to have a different kind of life from the world. The exhortation is
a present imperative, meaning that it is a continuing call to live in a
distinct way. It starts with one's thinking. Paul says there is an empti-
ness, a *futility*, in the way the world thinks. It approaches life without
engaging with life's substance. That kind of life is not for the
believer. This is a shortened form of three other texts: Romans
1:18–32; Colossians 3:5–10; and Ephesians 2:1–3. Futility is the way
Jews often describe connections to idols (Wis. 13 – 14), the exchange
of the worship of the Creator for the worship of the creature (Lev.
20:23; Deut. 18:9; Eccl. 1:2 LXX; Jer. 2:5; Acts 14:15; 1 Pet. 1:18;
4:3–4; 2 Pet. 2:17–19).

18. The description of the damaging approach to life in the
Gentile world continues: *they are darkened in their understanding,
alienated from the life of God because of the ignorance that is in them, due to
their hardness of heart.* There is no light to speak of here. God is
distant in this approach to life. So the Christian is not to live in that
world.

Several descriptions drive home the point. The *understanding* of
unbelievers is *darkened*. Spiritual darkness is a theme in the New
Testament (Rom. 1:21; 11:10; Eph. 5:8, 11; 6:12). The remark looks
back to 2:3. The reason for futility of thinking is that the mind
has been darkened. The perfect participle denotes a state that

characterizes Gentiles. Another effect is alienation from God (Eph. 2:12; Col. 1:21). The perfect participle again points to a state of living. A third impact is a life lived in *ignorance*. Paul is very full and direct in his critique of the Gentile state. Without discernment and solid reasoning of the mind, the Gentiles live in a world full of lack of judgment. The ignorance here does not leave them without excuse (Rom. 2:1). The term *agōnia* is used of an ignorance of which people are unaware (Lev. 5:18; 22:14; Eccl. 3:11; Acts 3:17; 17:30),[26] yet they are still responsible for the choices made. It is suppression of the presence of God (Rom. 1:21–25). They just do not see the error of the choices they are making. The responsibility for this ignorance is seen in *their hardness of heart*. There is no openness to considering another way; God is pushed away, to their own detriment. The picture in the word *pōrōsis* here is of a callous response that exists because the heart is impenetrable (Mark 3:5; Rom. 11:25).[27] The verb in John 12:40 speaks of eyes blinded as a result, while 1 Timothy 4:2 speaks of a seared conscience.[28] The opposite of this, enlightened eyes, appears in Ephesians 1:18. It is desires that are corrupted by a mind not operating as it should. The only reversal possible is to pay attention to the Spirit of God.

19. The situation escalates: a seared conscience leads to them giving themselves over to these desires. The consequences of the choice are a result of the suppression: *they have become callous and have given themselves up to licentiousness, greedy to practice every kind of uncleanness.* The result is a messed-up life. This is why it is so destructive to walk this way.

The callousness described here is an attitude that does not care about what one's behaviour means. The perfect participle (*apēlgēkotes*) means that Paul is again describing a state of being. A choice has been made to be consciously engaged in the acts described. They *have given themselves up* to this way of life. On the surface, there is a contrast with Romans 1:18–32, where God gives people over to this life. However, the point is that God lets them go

---

26. BDAG, p. 13.

27. Hoehner, pp. 587–588.

28. Bruce, p. 355.

this way. They make the choice. A divine judgment permits a self-judgment. It is a petrified heart that has no feeling or sensitivity to others.[29]

Three key terms describe the vices this lifestyle adopts. *Aselgeia* refers to a lack of restraint, abandonment into *licentiousness* (Gal. 5:19; 1 Pet. 4:3; 2 Pet. 2:2, 13–14).[30] The term is often sexual, but in this general context it refers to an array of choices for the self. *Akatharsia* refers to *uncleanness*, that which is vile or dirty (Gal. 5:19; Eph. 5:3; Col. 3:5).[31] *Pleonexia* is 'greediness', so it is self-focused desire (5:3; Col. 3:5).[32] Jesus warned against making such a choice (Mark 7:22; Luke 12:15).

20. Now the contrast comes in how they have been instructed as believers: *You did not so learn Christ!* When they came into the new man, that is, the new community, and sought forgiveness, they entered a new world. Christ did not teach them to be self-focused. They learned a different moral truth and a different way to respond (v. 21).

To *learn Christ* involves being affected by his person. The issue here is not only ideas, but also an approach to life. It means learning by example, reflective of the character Jesus reveals (Matt. 11:29; John 6:45; 1 Cor. 4:6; Gal. 3:2; Phil. 3:10; Col. 1:7). This requires a deep personal connection to Jesus, living by the power and enablement provided by the Spirit.

21. Paul assumes that they have been taught this new way: *if indeed you heard about him and were taught in him, just as the truth is in Jesus.* *Truth* tied to a person is what these believers had learned. John 8:32 speaks of knowing the truth, and that the truth will set people free. That truth is about what Jesus has done for people. It is interesting that *Jesus* is referred to in verse 21 rather than 'the Christ' or 'Christ Jesus'. The link to verse 20 tells us that we are still in the same place as Christ appears there: it is the Jesus who is the Christ we are considering. The opening instruction they received was about Jesus

---

29. Schnackenburg, p. 198.

30. BDAG, p. 141, 'licentiousness'.

31. BDAG, p. 34, 'immorality'.

32. BDAG, p. 824, 'greediness'.

and his life and work on their behalf. In that work, truth is found (John 14:6).

Paul is not expressing uncertainty about their having been taught these things. The rhetorical *if indeed* is not expressing uncertainty but confidence: 'you have heard . . . as I know you have' is the force.[33] The only question is whether they have paid attention to what they were taught. Paul is going back to the foundational teaching they had received, as the past tense of the verse looks back to their initial instruction in the church. They had been rooted in Christ and in the knowledge of him and his way. The gospel was called the 'word of truth' in 1:13 (cf. 1 Tim. 2:4; 2 Tim. 2:15). The thrust in the current text is that this truth is found in the activity and teaching tied to Jesus. In the end, truth is not abstract, but is tied to the example of a person.[34]

22. Paul presents the content of the teaching they received in a summarized form: *that you should put off according to your former way of life the old man being corrupted in accordance with deceitful desires* (author's translation). The first part of the teaching was to set aside *the old man* and their *former way of life*, which is what Paul has just described in verses 17–19. That life was lived in line with *deceitful desires*. That means that that life made promises that were not kept because it was a life focused on what the self could offer and was estranged from God. Such a way of life was to be set aside, *put off* permanently, like a change of clothes with a wardrobe to be left behind.

To get at the meaning of this verse and the two that follow, the role of the infinitives 'to put off', 'to be renewed' and 'to put on' needs attention. The first (*apothesthai*) and third infinitives (*endysasthai*) in verses 22 and 24 are aorist, while the one in between in verse 23 (*ananeousthai*) is a present infinitive. They all go back to the idea in verse 21 of being taught, making them indirect discourse infinitives.[35] The core question is whether these are to be seen as imperatival in force or indicatives. If imperatives, they would read: put off the old man, be renewed in your mind and put on the new

33. Best, p. 427.

34. Hoehner, p. 597.

35. Bock, '"New Man"', pp. 161–164.

man. If indicatives, the teaching would be: you have put off the old man, you are being renewed, you have put on the new man. With imperatives, it would be an exhortation. With indicatives, it states a fact. It is crucial to recall that this is about core teaching from the start of their faith walk, so it is not about what believers are down the road but what it is they have become in a transition.[36] Also crucial is the difference in the tenses and their order. Indicatives would make more sense if the order had been: you have put off the old man (position), you have put on the new man (position), now you are being renewed in your mind (continuing status). The current order favours imperatives: put off the old man with regard to your previous behaviour (aorist pointing to a resolve), be renewed in your mind (present tense looking to a continuing response), put on the new man (another aorist of resolve). The best support for indicatives here is the parallel of Colossians 3:9, where it is clear that the reality of the changed status is to motivate no longer lying. However, that passage does not have the reference to mind renewal that the Ephesians text has. It only speaks of the new man as having been renewed in knowledge. The claim that no imperatives appear in the chapter until 4:25 is technically correct, but misses the rhetorical force of both 4:1 and 4:17, which set the exhortative context of the entire section: to urge someone to walk worthily and that no-one should walk as a Gentile are imperatives in force if not in grammatical form. So it seems best to take these infinitives as imperatives. They represent the core exhortation, given with the response of faith, that summarizes what those just coming to faith were taught. It is out of that ground that the specific exhortations of verses 25–32 follow. Note how 'putting off' is repeated in verse 25 to link back to this text.

As was already suggested, we are in the midst of an image where a change of clothes has been urged. So the *old man* is to be set aside. The *old man* is not an image about what is inside a person, though the verse is often read this way. In the parallel in Colossians 3, when we

---

36. So Arnold, pp. 286–287, who argues that where Colossians stresses the already positional side of the tension between position and reality as a ground, Ephesians stresses the application into reality by appealing for a life lived in consistency with that position.

get to the description of the opposite image of the new man in Colossians 3:10–11, we are told that in the new man there is no Greek or Jew, circumcised or uncircumcised, barbarian, Scythian, slave or free. These are not qualities of the inner person; they are peoples in a community. The image is corporate and looks back to who people were before the new birth (2 Cor. 5:17). They were trapped in Adam. The ways of life from the old association with Adam are to be set aside. This is why it is described as the life of a former lifestyle. That way was left behind in the choice to pursue God's ways and embrace the forgiveness and cleansing Jesus provides. The old life in Adam involved a *corrupted* way of living, driven by *deceitful desires*. As with all of Paul's descriptions of the pre-conversion life, the view is quite negative, fitting the earlier description of pre-conversion life as involving walking death (2:1–3).

23. The exhortation continues with the call for an ongoing process of renewal: *to be renewed in the spirit of your mind*. The present infinitive possessing an imperatival force speaks to a continuing renewal as the transformation of the walk with God is an unending process that brings us closer to God until the goal is completed at glorification. Since the mind had been darkened in the previous life, with instincts and desires that were destructive, only a renewing of that mind into different ways of thinking can provide the reversal into a life of light, setting up the exhortation to come in 5:8. The exhortation of Romans 12:2 is similar and is a summary of the entire section here, with its call not to be conformed to the world but to be renewed in the mind. The human *spirit* is in view here because to speak of the Spirit of the mind needing renewal makes no sense. The Spirit is the agent that makes it possible, but renewal comes elsewhere in the person. Paul exhorts them to be open to what God is doing in them. Although not directly mentioned in 4:23, it is the work of the Spirit that enables our spirit to do this, as the Spirit is referred to elsewhere in the letter (1:17; 3:16; 4:3; 5:18; 6:18). Paul addresses this constant renewal in 2 Corinthians 4:16, where he says that the body may be dying but our inner person is being renewed. A constant walk with God is a walk in consistent response to him so he can do his work in us.

24. The concluding part of the exhortation is the call to put on the new man: *and put on the new man who has been created after God's* *image in the righteousness and holiness of the truth* (author's translation). The resolve is to walk in Christ, putting him on as one puts on clothes, by staying focused on what he represents and provides. The believer is to walk and live with others with a recognition that bearing Christ's name means living in a certain way. The allegiance to Christ and the view of self that identifies with him and his cause drives the believer to respond in ways pleasing to him. Paul wants their identity and connection to Christ to run this deep.

Just as 'the old man' is a corporate image tied to Adam, so *the new man* is a corporate image tied to being in Christ. The 'new man' parallel in Colossians 3:10–11, with its mention of barbarians and Scythians, shows the corporate nature of the image since an individual's human nature does not contain a differentiation of peoples within it. It is not the new nature that is meant, but the connection to and character of the new community to which believers belong as a combination of peoples and which they represent. The community of Christ into which believers have been placed has been created *after God's image* or likeness. They are being urged to identify with and reflect that likeness. That likeness also shares two core attributes, *righteousness* and *holiness*, that come out of the *truth* these virtues represent. The combination of righteousness and holiness is common in the New Testament (Luke 1:75; 1 Thess. 2:10; Titus 1:8; Rev. 16:5). This is a reference to personal piety or a virtuous life. The *truth* here from which these virtues emerge is again not just ideas, but an authenticity, a genuineness that is part of the character that reflects God and the Christ. It contrasts with the deceit that drove the life in darkness (vv. 17–19). One cannot overemphasize how ethical this entire section of exhortation is. Paul is calling them to a kind of living that is authentic and honours God. It is rooted in all God has provided in Christ. Ephesians 5:9 will elaborate on this theme by associating goodness, righteousness and the truth. Whatever we lacked to be able to honour God before coming into Christ is now remedied in what God has provided through him.[37] Romans 13:14, with its call to put on Christ, makes a similar point.

---

37. Fowl, p. 153.

25. Now Paul gives specific exhortations to elaborate on what his general encouragement means in practice. There is a series of exhortations running through verses 25–32. It has a consistent structure of 'do not do this but do that'. The first treats veracity: *Therefore, having laid aside falsehood, each one of you speak the truth with his neighbor, for we are members of one another.* The term *falsehood* has an article and looks back to the cunningness and deceit of the wayward life described in verses 17–19. That is to be put aside and a genuineness and veracity of character in speech is to be the result. The idea of putting off echoes verse 22. This is one of the practices of the old man to be left behind. The call to *speak . . . truth* to one's *neighbor* uses language that matches that of Zechariah 8:16. The present tense imperative of *laleite* ('speak') points to a constancy to this honesty. *Truth* echoes verse 24. The Zechariah citation is appropriate here because in the pressure of exile, the call was to be faithful to each other. Their connection to each other as fellow body *members* is the rationale here. That rationale is deeply relational. Paul does not allow believers to think of themselves as independent agents (Rom. 12:4–5; 1 Cor. 12:14–26). Colossians 3:9 has a similar exhortation. Even though the exhortation focuses on others within the community, Paul is not suggesting that they are free to lie otherwise. This is an exhortation of the sort 'do this especially among those of the faith' (see Gal. 6:10).

26–27. Paul now turns to the topic of anger: *Be angry but do not sin. Do not let the sun go down on your provocation nor give opportunity to the devil* (author's translation). The unusual nature of the exhortation means we do not get the 'do not do this but do that' pattern of the section. Instead, we have a 'do it this way' exhortation.

There is a kind of anger that is legitimate, but letting it simmer is what Paul urges them to avoid.[38] The key to this verse is understanding that a righteous anger is in view. It is found in the term *parorgismos* (*provocation*) and it defines what is being covered in the teaching. *Provocation* refers to being provoked to an angry response (e.g. God angered by sin, 3 Kgs 15:30 LXX; 4 Kgs 23:26 LXX).[39] Some

---

38. Foulkes, p. 139.

39. BDAG, p. 780.

argue that the exhortation is about all sorts of anger,[40] but this term's being in a coupled pair (anger and provocation) limits the context of the opening part of the linked exhortation. The anger being discussed is one that includes provocation. Anger for anger's sake is never right, but a righteous anger might be justified. Ephesians 4:31 tells us to put anger aside, as does Matthew 5:21–22, so a general remark here is unlikely as the general remark appears in this later verse. Simmering anger, even when justified, erodes bodily health. When anger simmers the devil gets an opportunity to divide and conquer.

The exhortation about being angry yet not sinning replicates Psalm 4:5 LXX. The term *orgizomai* ('am angry') is always passive in the New Testament (Matt. 5:22; 18:34; 22:7; Luke 14:21; 15:28). Interestingly, in one of those texts, Matthew 5, Jesus urges that if someone has something against a brother, it is to be resolved before bringing an offering to worship God. The principle here is one directly tied to Jesus' teaching. Part of the point is that there is a way to be angry and a way not to be angry. So the two commands – be angry but do not sin – very much work together as a pair.

Part of the check on justified anger is to not let it linger. The explanation is seen in the next command not to allow the *sun* to *go down* on one's anger, which is a metaphor for not letting that reaction hang around. The present tense tied to the exhortation 'do not let the sun set' (author's translation) means that this is to be a consistent response. Anger may come, even for good cause, but it is not to hang around like a cloud over relationships. When anger lingers, *opportunity* comes to the *devil*. That is to be avoided. No place is to be given to him; the devil should not be allowed to stir the pot.[41] The devil has no place at the table of relationships emerging out of the community, a point that fits the larger context of the pursuit of unity in the community. The church is to seek to be a refuge of *shalom*. Romans 12:19 sees the resolution of justice in proper

---

40. For example, Lincoln, p. 301. Interestingly, despite the differences in how some see the verse, in the end the ultimate point is not to let anger linger.

41. Best, p. 451.

avenging as ultimately God's job, as his wrath is one that resolves issues and prevents the need for one to avenge on one's own. After a call to be slow to anger, James 1:20 teaches that human anger does not achieve the righteousness of God. So we are dealing with a theme consistently set forth in the New Testament.

28. This is the third exhortation in this unit. We have moved from lying to anger to stealing: *The one who steals must steal no longer; rather he must labor, doing good with his own hands, so that he may have something to share with the one who has need.* This exhortation is interesting for it represents the swing in lifestyle in a single topic. Instead of stealing and looking out for what one can have and take, one is to *labor* so as to be able to give and *share* with those who have *need.* Part of what we gain is not to be treated as our own to hoard but as a resource to be used to serve.[42] Who is in view here? It was probably labourers desperate to survive or shopkeepers who may have cheated others.

The call not to *steal* is not a surprise as it is a reflection of one of the Ten Commandments (Exod. 20:15; Deut. 5:19) and part of lists repeated in the New Testament (Mark 10:19; Rom. 13:9), and it is tied to the note about greed in verse 19. Lying and stealing appear next to each other in Leviticus 19:11. In contrast to this kind of taking, there is a call to work and to give. The verse simply suggests that the purpose of work is to provide gain that puts one in a position to be of help to others in need. Paul was an example of this, working as a tentmaker and doing so in part not to be a burden on those he served (1 Cor. 9:1–17; 1 Thess. 4:11–12; 2 Thess. 3:6–12). The idea that this verse has no theology of work is simply wrong.[43] It is true that it is not comprehensive, but the verse does affirm a purpose for labouring, which is to steward resources well in terms of others (Acts 20:35; 1 Tim. 6:18; Titus 3:14). The Old Testament and Judaism valued work, as tending the creation was a call in Genesis 1:26–28 and the text honours labour (Exod. 20:9; Prov. 6:6; 28:19; Sir. 7:15). *Didache* 4:7–8 makes a similar point: to give and not despise doing so, to not say 'this is mine' but to meet

---

42. Hoehner, p. 624.

43. But so Best, p. 454.

needs, for if you share in imperishable things, so also in perishable things (author's summary). Lincoln summarizes the transition of the verse well: the exhortation is a call to go from thief to philanthropist.[44]

29. Fourth, Paul turns to speech: *let no unwholesome word come out of your mouth, but only what is beneficial for the building up of the one in need, that it may give grace to those who hear.* Speech is a gift and has power (Prov. 10:11, 31–32; Jas 3:6–12). It can tear down or build up. Paul urges that it might build others up and be *beneficial*.

The term *sapros* (*unwholesome*) means putrid, rancid, or rotten, decaying (Matt. 12:33; 13:48).[45] This is speech with a stench. The present imperative of the verb points to something that is to stop or not continue. In contrast, speech should be good (*agathos*) and for the edification of the needy. It should lift up, and meet needs. The result is an encouragement, the giving of *grace to those who hear*, conveying some type of spiritual benefit. This is why one can say that speech, when used properly, is a gift. If we think about this and the previous exhortation, they show that a believer is supposed to be a dispenser of gifts that lift up and strengthen others.

30. Fifth, and in an exhortation that begins to summarize, Paul turns to our representation and reflection of God: *And do not grieve the Holy Spirit of God, by whom you were sealed for the day of redemption.* Our allegiance to God should make us sensitive to not grieving the Spirit he sent and who has marked us for redemption. Again, the present imperative of the phrase *do not grieve* points to not continuing to do something. The things Paul has exhorted the Ephesians not to do are the types of actions that grieve the Spirit. There is more than speech in view here, although the link *kai* (*and*) at the beginning of the verse tells us that speech is a key part of this exhortation. The remark serves to summarize the section. Note that the Spirit is described as a personal agent. There is a relational offence at work here.

The language parallels Isaiah 63:9–10, where acts that produced grieving by the Spirit were preceded by acts of good faith by God.

---

44. Lincoln, p. 304.
45. BDAG, p. 913.

The allusion may also hint at a risk in doing so. Believers are accountable to God, who can respond with discipline. Psalm 78:40–72 shows how these themes can be juxtaposed.[46] The offence is a significant one since they are called to reflect and represent God's presence in the world. The idea of grief also points to the pain or loss that such misrepresentation produces. Some hesitate to give emotions to God, but he also loves, has anger and rejoices. These acts that cause grieving are counter to why the Spirit indwells them and seals them for their day of deliverance (1:13–14). It is inconsistent with why God took the initiative to save them and with where God is taking them one day.

31. In a summary exhortation, Paul now states things negatively then positively in this and the next verse. First comes the negative: *You must put away every kind of bitterness, anger, wrath, quarrelling, and evil, slanderous talk, together with every kind of malice* (author's translation). Certain behaviours and responses are beneath what should be reflected in a walk with God. Hostility is to be distant in all the forms it might take.

There is a variety of responses to be avoided (1 Pet. 2:1). *Pikria* (*bitterness*) refers to resentment that leaves a sour attitude or animosity towards someone (Rom. 3:14; Jas 3:14).[47] It is a harboured resentment that prevents reconciliation.[48] *Thymos* (*anger*) and *orgē* (*wrath*) are paired and deal with how bitterness can express itself (2 Cor. 12:20; Gal. 5:20; Col. 3:8; 1 Tim. 2:8).[49] Animosity is the fruit of these responses. Another way these emotions express themselves is as *karaugē* ('clamour') and *blasphēmia* ('slander'), anger verbalized in ways that attack people (Exod. 12:30; 1 Sam. 4:6; Mark 7:22; Col. 3:8; Jas 1:19–20).[50] Such themes fit exhortations from the Old Testament (Prov. 15:1–4; 16:32; 29:8, 11). These behaviours plus any other form of *malice* need to be *put away*. Where present

---

46. Arnold, p. 306.

47. BDAG, p. 813.

48. Foulkes, pp. 142–143.

49. BDAG, pp. 461–462, 720–721. We have an unjustified human anger here, as opposed to a justified divine wrath.

50. BDAG, pp. 565–566, 178.

imperatives have dominated this section, here we have an exhortation in the aorist, where the force is to change one's behaviour with
a resolve to get it done. It may be that the force of the shift in tense
is: 'This needs to be done now.' Where these negative traits
dominate, division and conflict reside. They do not breed the
maintenance of unity.

32. In contrast to bitterness and malice, the community should
display positive virtues: *Instead, be kind to one another, compassionate,
forgiving one another, just as God in Christ also forgave you.* Here we have
a series of virtues that reflect a bearing up of one another tied to
the example of what God did in Christ as the standard for response
in the community. It is a powerful base from which to give the
command.

The core virtues that should reflect the image of the church are
kindness, compassion and forgiveness. Colossians 3:12–13 adds
mercy, humility and gentleness. These virtues describe what it takes
to walk in love (Eph. 5:2). The term *chrēstos* (*kind*) communicates
the idea of benevolence and mirrors the attribute of God (Luke
6:35–36; 2 Cor. 6:6; Gal. 5:22; 1 Pet. 2:3).[51] The idea of *eusplanchnos*
(*compassionate*) speaks to an ability to identify with another from the
'gut', since the term *splanchnon* refers to the intestines (Acts 1:18).[52]
The term points to tender or sensitive feelings and is a quality
members of the body are to possess (1 Pet. 3:8). Forgiveness is the
core divine attribute that brought us into God's community (Eph.
1:7; Col. 3:13). Christ's willingness to take on that which we deserved
cleared a fresh path to a new life. The present participle (*forgiving*)
looking back to a present imperative (*be . . .*) points to the continuing
character of this forgiveness (cf. Matt. 18:21–22; Luke 17:3–4). Built
into the idea of being forgiving is being gracious to one another.
We are to show these same attributes to those around us. Galatians
6:10 speaks of doing good to all, especially to those of the faith.
Although the term is not present, these virtues together reflect a
deep love (John 13:34; 1 John 4:10, 19). When Paul spoke of the
new man being renewed in the likeness of God (4:24), it was these

51. BDAG, p. 1090.
52. BDAG, p. 413.

relational traits that were partly in mind. Forgiveness is so central that Jesus taught about it in detail, making it a point of the prayer he taught the disciples (Matt. 6:12; Luke 11:4) and teaching a parable on the theme (Matt. 18:23–35).

Theology
So what does the walk of this new way in Christ look like? It is not like the world's walk. It sheds the hostility and selfishness that are common in the world. It does not pursue paths of self-destruction. When the Ephesians came to Christ, they took on a new life and a new allegiance. Their connection to Adam and his ways was severed as the dominant force in their lives. They became a people who now had put on and were to represent God and his character – and the same is true for all believers. So lying, anger, stealing and negative speech, along with all forms of bitterness, are to be abandoned. Instead, there is to be integrity, an avoidance of that which divides, labouring with open hands to help others, and speech that builds up. In place of bitterness and malice there is to be kindness and grace, a willingness to forgive. Our new identity in Christ and loyalty to it is to drive this different way of living. We represent him wherever we go, and are to live accordingly. All of this is possible because our acceptance by God means we have nothing to earn from anyone else.

This section is highly relational. The example is that provided by God in Christ. Believers are never to forget where they came from and how it was God who brought them there. They are to treat others in a similar way. Love, kindness and graciousness are to drive our responses. Our speech is to reflect that core, all of which is rooted in the Spirit who resides within us.

iii. Walk in love (5:1–6)
Context
This short section is a transition and summary of the previous unit, so much so that some interpreters divide the section after 5:2. However, the theme of the 'walk' appears to set off units and the term 'therefore' that opens 5:1 corresponds to 4:1 and 4:17. Here the call is to be an imitator of God and walk in love. The theme closing 4:32 is reviewed and developed here. The repetition shows how important these relational ideas are to Paul.

Comment

1. In sum, the believer is to be an imitator of God, reflecting his character to the world: *Therefore, be imitators of God as dearly loved children.* Not only are we to reflect his character; we are to look like his sons and daughters in how we live: like father, like son and daughter. The call to be *imitators of God* is aimed especially at the love, compassion and forgiveness Paul has just named (4:32) or will name (5:2). In 1 Corinthians 11:1 Paul calls on people to imitate him just as he imitates Christ (see also 1 Thess. 1:6). According to 2 Peter 1:4, we can partake of the divine nature, escaping corruption and evil desire. Hebrews 6:12 calls on believers to imitate those who by faith and perseverance inherit the promises, while 1 Peter 2:21 calls on us to follow the example of Jesus in his sufferings. The roots of this call go back to the idea in the Old Testament of being holy as God is holy (Lev. 19:2) and to Jesus' teaching to mirror God's character (Matt. 5:44–45, 48; Luke 6:36). Our adoption as God's children takes place as we embrace his work and receive the Spirit (John 1:12; Rom. 8:15; Gal. 4:5–6).[53]

2. Paul calls on them to live in love: *and walk in love, as Christ also loved us*[54] *and gave himself for us, an offering and sacrifice to God for a pleasing fragrance* (author's translation). To love and give is a refrain in Scripture. John 3:16 says, 'For God so loved the world that he gave his only Son.' To love is to give. So living a life that looks to others and meets needs is the call for the believer's walk. The call to love reflects the exhortation of 4:15–16 and is much like Colossians 3:14. The fact that love is essential appears in 1 Corinthians 13, while 1 John 3:16 expresses a very similar sentiment (also 1 John 4:10–11). This call is deeply rooted in Christian teaching. The *walk* theme recalls 4:1 (walk worthy of the calling) and 4:17 (walk in holiness). Christ giving himself is also another key New Testament theme (Rom. 4:25; 8:32; Gal. 1:4; Eph.

---

53. Schnackenburg, p. 212.

54. In both uses of the plural here there is a textual question regarding whether 'us' or the plural 'you' is to be read. In the second case, the attestation for 'us' is stronger and it is likely that the two readings are the same, so we read 'us' in both cases.

5:25; I Tim. 2:6; Titus 2:14) and will be noted again in 5:25 and Galatians 2:20.

The portrait of a fragrant offering points to a pleasing sacrifice (Gen. 8:21; Exod. 29:18, 25, 41; Lev. 1:9, 13, 17; 2:9; 3:5; Ezek. 20:41; Rom. 12:1–2; 2 Cor. 2:14–16; Phil. 4:18; I Pet. 2:5). God accepted what Jesus accomplished in his death for us. We are the beneficiaries of that act when we embrace what that death means for our forgiveness. It gives us an identity in Christ that is secured by the surety of Jesus' death.

3. Paul treats what should not be attached to believers: *Let not immorality, all uncleanness, nor greed be named among you even as is proper for saints* (author's translation). The alternating focus on what believers should and should not do has been a consistent part of these exhortations. The focus here turns to what we should not do. There is a range of vices here, from sexual issues, to morality in general, to avarice.

The term *porneia* is a general term for all kinds of sexual immorality (I Thess. 4:3).[55] It is a broader term than adultery. It deals with any sex outside of marriage, consensual or not. Another broad term is *akatharsia* (*uncleanness*).[56] It refers to anything that is morally vile and contrary to the will of God, who is holy (Mark 7:20–23; 2 Cor. 12:21; Gal. 5:19; Col. 3:5). It is the opposite of piety. The final term in this list, *pleonexia* (*greed*), refers to that which causes us to take advantage of people and to hoard things for ourselves (Mark 7:22; Eph. 4:19; 5:5; Col. 3:5).[57] With this term the verse moves beyond sexual selfishness to deal with all forms of avarice and coveting. The selfishness and self-indulgence of these activities and their destructiveness make them inappropriate for *saints*, those who have been set apart and sanctified to God. These vices are so serious that they should not even be mentioned among them. Such activity undercuts the credibility of the church. We have in this verse and the next core vices that have no place among God's people. The details fit the earlier call not to walk as the Gentiles

---

55. BDAG, p. 854, 'fornication'.

56. BDAG, p. 34, 'unclean, impure'.

57. BDAG, p. 824, 'greedy'.

do (4:17). The exhortation in 1 Thessalonians 4:3–7 is parallel in emphasis.

4. Paul now takes on damaging speech, which also is inappropriate: *Let there be no vulgarity, and foolish talk, or coarse jesting, which are not appropriate, but rather thanksgiving* (author's translation). It is not only what we do that harms, but also what we say. So certain kinds of language are also not to be named among believers. The verb to not let these things be named among them is shared with those elements exhorted against in verse 3. Certain activities and certain kinds of speech are not to be a part of the Christian walk. The term for *vulgarity* (*aischrotēs*) appears only here in the New Testament.[58] It can describe that which is shameful or foul language since it refers to that which shames. It is probably a broad term here that covers more than speech, since a specific term for vulgar speech existed and is used in Colossians 3:8. *Foolish talk* (*mōrologia*) describes that which does not have any merit or which makes no sense.[59] It is 'the language of fools'.[60] Impious language is in view. This term also appears only here in the New Testament. The third kind of speech to be avoided also uses a word that appears only here in the New Testament, *eutrapelia*.[61] It means *coarse jesting*, humour that is in bad taste, smutty talk. This kind of speech is not fitting for believers and is not to be named among them as it degrades others. Rather, they are to be characterized by *thanksgiving*, reflecting an appreciation for what God has done for them by grace (5:20; Phil. 4:6; Col. 2:7; 3:15; 4:2; 1 Thess. 5:18). A core attitude of appreciation is an antidote to the kind of bitter speech described here. Ephesians 4:29 made a very similar point, but spoke of speech that edifies. In these last two verses six vices have been highlighted: immorality, that which is vile, greed, vulgarity, foolish speech and coarse jesting. These things are not to be found among believers.

5. There is a certain kind of character that is not fit for the kingdom to which Paul's readers belong: *Be sure of this: that no*

---

58. BDAG, p. 29, 'behavior that flouts social and moral standards'.

59. BDAG, p. 663, 'silly talk'.

60. Best, p. 478.

61. BDAG, p. 414, 'coarse jesting'.

immoral, impure or greedy person, who is an idolater, has an inheritance in the kingdom of Christ and God (author's translation). If there is no place for such a person among God's people, why would anyone in the kingdom display such traits? Paul's point is that these traits do not fit the position and identity believers possess. This is why he will urge them in 5:6–7 not to be partakers with the 'sons of disobedience' in such things. 'Different from the world' is the refrain of these exhortations extending back to 4:17.

Three more types of people are described as not having a place in God's kingdom. They are the *immoral* person, the *impure* person and the *greedy* person, who is an *idolater*. The term for *immoral* is *pornos*.[62] It is related to the sexual immorality prohibited in verse 3. This is the sexually immoral person (1 Cor. 5:9, 10–11; 6:9; 1 Tim. 1:10; Rev. 21:8; 22:15). The texts from the book of Revelation describe this person as experiencing the second death and being outside the city of the redeemed. The *impure* person is *akathartos*, another mirror of verse 3.[63] Contextually this is an unclean, immoral person, whose actions are an offence (Rev. 17:4). The term is used of unclean spirits or demons (Mark 1:23; Luke 4:36), those not aligned with God. The third person on the list is the *greedy* person (*pleonektēs*), a third mirror of verse 3 (1 Cor. 5:10–11; 6:10).[64] Such a person is seen as an *idolater* because in a sense the world revolves around that person. There is a self-focus that tries to makes all things revolve around what he or she wants. The creature has the honour, not the Creator (Rom. 1:21–25). The picture here is like the parable Jesus told about the rich fool in Luke 12:15–21. The fact that this term appears in the Corinthian texts indicates the presence of a core vice that is consistently condemned. For those in Corinth there was an additional reminder that they were such people in the past, but that the washing tied to salvation's forgiveness had changed things. Also similar is the exhortation in Colossians 3:5. It is inconsistent to claim association with God and live this way. Lincoln notes that there is a trinity of vices in view here: sex, excessive focus

---

62. BDAG, p. 855, 'fornicator'.
63. BDAG, p. 34, 'impure'.
64. BDAG, p. 824, 'greedy person'.

on riches, and power.[65] Such behaviour does not fit the rule of God's people that comes from God through Christ.

This is a warning of sorts not to be one who merely professes the name of Christ, but to reflect a life that shows that the Spirit resides within.[66] Paul exhorts the believers not to be the odd person out that Jesus warns about, one who utters the name of Jesus but does not know him (Matt. 7:21–23; 25:31–46; Gal. 5:19–21). This verse is not about indiscretions, but about those whose lifestyles are set in this ungodly direction; this is who these people are. Paul is saying that this kind of life orientation is not what the kingdom of God and his Messiah is about. He clearly sees his audience as not in this category (1:13–14), yet the issue becomes whether the idolatry this kind of immoral life reflects in fact represents someone who has the Spirit. It is not that salvation is a reward for behaviour – that is precluded by 2:8–10 – but that one who has the Spirit is affected by that divine presence. Paul is seeking to invoke and vitalize that spiritual connection.

6. Paul now warns about being deceived that such a lifestyle gets a free pass: *Let no one deceive you with empty words, for it is because of these things that the wrath of God comes upon the sons of disobedience.* Those who live this way show themselves to be *sons of disobedience* and are subject to God's *wrath*. That is not who the Ephesian believers are, as verse 7 will make the application for them not to be partakers with such people. Those whose identity is in Christ will see and respond as children of light (5:8).

The vices Paul has just listed result in wrath for the *sons of disobedience*, a reference to unbelievers. Paul precedes that point with a statement that urges them not to be *deceive[d]* with words that are *empty*, meaning 'not true'. Apparently some people were suggesting something to the effect that 'it makes no difference how you live'. The concern is something like what Paul expresses in 1 Corinthians 6:12–20 (cf. 2 Pet. 2:1–3). Right before that 1 Corinthians passage comes a vice list just like the one we have here in Ephesians 5:3–5. Paul is making it utterly clear that these activities do not please God,

---

65. Lincoln, p. 324.
66. Hoehner, p. 662.

so they should not exist among God's children nor be advocated as in any way insignificant. If God judges these things (Eph. 2:2–3), his children have no business doing them. Colossians 2:8 says this in a way that looks at why such an approach to life is destructive. In a sense, this says in another way what Ephesians 4:17–18 asserts: 'do not live in ways that are like those of the world.' The present tense meaning of wrath 'coming' shows a relationship between the activity and the displeasure of God, something like a debt being stored up that one day God will assess because accountability is on the horizon (see Luke 12:54).[67]

Theology

For Paul, our relationship to God and our position as his children means we are to reflect his character as we represent him in the world. So we must avoid these vices as we walk in love and imitate God (5:1–2). In fact, loving God and imitating him means that these vices will be avoided. Those vices cover sexuality, moral impurity of any type, greed, and the speech that can accompany them. Sex, misuse of money and power that is self-directed are in view. People who act with such self-focus are guilty of idolatry and will be judged by God. So such activity is not even to be named among those who believe. It is not worthy of their cleansed relationship before God. How we live does matter very much to our own well-being as well as to God. As our new relationship to God was rooted in Christ's sacrificial death, it is also an insult to his work not to pursue the life he died to provide. His example of loving and giving should be followed. To be a child of God means something for the way we live.

iv. Walk in light (5:7–14)

Context

Who the Ephesians have become in Christ now drives the exhortations that follow. Believers are children of light so they should walk as such children and not be partakers of the kinds of practices that point to darkness. Light consists of goodness, righteousness and

---

67. Thielman, p. 335.

truth – a truth that is not only conceptual but authentic in its practice. This walk pleases the Lord and mirrors Christ. Light is to expose and contrast with darkness by showing it up. To be connected to Christ is to be connected to light. The resurrection life is designed to bring us to light.

Comment

7. Paul applies the point about walking in love (5:2) and gives a rationale for it in this entire section. As is common, he first makes his point with a negative: *Therefore do not be partners with them* (author's translation). The lives of believers are not to look like those of the world, nor are they to share in the practices of the 'sons of disobedience' (5:6). That was a world to which they once belonged, but no longer. The verse begins with an applicational use of *therefore*: 'Therefore, this is what you are to do.'

The key term in this exhortation is *symmetochos*, 'fellow members'.[68] The term appears in a positive context in 3:6 of Gentiles being co-members of the benefits of the gospel. The exhortation here means to not be fellow partakers with them, not sharing in what they do with regard to the vices listed in the context. It is important to be clear here as some translations say 'do not associate with them' (RSV; cf. NRSV), which is not the point. Christians are not to be withdrawn from the world in terms of engaging with others, as the Great Commission (Matt. 28:18–20), along with Jesus' additional teaching, makes clear (John 17:15). Paul's words in 1 Corinthians 5:9–10 show that engagement with unbelieving sinners is not in view. Here Paul has in mind moral action, namely, sharing in their immoral actions by doing the same things that take place in the world. Lincoln says it well: 'The context here in Ephesians makes clear that what is involved is not a general distancing from all aspects of life in the Gentile world but in particular a separation from its immoral aspects.'[69] Thielman says it this way: 'Paul's point here is that fully participating in the worldview and conduct of unbelievers in matters of sex and money is incompatible with

---

68. BDAG, p. 958, 'sharing with them, casting one's lot with them'.
69. Lincoln, p. 326.

membership in the people of God.'[70] A similar point appears in 2 Corinthians 6:14. The elaboration comes in Ephesians 5:11, where the deeds of darkness that these disobedient people engage in come into view.

8. The justification for the exhortation not to be partakers involves the core change of association believers now possess: *for once you were darkness, but now you are light in the Lord; walk as children of light.* The opening term of the verse, *gar* (*for*), tells us that Paul is explaining the rationale for what he has just said. The call is to reflect the connection they have to the light. The 'formerly but now' transition parallels what we saw in 2:2–3, 11, 13; see the larger such transition in Romans 1 – 8. They were formerly of *darkness*, a metaphor for the presence and power of sin and moral failure that does not illumine life but obscures the way. To be in and of the dark is as good as being blind.

However, things have changed. Behaviour is to reflect association and allegiance, and these are now tied to the believers' position in the light. *Light* pictures an illumined way of life, where the path of how to live is clear (John 8:12; 9:5; 12:46; 1 John 1:5). It is a rich metaphor with roots in the Old Testament (Ps. 43:3; Isa. 9:2; 42:6; 60:1–2). The light of life is found in the *Lord*. So another present imperative appears, as in verse 7, that issues a call to make this application to life and continue to live this way. They are to walk as *children* of that to which they belong. Once again, a deep sense of identity and self-understanding about who we are is to drive our response. This is the fourth time the *walk* has been invoked (4:1: walk worthy of the calling; 4:17: do not walk as the Gentiles; 5:2: walk in love). The contrast between light and darkness appears elsewhere in the New Testament as well (Matt. 5:14; Acts 26:18; Rom. 13:12; 2 Cor. 4:6; Phil. 2:14–16; 1 Thess. 5:5; 1 Pet. 2:9) and was a common image in Judaism and at Qumran. At Qumran there was a contrast between sons of light and sons of darkness (1QM 1:1). The frequency and widespread use of the image means that the meaning would have been immediately understood. The new feature is the tie to the Lord as an extension of the tie to God.

---

70. Thielman, pp. 335–336.

9. What light is makes for the benefit that comes from following it: *for the fruit of the light consists in all goodness, righteousness, and truth.* So the exhortation is a call to reflect these three core virtues: that which is good, right and true. The rationale for walking as children of light is found in what light is and what it produces (*gar, for*). This list of virtues is a short form of Galatians 5:22–23 and its articulation of the fruit of the Spirit. *Goodness* (*agathōsynē*) is looking after the welfare of and acting on behalf of others (cf. Rom. 15:14; Gal. 5:22; 2 Thess. 1:11).[71] *Righteousness* involves the piety of a morally consistent life, upright behaviour (Mic. 6:8; Matt. 6:33; Phil. 1:11; 1 Pet. 3:14).[72] As we saw in 4:21, 24, the *truth* in view here has both content and ethical dimensions to it, forthright and honest behaviour.[73] It is both thinking and acting in accordance with a true and authentic way of living. These virtues are what comes from light and drawing on what God has provided (2:10; cf. Col. 1:10).

10. The living out of a righteous life in the midst of a problematic world requires discernment: *testing what is pleasing to the Lord* (author's translation). The bearing of fruit does not come naturally but requires staying connected to the light. Living in this world is a test that requires judgment. Fruitfulness is a product of such discernment. The *testing* is examining and discerning what is pleasing to the Lord. This is about more than learning; it is an acquired skill of discernment. This is how one accomplishes a walk in the light.

The idea of *testing* or 'approving' (*dokimazō*) is common in the New Testament.[74] People can discern the weather but are less able to be spiritually aware (Luke 12:56). The law helped the Jews determine God's will (Rom. 2:18). Believers are to test what God's will is (Rom. 12:2). Self-examination is to accompany participation in the Lord's Supper (1 Cor. 11:28). What was pleasing in Judaism was tied to wisdom (Wis. 4:10; 9:10). Through embracing wisdom one sees what is *pleasing* to God. The transformation of the mind from our old instincts is pleasing to God as we determine his will (Rom. 12:2).

---

71. BDAG, p. 4, 'goodness'.

72. BDAG, p. 248, 'uprightness'.

73. Thielman, p. 340.

74. BDAG, pp. 255–256, 'examining'.

For example, children and slaves are to live in ways that are pleasing
to their parents and masters (Col. 3:20; Titus 2:9). To be pleasing to
God is a goal of the Christian walk (Rom. 14:18; 2 Cor. 5:9;
Phil. 1:9–10; Heb. 13:21). Believers are called to self-examination
(Gal. 6:4; 1 Thess. 5:21). It takes discernment to live in goodness,
righteousness and truth. It also takes discernment to live with
a freedom that is responsible and not self-destructive, because not
all freedom builds up (1 Cor. 6:12).

11. Paul now issues a contrastive exhortation: *Do not share in the
unfruitful works of darkness, but rather expose them* (author's translation).
Paul plays with the image of light. Light makes things evident, and
believers' lives are to shine in contrast to the deeds of darkness. We
are not to share in those acts but rather to live in such a way that
those acts are shown for what they are.

The verb *share* used here (*synkoinōneō*) refers to participation with
someone in an activity.[75] The present imperative continues the pattern of the section by urging a response that is to be a consistent
pattern. In the context, these *unfruitful works of darkness* are the vices
that have been mentioned and which are the exact opposite of
the fruitful deeds noted in verse 9. These vices reflect an identity the
Ephesians have left behind, according to verse 8. Those dark deeds
yield nothing of value. Instead, there is a call to *expose* them. The
verb *elenchō* can mean 'rebuke verbally' or 'expose'.[76] The context of
'light' favours 'exposure', as light reveals (John 3:20). That may
involve speaking about these deeds, but the point is broader. In fact,
the next verse says it is shameful even to speak of such things, so
giving excessive attention to the destructive acts is not the point.
Exposure means that believers neither participate in nor condone
these works. It is in the believers' contrastive way of living, by
showing a different path, that such exposure must take place.[77] This
is why it is so important for believers to live in a contrastive manner
in terms of how they talk about, interact with and treat others. The
debate as to whether we are speaking of believers or unbelievers

---

75. BDAG, p. 952, 'be associated with'.

76. BDAG, p. 315, 'to examine or scrutinize carefully'.

77. Schnackenburg, p. 226.

here is rather pointless; it is the deeds that are in view. If these deeds are present, they are to be dealt with and exposed. It is clear from all that Paul has said that these deeds are not to be the actions of believers, but the fact that he has to exhort them about such activities shows that it might be something the community is doing that they need to avoid. Another point is important: this is not a prohibition of having relationships with unbelievers, but only of sharing in their deeds. The call of the Great Commission assumes engagement with those outside the faith.

12. Yet another reason (*gar, for*) exists for not walking in darkness: *For the things they do in secret are shameful even to mention.* The term *aischros* (*shameful*) describes activities that, when weighed morally, it is unacceptable to speak about and which bring dishonour on those tied to them.[78] That judgment may not be the one that exists among those who practise such deeds, but it is how God sees it, and that is what matters for believers. Paul says that it is the things they do in *secret*, when they think no-one sees and knows, that are shameful to speak about. Of course, God knows about these actions, so nothing is ever hidden or secret. Isaiah 29:15 records a woe to those who do things in secret. Until it becomes brazen, darkness seeks to conceal (John 3:19–21; Rom. 2:15–16). The people referred to here are those who perform the deeds Paul is condemning, again whether believer or unbeliever. It is nearly impossible to challenge what believers may be doing in this regard and not also imply what it means for outsiders. One can see the mix even in this exhortation (also Rom. 13:13). So Paul may be especially concerned with how believers behave, but the challenge of exposing these deeds is general. Such activity is so shameful that it should be avoided and should not be attached to anyone of faith. As the previous verse noted, these actions are not to be ignored but exposed, because they are damaging to people. Paul covers this so quickly he makes no effort to identify the specifics. In terms of identification of the deeds, the best we have is the categories of verse 3. He assumes his audience knows what he means and expresses it hyperbolically when he speaks of never saying anything about it.

---

78. BDAG, p. 29, 'being socially or morally unacceptable'.

13. So Paul turns to the idea that light exposes: *But all things being exposed by the light are made evident.* Paul looks back to what he said in verse 11: the call is to expose such deeds as opposed to sharing in them. We are taking the prepositional phrase *by the light* to go with the idea of exposure, and the verb in the sentence as passive (*made evident*).[79]

The imagery here has parallels in the Gospels. John 3:20–21 pictures how light exposes, as does Luke 8:17 (also Mark 4:22). In the Lukan text a day is coming when all will be exposed. The idea of exposure was introduced in Ephesians 5:11. It is the *light* that does the exposing. Paul states a principle of divine activity. Light reveals evil so it works to bring good. It also shows things for what they are, without any obscurity. With the exposure also comes the opportunity for a change in direction (John 16:8 of the work of the Spirit; 1 Cor. 14:24–25). The language mirrors an image Jesus gave when he spoke of disciples as light (Matt. 5:14–16; cf. Phil. 2:15). Believers and their lives are seen as light that is to be a contrast to the world and that exposes by showing a different, more beneficial way to live and to relate to others (1 Pet. 2:15).

14. Paul supplies an explanation for the principle he has just described and then cites a Christian text of some kind, possibly a hymn fragment, to drive home the point: *For everything made evident is light, and for this reason it says: 'Awake, O sleeper! Rise from the dead, and Christ will shine on you!'* Not only is light seen as exposing here, but that light is now seen as transforming through a call to rise from the dead and recognize what is exposed, and by so doing receive the benefit of what Christ is as light.

The expression *for this reason it says* introduces a citation of something familiar to both the author and the reader. The citation is not seen as Scripture, since it does not match any specific text. It is likely a piece tied to the community and its worship, which is why, given the parallel structure, many assume a hymn fragment. Best speaks of the possibility that the words were part of one of the spiritual hymns mentioned in 5:19.[80] The imagery alludes to texts like Isaiah

---

79. Hoehner, pp. 683–684, has a detailed discussion.

80. Best, pp. 497–498.

26:19 and 60:1–2, passages that describe restoration and light in the midst of darkness and death. The call to arise is a call to experience the benefits of resurrection. It is here that Christ's light illumines them and the way into a flourishing life (John 8:12). The citation supports the idea that *light* makes things *evident*, so it is a rationale for participating in and living in the light, reflecting its value and brilliance.

The context for the remarks is broad and flexible. It could simply be a description of what the gospel itself offers to those in darkness. It also could be a call to come back into the light for those among the community who have compromised their walk by engaging in such deeds. More naturally the remarks have the former meaning of an original call into light, but the application can extend into the second possibility. By contending that Paul is focused on the deeds and being separated from them, the concern in citing the poetic piece is not with a particular status of the audience. The text can also apply in either direction, although the point is an exhortation to the church not to live inconsistently with what their salvation means and has called them to become (5:8). The call to *awake* from sleep is an image Paul uses elsewhere to remind believers of their calling (Rom. 13:11–14; 1 Thess. 5:5–6). Romans 6:13 makes the same point with different imagery, as does 2 Corinthians 4:6.[81] The one who responds is drawing on the light and experiences the practical benefit that being connected to Christ provides. In essence, practice in life that honours God shines.[82]

Theology

There are two key themes in this section. The first treats identity. The fact that believers have moved from darkness to light should define how they react to the choices they are faced with. The second is that by recognizing their allegiance to light, they should live in a manner that is separated from the deeds of darkness and reflects the goodness, righteousness and truth of that light. Not only that, this distinctive life serves to contrast with and expose what darkness is

81. Arnold, p. 335.
82. Lunde and Dunne, 'Use of Isaiah', pp. 87–110.

like. Maturity pursues what is pleasing to the Lord. It takes a concentrated effort not to walk by past instincts. To live a righteous life takes discernment. Believers do not withdraw from the world but live distinctively in its midst. This section continues to elaborate the call of 4:17 not to walk as Gentiles do. Such a walk reflects and honours God. Those who are open and responsive to the walk of light experience the blessing of Christ shining on them, the benefit of a life lived with empowerment from him and in a way that is flourishing.

v. Walk in the Spirit (5:15–21)

Context

The walk in the light is also a walk of wisdom in the Spirit. Wisdom is the topic of verses 15–17, while the walk in the Spirit is treated in verses 18–21. The discernment Paul has mentioned shows itself in a wise use of time, avoiding the evil that can accompany any day. At the core of such a response is following the will of God and being controlled by the Spirit of God. That means living with a sense that God's direction and way must be followed and his strength be drawn upon in order to avoid being controlled by more destructive desires. Placed around the commitment to follow the Spirit is an atmosphere of praise and gratitude for what God has done that supports the connection to God's way. Also building that spiritual walk is a mutual submission that not only serves another but also sets up the unity that Paul appealed for earlier in 4:1–3 and the love he urges them to have in 5:1–2. Once again the stress is on the relational goal of the spiritual walk. How believers get along is a test of how well we are walking with God.

Comment

15. If one is to walk in the light, one needs to have an awareness about what such a walk requires. The challenge of living in a world filled with darkness and living distinctly from it requires wisdom and a walk filled with care: *Look carefully then how you walk, not as unwise men but as wise.*[83] The present imperatives *look* and *walk* point

---

83. The term 'carefully' goes with the exhortation to look. Some manuscripts invert the terms so that it would link to how one walks, but the evidence

to a continual need. The idea of taking care suggests something that does not come naturally or instinctively, but a way of life that requires some concentration. The Christian life is a thoughtful, reflective life that takes the road less travelled. As in several other sections of application in this letter, the call is to walk, that is, to live, moment to moment in a certain way (4:1, 17; 5:2, 8).

The exhortation here is like that in Colossians 4:5. Part of the discernment of wisdom is the ability to see the opportunity and work through it, even though the situation may be challenging. Living life in a setting filled with bad choices is not easy, especially when there are efforts all around to draw one into those bad choices (Eph. 4:14; 5:6). So the call is to live wisely. Required is a sensitive perception that has ethical insight into God's will in the face of circumstances that often are not ideal.[84] The assumption of the text is that we cannot isolate ourselves from the world in a way that inoculates us from such choices. The text assumes engagement, as does Colossians 4:5 more explicitly, but it is interaction made with careful choices. As other texts note, we are to be wise with what is good and innocent with what is evil (Rom. 16:19). Wisdom is seen in doing what is good in the gentleness that comes with it (Jas 3:13). Divine wisdom is not like our wise instincts (1 Cor. 1:19; 2:6–8); it must be learned with a renewal of the mind (Rom. 12:1–2).

16. Part of the discernment is seeing the opportunity and path in the midst of the evil: *making the most of the time, because the days are evil*. The verb translated *making the most of the time* normally means 'redeeming' (*exagorazō*), an economic term with the idea of purchasing.[85] The figure of wisely redeeming the time looks at using well the opportunities we have, because the threat to do otherwise is great. Taking advantage of time is the point.

---

in the manuscripts for this alternative is not as strong, as p[46], ℵ and B tie the adverb to 'look'. Arnold, p. 345, notes that the adverb is uncommonly linked to either verb, so there is no internal, stylistic rule that favours one reading over the other.

84. Lincoln, p. 341.

85. BDAG, p. 343.

So what does a wise walk look like? Besides being discerning, as Paul has already indicated in verse 10, the wise walk cashes in on opportunity by making the right decisions across time (Col. 4:5). It 'snaps up every opportunity'.[86] It steers clear of evil days, not by escaping, as that is not possible, but by living distinctively, showing the way of light. The threat has already been noted in the picture of light living in darkness and in the remarks of 2:2 (cf. 4:17–19, 22; 6:13; Gal. 1:4). Fear is not necessary because believers have been given what they need and a model for how to live in such a dangerous context (Pss 49; 90:12; 1 Pet. 3:13–18). Two examples come to mind: how Joseph handled his brothers' betrayal in Genesis 37 – 50 and how Paul viewed and approached his imprisonment (Phil. 1:12–14). The call is to serve the world through good choices (Gal. 6:10; Eph. 2:10). As we shall see, the Spirit has been provided to give us the enablement to do this.

17. As a result, a wise walk is not just an option, but an imperative: *For this reason do not be foolish, but be wise by understanding what the Lord's will is.* Given the danger that lurks in each day and the need to be wise (*for this reason*), it is imperative to do things God's way. That will be defined by what Paul says next about drawing on God's Spirit. It shows itself primarily in relating to situations and people well, reflecting the virtues that the Spirit gives.

The idea here repeats what was said in verse 10, doing what is pleasing to the Lord, and in verse 15, not doing unwise things. In Scripture, the fool does unwise things and does not go the way of God (Prov. 1:22; 10:18, 23; 17:18; 24:7, 30). This theme is especially present in Proverbs, where wisdom is the theme and a lack of it is the foil (Prov. 1:7; 2:1–4; 8:1–36; 14:16). Colossians 1:9 calls us to be filled with an understanding of God's will. This truth is found in the ethical way of Jesus (Eph. 4:20–21). Central to this is identifying with 'the new man' and representing Jesus and his church in appropriate ways. Doing God's will affirms one's status in his family (Matt. 12:50). To seek holiness and be thankful in spirit are key parts of the will of God (1 Thess. 4:3; 5:18). Such discernment takes a renewal of our minds because our instincts certainly do not take us

---

86. Hoehner, p. 692.

there (Rom. 12:1–2). We are speaking here about practical wisdom and habits that draw us closer to God as we draw on what his enablement provides, and that theme is where Paul goes next.

18. So what should control believers and drive our lives? Not what we drink; that can take control of us and cause us to have poor judgment. Rather, it is the Spirit of God: *And do not get drunk with wine, which is debauchery, but be filled by the Spirit.* A person should draw on what the Spirit provides. That person will be wise and do the right thing, following the will of God.

Paul negatively warns about vice and positively speaks of virtue, the third time this structure appears in this section. The negative exhortation involves not getting *drunk* with drink. Sometimes there is discussion about how much alcohol ancient wine possessed compared with wine today. The argument is that wine was more diluted then, but a key thing this exhortation shows is that ancient wine still could get people drunk and take control of them so that they did destructive things. To fall under the control of wine is described as *debauchery* (Prov. 20:1; 23:31–34; Sir. 31:29). The term used, *asōtia*, refers to something that leads to recklessness or wild living that brings nothing of value (Titus 1:6; 1 Pet. 4:4).[87] A picture of the term's force is found in 2 Maccabees 6:4, which describes a wild party. The prodigal son was said to have been guilty of this kind of life (Luke 15:13). These kinds of scenes were common in the ancient world.

Instead of being controlled by a drink, believers should be directed by God's *Spirit*. The passive *be filled* implies that God does the filling. They are permitting this filling to take place by pursuing God's will and drawing on God's enablement. Just as one consciously takes a drink, so they are to take in the Spirit, letting him work from the inside out. The idea of filling in this context describes an effective, controlling presence. Again, the present imperative speaks of a habit of life (Rom. 13:12–13). This exhortation probably refers back to being filled with God's power in Ephesians 1:23 and the call to be filled with God's power in 3:19. Another way to say the same thing appears in Colossians 3:16 where

---

87. BDAG, p. 148, 'dissipation'.

the 'word of Christ' is said to 'dwell' in us 'richly'. In Colossians 3, it is the content that is stressed (the word of Christ), while here it is the agent who makes that word effective (the Spirit himself). The sharing of roles between Christ and the Spirit in this kind of language reflects the intermix of activity within the Godhead, where roles are shared, not so much differentiated. For Paul, the Spirit of God is a key enabler of the spiritual life (Rom. 5:5; 8:4, 9–11; 1 Cor. 2:12; 3:16–17; 6:19; 2 Cor. 5:5; 6:16 [God living in them]; Gal. 3:14; 4:6; 5:13–18, 22–25; Eph. 2:22; 2 Tim. 1:7).[88] Filling goes beyond indwelling by the Spirit. Indwelling refers to the Spirit taking residence within a believer, while filling is the direction or control the indwelling Spirit possesses as the believer draws on his presence. The expression *by the Spirit* is governed by the preposition *en* and refers to the means by or sphere in which this activity takes place, but the contrast with wine shows that this is not an abstract comparison. It is a contrast with the Spirit active in the environment in which the believer resides. We are to draw on the enablement God has placed within us. The presence and power of the Spirit of God is what the promise of the new covenant was all about, as it leads into doing God's will from the heart (Jer. 31:31–35). As the next verses show, the opportunity to draw on such power is often tied to the worship of the community and the way that draws us near to God in reflection and teaching. In contrast to the drunken feasts of the culture, believers are to draw on the Spirit in the context of their gathering together for encouragement and the pursuit of unity Paul stressed in 4:1–6.[89]

19. There is an environment conducive to drawing on the Spirit: *speaking to one another in psalms, hymns, and spiritual songs, singing and making music in your hearts to the Lord.* These participles that follow the exhortation to 'be filled with the Spirit' probably communicate what is called 'attendant circumstances', in this case the kinds of

---

88. Hoehner, p. 705.

89. An article by Collins, 'What Does πληροῦσθε εν πνεύματι Mean?', pp. 12–30, argues that filling is simply about gift enablement in the context of worship. That may be too narrow, but it certainly is part of the point.

situations that can spur a spiritual response. In other words, it is these kinds of situations that can encourage the heart to draw near to God. They are not the means by which one is filled with the Spirit, as that is too mechanical a way to read the exhortation; rather, the passage is more likely about the kind of environment where access to the Spirit is encouraged. Means is the next most likely possibility for what is meant here, but one cannot mechanically be filled with the Spirit. Paul is not giving us a formula that says that if you do these things in this way, spirituality will follow automatically. Spirituality requires an open heart and is not solely dictated by outside circumstances. Against the idea of attendant circumstances it is sometimes contended that aorist verbs and participles are normally used in such a construction, but in these exhortations the present tense has dominated throughout, so an exception, using the present, is quite possible here. The difference between the two options is very slight, being the nature of the connection – whether direct (means) or indirect (attendant circumstance).[90] Participles of result are also possible, whereby the meaning would be that the filling of the Spirit would result in what the participles describe. However, that category for a participle is rare, making that sense unlikely. More than that, the result Paul is after in urging filling is not merely about worship but about behaviour in the world. So the praise and worship of God, a spirit of gratitude, and relational humility and well-being contribute to a setting in which we can draw near to God and, by doing so, live differently.

The list *psalms, hymns, and spiritual songs* parallels Colossians 3:16. Music and praise in song were a part of the earliest worship in the new community. Pliny the Younger spoke of the church singing a 'hymn to Christ as to God' when writing to the emperor Trajan in the very early second century from Bithynia, in what is now northern Turkey (*Epistle* 96). Singing also appears in heaven in Revelation 4 – 5, as it did in the Jewish temple. It suggests that singing is appropriate in sacred space. This musical address to God acknowledges his goodness and opens the heart to appreciate all

---

90. Arnold, pp. 351–352, opts for means, but sees it similarly as described above, by rejecting a mechanical formula as present.

that God has done. It is part of a context that causes one to turn to and respond to him. Its corporate nature means we share in this approach to God, as the spiritual life was never meant to be a strictly private affair. There is probably little difference between the three terms *psalms*, *hymns* and *spiritual song*s, given the author's tendency to pile up related words in places (e.g. 1:21). Josephus used songs and hymns together to describe David's compositions (*Ant.* 7.305; also 12.323 of Jewish worship in the Maccabean period). These involved poetic and lyrical praise. So the listing likely includes a reference to the psalms of the Psalter and also hymns or songs sung with or without some form of musical accompaniment. Instruments much like a harp were used in the period.[91] This music is characterized as *spiritual* because of its content and goal: to bring one's spirit closer to God. We see examples here and there in Paul of what the wording might have been like (5:14; Phil. 2:5–11; Col. 1:15–20).

The result is congregational singing, *making music in [their] hearts to the Lord*. Worship is an offer of the self to God of the group's awareness of his presence, goodness and power. It comes from deep within. In contrast to the drunkenness noted earlier, it is done in full consciousness. It is done together as the community affirms its connection to God.

20. There is a gratitude that comes with focusing on who God is, what he has done and how he has graced us: *always and for everything giving thanks in the name of our Lord Jesus Christ to God the Father.* So not only is praise and rejoicing present, but also a spirit that appreciates what God has done in giving us the honour of being his children.

We live under the sovereignty of God who through all that he does works *everything* together for good for those who love him (Rom. 8:28). This does not mean that everything that happens is good, but that some events placed alongside other things eventually work out to be positive. One can even appreciate hard things in life (2 Cor. 12:5–10; 1 Pet. 1:3–9). There is a trust and awareness in our thanksgiving. Truly understanding grace and how we get access to the Spirit through the cross engenders gratitude, as does having the

---

91. Hoehner, p. 708.

honour of walking with and knowing God. Those who appreciate how much God has done and that it was not deserved develop gratitude (Luke 7:47). The size of our cancelled debt produces gratitude (Col. 1:12). There is also much to be thankful for in the world we live in that God created. Our thanks are directed to *God the Father* through the *Lord Jesus Christ* for the provision that has come from God through the Christ. Colossians 3:17 expresses a similar sentiment about thanksgiving. This letter to the Ephesians opened with such sentiments (1:3–14), while most of Paul's letters open with a note of thanksgiving and prayer (Col. 4:2; 1 Thess. 5:18; 1 Tim. 2:1). To refer to God as *Father* points to an intimacy of relationship that stands at the centre of the Christian faith. It is with gratitude that believers have a place in God's family. The functioning in that family involves the plan of the Father, the sacrifice of the Son and the provision for enablement by the Spirit, as this passage has shown.

21. Paul finally turns to the relational part of what leads to deeper spiritual openness: *and submitting to one another out of reverence for Christ.* The work of Jesus has made the community into a family, so there is a mutual respect that is to be shown out of honour for Jesus. This verse is important for it acts as a transition to the list of family relationships Paul will turn to next: wife and husband, children and parents, slaves and masters. Without mutual submission and a respect for God, these relationships can break down into power plays that bring dysfunction.

The key issue in this verse is where it fits. Does it conclude the context of the exhortation about being filled with the Spirit, or does it belong as the introduction to the exhortation to wives to submit, framing marriage as an act of dual submission? The answer is 'both'. It is a transition verse, belonging to both contexts.[92] The participle *hypotassomenoi* ('be submissive') connects it back to the other participles of verses 19–20 and to the call to be filled with the Spirit in verse 18. However, verse 22 lacks a verb and takes its meaning from this participle here in verse 21. Submission describes

---

92. On this verse as a 'hinge' verse, see Merkle, 'Start of Instruction', pp. 179–192.

the placing of oneself in response to another or to something. So one submits or fails to submit to God's law (Rom. 8:7; 10:3), to masters (Titus 2:9; 1 Pet. 2:18), to government (Rom. 13:1) or to husbands (Col. 3:18). It is a term designed to give order to social relationships, but is also one that in a Christian context gets reframed in relationship to humility. As Calvin said,

> God has so bound us to each other, that no man ought to avoid subjection. And where love reigns, there is mutual servitude. I do not except even kings and governors, for they rule that they may serve. Therefore it is very right that he [Paul] should exhort all to be subject to each other.[93]

When in the next verse Paul tells wives to submit, the idea comes from this verse so that its context is one of mutual submission to one another. It is an important framing because it means that the marriage is to mirror relationships in the church and that the humility involved in submission is to apply to both partners in the marriage, even as rank is also discussed. The details of how that works will come in the following verses. Submission requires humility, which is a core virtue for believers. What such humility looks like is shown in the example of Jesus described in Philippians 2:5–11, where Jesus did not cling to his divinity but emptied himself to take on humanity, die for sinners and serve people despite his rank. In other words, rank meant little in relating and serving (Mark 10:35–45). Jesus told the disciples that they had rank but were to exercise it in a way distinct from the world. Rank is not focused on status or power, but on service. The *reverence* or respect *for Christ* that is to accompany mutual submission points not only to regard for him but to an awareness of his example as our model (so also in 1 Pet. 3:13–18). In the following lists, that husbands, parents and masters would be addressed at all concerning their responsibility to serve would be a surprise to a Gentile world where rank meant freedom to exercise power, 'to lord it over' others, as Mark 10 puts it. Jesus and Paul have in mind something quite different from that. The result is that both headship and submission get reconfigured.

---

93. Calvin, *Epistles of Paul*, p. 204, also noted in Arnold, p. 357.

Our walk is to have a sensitivity towards and empathy for others. Relationships are built on one's ability to be aware of others. Service means being connected to the needs of others. So there is an orientation towards others that means that our attention is not on us but on them. That kind of mutual awareness ties people together and makes them a body. It is better to have people look out for each other than for one to have to look out for oneself. The verse calls for a deference to each other; but, at the same time, Paul places his statement in a context where there are also roles in how that deference is to work. Both parts of relating are important, and the burden is placed later on the one who has 'rank' yet who is not to play the rank card because of this sense of mutual care. In such a context, power is redefined and used in ways that serve. As Thielman says, 'Authority is tempered by an attitude of service.'[94] Fowl speaks of 'some relativity of authority within the Spirit-filled body' that 'requires a disposition of humility similar to that described in Phil. 2:3–4, where others are considered to be of higher status, and people attend to the interests of others rather than their own'.[95] The fact that this verse transitions into the household codes that follow, in which standard ways of dealing with social status are challenged, shows the importance of the verse. This attitude is also seen in texts like Romans 12:10; 2 Corinthians 4:5; Galatians 5:13; and Philippians 2:5–8. It also repeats the theme introduced in Ephesians 4:2–3. The ideas of submission or related concepts reappear at various points in the household code (5:22, 24, 33; 6:1–2, 5). So the mutuality of submission drives relationships in a community where all follow the example of Christ, who served from on high.

The call to be filled with the Spirit is set within a context that has appealed to worship, gratitude and humility (vv. 18–21). These positive approaches to life open up the heart to be responsive to God.

Theology
The call to the wise walk is necessary because our instincts do not, on their own, take us in God's ways. In a world that can seduce us into

---

94. Thielman, p. 373.
95. Fowl, p. 187.

making destructive choices, it takes wisdom and discernment to walk in ways that lead to flourishing. So the call is to be controlled by God's Spirit, who points the way and supplies the enablement to discern and walk in ways that please God. In fact, none of this is possible without the Spirit of God. There is an environment conducive to such a walk. It involves a heart, body, mind and soul worshipping God in community, a gratitude for what God gives us, and a mutual submission that gives oneself to others. So there is a theology of corporate worship embedded in the text that is said to influence spirituality. This is the theology of the passage: a theology of relating to God and others that mirrors the call to love God and others as well as to reflect the humility that follows the example Christ gave in his service to the world. One of the key fuels for this walk is corporate worship.

vi. Walk in core relationships (5:22 – 6:9)

Paul introduces what has been called a 'household code', a Graeco-Roman ethical discussion of how the home is to operate. There is a series of relationships: wives–husbands (5:22–33), children–parents (6:1–4) and slaves–masters (6:5–9). In each case a mutual ordering is present, but in a way where power is not abused and sensitivity is urged. When believers have mutual regard for one another, the activities of life can advance. Such codes appear in various other texts: Colossians 3:18 – 4:1; 1 Timothy 2:8–15; 6:1–10; Titus 2:1–10; and 1 Peter 2:18 – 3:7. The root of seeing family structures this way goes back to Aristotle (*Politica* 1.2.1 §1253b.1–14), who has the same three groupings.[96] Josephus (*Contra Apion* 2.199, 206, 215–217) and Philo (*Decalogue* 165–167; *Special Laws* 2.225–227) have similar discussions. These texts deal with the existing social realities in the ancient world. In particular, they do not endorse slavery. This point emerges when one considers texts such as Philemon, where Paul undermines the custom by promoting in status Onesimus, a slave, to Philemon, his owner. Onesimus is not only equal to a brother but is to be treated like the apostle himself. These instructions are not mere mirrors of the culture but reconfigurations of it, as the example of Christ shows a different

---

96. Balch, *Let Wives Be Submissive*, pp. 33–49.

way to handle these relationships, placing more burden on the person with social power.[97] In other words, lines of authority exist, but they are redefined such that care for the other person should drive the use of power, rather than the possession of status driving the relationship.[98] This distinct use of power produces the ability to function with a united household. These relationships also preview how structures of relating should work in any context when they are filled with Christian principles whereby power is used with care and responded to with respect. The order of discussion always starts with the person in the responsive position, then it takes on the role of the person having responsibility to guide. These exhortations were designed to stabilize potentially disruptive dynamics in relationships and transform the way such social roles worked in the ancient world, serving as lessons for us as well.

a. Wives and husbands (5:22–33)
Context
The first core relationship is that of husbands and wives. Here submission and love are paired in such a way that the wife is responsive to a husband who cares for her as Christ cared for the church. The passage engenders much debate today because of the idea of submission, but it actually places a burden on the husband not to defend a rank, but to serve and give as Christ did. In doing so, it changes the way power is seen and shows the distinctive way of Christ. There was an array of pressures in the ancient world where women were exercising more independence,[99] especially in Ephesus,

---

97. This is nicely covered by Keown, 'Paul's Vision of a New Masculinity', pp. 47–60. He argues that Paul is redefining how the *paterfamilias* is to function in a Christian context. The man was the 'head' of the household in the Graeco-Roman world.

98. In particular with marriage, the exhortation works to build a marital unity and an approach to headship that is counter-cultural to the Roman, Hellenistic and Jewish models of the time: Gibson, 'Ephesians 5:21–33', pp. 162–177.

99. Arnold, pp. 372–380. Some details on these pressures appear in Winter, *Roman Wives, Roman Widows*; and Paul Trebilco, *Early Christians*, pp. 507–552.

yet Paul's instruction calls for mutual respect in an orderly manner that can engage with such pressure without breaking up the family order.

Comment

22. Paul exhorts wives to submit to their husbands: *Wives, to your own husbands as to the Lord* (author's translation). We have omitted the verb on purpose to show the construction. The idea of submission comes from verse 21 and is repeated for clarity in verse 24 (also Col. 3:18; Titus 2:5; 1 Pet. 3:1–6). The submission is limited to the husband and is not to all men (*your own husbands*). The comparison is that just as the woman submits to the Lord, so also in her marriage. Her submission to the Lord is used as an analogy, with the recognition that the husband and Christ are not the same but are related to each other in how the home is run. The idea is 'just as you did it for them, you did it for me' (see Matt. 25:40).[100] Part of a wife's response to her husband is tied to the order Christ has set.[101] Thus the point is like that of Ephesians 6:1, 5, 7 (cf. Col. 3:18). Christ is the wife's ultimate authority, and it is he who is calling for this kind of ordering in the home.[102]

The exhortation to the wife focuses on being supportive, as the term 'respect' is used in verse 33 as a summary for the idea here. The imperative is formulated in the middle voice, which means that the wife chooses to undertake this response. There is no suggestion that the wife is being forced to submit, which is what the passive voice would suggest. That also fits the exhortation of verse 21, where mutual submission is a response to an exhortation to be submissive. The wife is to respect the husband's role and support it, as the husband is sensitive to his wife. This is not an endorsement of the patriarchy that surrounded them in the culture; the call for husbands to have concern for their wives was missing in the larger culture. It is also significant that what Paul focuses on here is not the rights a person has in the marriage but on his or her

---

100. Hoehner, p. 737.

101. Fowl, p. 187.

102. Thielman, p. 376.

responsibility to the other person. The exhortations are ultimately focused outwards. They are not to be read or applied selfishly, but selflessly.

The wife is not told to 'obey' her husband, as is the case with children and slaves in the next listings. This might be significant. It seems to indicate a place for give-and-take discussion in marriage when a decision is reached. She chooses to be respectful as a way to bring stability to the home. The assumption of the text as a whole is that the husband also is sensitive, though the text does not qualify the wife's response as being dependent on the husband's care. There is a balance in this text that makes for the stability being sought. The love and care required of the husband, who in the Graeco-Roman culture would have been seen to have absolute power, shows the effort to convey a balance in the relationship. Marriage works best when sensitivity works in both directions, as the husband leads with a caring, nurturing love and the wife responds with submission. Perhaps this sensitivity is also seen in how children are called to honour both parents in the union in the Ten Commandments (Exod. 20:12; Deut. 5:16). In other words, the submission–love combination is not to be seen in terms of power or rank, as it often is portrayed, but as a form of cooperation in reaching for a shared goal. Even children are to see their parents as a team sharing honour.

If there was any doubt that submission is the term in view, verse 24 shows that it is, as does the comparison to *the Lord*. The text does not say that the husband is his wife's lord, nor that communication in a marriage is only one-way. It looks to how the team in the marriage is structured to work. The wife is called to respond to the lead of her husband. The husband is told in verses 25–32 to lead with care, compassion and support towards his wife because that is how Christ served the church. If we consider the amount of time spent discussing each role, the stress is not on how the wife responds but on how the husband loves. Power and rank are reconfigured by the way the entire passage works. The social hierarchy is present but with additional elements that change it from being a mere paradigm of personal power. Most of the description of activity in the passage as a whole deals with love, care and sensitivity towards the one cared for in the marriage. Nonetheless, the wife is told to be responsive to and supportive of her husband. What all of this means practically is that couples have an array of options as to how they design their unique relationship, given how the husband is to be sensitive towards his wife and the wife supportive of her husband – principles that allow for a couple to work out its dynamics in a mutually agreed way in which love and submission work together.

23. Paul explains his rationale for the exhortation to submission: *because the husband is the head of the wife as also Christ is the head of the church – he himself being the savior of the body.* The role of the husband involves headship. Paul defines that headship as being mirrored in *how* Christ serves as head and saviour. This also is a balanced declaration. Yes, Christ has authority, but he uses it to save, sacrifice and serve. Again, power and rank are present, but they are contextualized and reconfigured by considering how that power is used and applied, not merely presented in isolation.

The key term in this verse is the idea of the husband being the *head* of the wife as Christ is of the church. An extended discussion surrounds *kephalē*, the term translated *head*. Does it mean 'source' or does it point to 'authority'? The case for 'source' was made by Bedale.[103] His work showed that the term could mean 'source'. Genesis 2:21–24 is the text associated with the meaning: the woman was originally 'sourced' in the man. However, the term can also point to the meaning of 'authority'. Ephesians 1:19–22 has Jesus as 'head' over all rule and authority. In that context, 'source' does not make sense. That text is the basis for the analogy here, since there Paul is also discussing Christ as head of the church (cf. Col. 1:18; 2:10).[104] It has been suggested that the term 'head' in Ephesians

---

103. Bedale, 'Meaning', pp. 211–215.

104. Lincoln, pp. 368–369, is clear on this, as is Arnold, pp. 381–382. This
    is about more than simple pre-eminence given the backdrop of Eph.
    1:19–22. That is the third option which Hoehner, p. 739, supports. The
    point made here undercuts the kind of argument for 'source' made by
    Martin, 'Performing the Head Role', pp. 69–80. His article shows that
    'source' can be a meaning, but his primarily lexical path alongside his
    look at anthropology negates the influence of Eph. 1:19–22 in defining

4:15–16 means 'source' in terms of nurturing, but that makes little sense here as a reason to submit. The earlier use of the term is better for this context. The point is that the husband has authority in relationship to his wife, just as Christ does in relationship to the church. This is immediately qualified by the reference to Christ as the *savior of the body*.[105] So it is an authority that serves, something verses 25–33 will also stress. As Schnackenburg says, 'A one-sided "domineering" understanding of the "Head" is excluded by the attribute.'[106] So there is a reconfiguration from the way power is normally seen in the culture, where the father, with *patria potestas* ('power of a father', a Latin legal term), had total authority over a family, even having the right to put his children to death if he desired.

The idea that the husband is the saviour of his wife is not in the passage. Only Christ is saviour. Yet this one saviour, Jesus, provides the example for the husband's role as head by the way Jesus cares for the church and honours her as his bride. The elaboration of this point comes when the husband is directly addressed in verses 25–33. Though some discuss the husband's role in terms of protection, Paul elaborates it in terms of service, nurture and care, so it points to more than that. Christ as saviour is almost a refrain in the New Testament (Luke 2:11; John 4:42; Acts 5:31; 13:23; 2 Tim. 1:10; Titus 1:4; 2:13; 2 Pet. 1:1, 11; 2:20; 3:2, 18; 1 John 4:14).

24. Paul closes his instructions to wives with a summary exhortation: *But as the church submits to Christ, so also wives should submit to their*

Paul's use in the letter. See also Mouton, 'Reimaging Ancient Household Ethos?', pp. 163–185, who also sees 'head' as 'source' but analyses the counter-cultural ring of the passage well in the context of discussion with feminism and colonial theology.

105. Bruce, p. 385, says the relevance of this addition is not obvious. We beg to differ and argue that it is an important and clear point being made and then reinforced contextually.

106. Schnackenburg, p. 247. Also Cohick, 'Tyranny, Authority, Service', pp. 74–89, shows how Paul's remarks undercut ancient social norms and reconfigure the discussion away from categories of power to those of service.

husbands in everything. The contrast opening the verse simply draws attention back from the rationale of the previous verse to the exhortation. It is merely resumptive. Again, the Christological analogy, not the culture, is the mirror through which all this is seen. The church is responsive to and follows the lead of her Christ. So the wife is to be responsive to the husband with respect to all issues in the marriage.

The verse repeats the core exhortation of verse 22 and adds one element. That is the call to submit 'with respect to all things' (author's translation). This call is like what is said to children and slaves in Colossians 3:20, 22. The remark is to a degree rhetorical as the call would not be for a wife to submit to a husband who asks something of her that violates the command of God. Acts of sin, being subject to abuse or subjecting the wife, a child or others to immoral or dangerous circumstances are not at all in view here. Its thrust is that as long as what is asked is morally appropriate and not harmful, submission is the response.[107] None of this excludes the give and take that is part of a partnership, but it does indicate an orderliness in how resolution can result. It is important that what is said here is part of a pairing that urges a husband to relate to his wife with care and sensitivity.

Two important additional observations need to be made.[108] First, despite the balance the passage seeks, nothing said here requires that the wife submit only if her husband loves her, or that her husband must be a believer (1 Pet. 3:1). The passage is working to make sure that a marriage is not a constant battleground. Second, obedience is not something that the husband is to demand. In his love he is to show concern for the needs and the well-being of his wife.

25. Paul now turns to the husband: *Husbands, love your wives just as Christ loved the church and gave himself for her.* The husband is to *love* his wife, not lord it over her. The present imperative makes this a constant responsibility. The husband's love is illustrated by his

---

107. The 'in all things' and how to qualify it is discussed in Tracy, 'What Does "Submit in Everything" Really Mean?', pp. 285–312.
108. Hoehner, p. 746.

sacrifice on behalf of his wife. He is to be a giver and server, looking out for her growth and best interests. Each partner in this exhortation is looking at how to give positive energy to the relationship. Paul spends a full eight verses in his instructions to the husband, versus the three about the wife (125 words to 41).[109] The husband is especially urged to follow through on this call. There is no prerequisite for this love coming from the wife. This is what he is supposed to be: loving and giving.

The exhortation here differs slightly from that in Colossians 3:19. There the call is to love and not be embittered against wives. That states the love principle by looking at the opposite possibility. Again, *Christ* and the *church* are the mirror and example for the relationship. This is something Paul does elsewhere (2 Cor. 11:2–3), but there it is relationships in the church that are in view. The idea of sacrifice on behalf of the bride points to a specific kind of love for the husband. One might have expected a call to rule the wife here, in contrast to the submission asked of the wife, but that is not the case.[110] So it is not headship by self-assertion, but by self-offering. Sacrifice for others and their well-being follows the example of Christ (Phil. 2:5–11). This kind of exhortation to love is rare in household codes (cf. Pseudo-Phocylides 195–197; and the much later Talmudic text *b. Yeb.* 62b).[111] To love in this manner points to Christ, who *gave himself* up for the church (John 10:11, 15, 17; 15:13; Eph. 5:2). One could well argue that if the call of the Christian is to love one's neighbour (Lev. 19:18; Matt. 19:19; Gal. 5:14; 6:10), certainly the wife qualifies!

26. The goal of Christ's activity undergirds the example of love: *that he might sanctify her, having cleansed her by the washing of water with the word.* Jesus' death had a purpose: to make the church into something

---

109. Hoehner, p. 746.

110. Lincoln, p. 374.

111. Lincoln, p. 374; Thielman, pp. 381–382, adds a few more texts, including Plutarch who calls a marriage of love an intimate union like the organic unity of a creature (*Conjugalia praecepta* 142e). This text is cited in the discussion on 5:28. Usually the wife is urged to care for the home and free the husband from concerns about the house.

special, to set her apart and cleanse her by the word. His service was for her and for her edification. Thus Paul completes his definition of love.

Sanctification is the first of three goals of Christ's love for the church, as verses 26–27 will note. The idea of being sanctified means being set apart for something, no longer being common or profane. In this case, it is for service to God. Such a setting apart required a cleansing that Christ achieved for the church in his death, an act pictured as a *washing*. Paul reinforces the idea of cleansing with the image of a bath. Though often connected to baptism, the corporate nature of the remark runs counter to this idea, since baptism is individual. It is best to see it as an extension of bridal imagery tied to the bath a bride took before her wedding. The bath cleansed her and made the presentation at the wedding an event where she could be at her best. This is pictured in Ezekiel 16:4–14 (cf. Ezek. 36:25–27). Purification appears in many contexts in Judaism: for lepers, Nazirites, women after their menstrual cycles and people who bring sacrifices to the temple.[112] The image is a common one.

So we have a cleansing that Christ makes possible and that prepares his bride, the church, for its union with him. The cleansing and sanctification occur together. The cleansing probably points to regeneration and the indwelling presence of the Spirit (1 Cor. 1:2; 6:11; 2 Tim. 2:21; Titus 3:5; Heb. 10:22). That cleansing is also tied to the *word* of God, a reference to the promise and plan of God tied to salvation, looking at the response and embrace of that message and its promises (John 15:3; 17:17; Rom. 10:8, 17; Eph. 1:13–14; 6:17). Although this cleansing starts with faith and is the focus here, it will be completed when salvation is consummated (Rom. 6:19, 22; 1 Thess. 5:23). As a result of Christ's loving act, the church is set apart and cleansed from sin. Such care and provision is a model for the husband's love for his wife.

27. There is a goal in this sanctification and cleansing: *so that he may present the church to himself as glorious – not having a stain or wrinkle, or any such blemish, but holy and blameless.* The goal of the cleansing is

---

112. Arnold, p. 387.

a marvellous presentation of the prepared bride. The term *endoxos* looks to something splendid, thus *glorious* (Luke 7:25).[113] The scene is like the moment at a wedding when a bride begins her walk down the aisle and everyone exclaims, 'How beautiful!' In this case, it is Christ's work that is seen as responsible for this exclamation. The image is like the one Paul used in 2 Corinthians 11:2 where he speaks of presenting the local Corinthian church as a pure virgin to Christ, much as a father or the bridegroom might.[114] There Paul speaks of his own work in one location, but the goal is the same as the one Christ has for all the church. The Ephesian text looks at the entire church, not just one location. The image gets more concrete in the parallel of Colossians 1:28, where the goal is to present everyone perfect in Christ.

There is a question as to when this take places: in the future with Christ's return,[115] or with the incorporation of the church at the time of Christ's work?[116] In the New Testament as a whole the answer is 'both', depending on the text and context (begun with Jesus' work: Acts 15:9; Rom. 6:1–11; 1 Pet. 1:22–23; mostly future: Matt. 25:1–13; Rom. 8:18–39; 1 Cor. 15:35–58; Rev. 19:1–10; 21:9). In 2 Corinthians 11:2 it is a future presentation that is in view. Many see that as the case here as well, but the context's imagery is against that idea. The washing has already taken place, as has Christ's work in his self-giving in death. The act is an example to be followed, not merely anticipated. The marriage of Christ and the church has already taken place. They are functioning as one flesh (Gen. 2:24 in Eph. 5:31). So we have in view what Christ has made the church to be with his death. This is why believers can already be called saints. What Christ has made the church to be is also what it will fully become in the consummation, but Paul has the start and design of that journey in mind here. The reference is to the present. The bride *is* holy (and thus should live that way!). The future presentation mirrors the goal of the act in view here and is when that reality will

---

113. BDAG, pp. 332–333.

114. Bruce, p. 389.

115. So Hoehner, p. 761.

116. So Lincoln, p. 377.

become permanent. The picture reflects the description of a real bride in Psalm 45:13 or the image of how God cared for and presented Israel as a wedded spouse in Ezekiel 16:10–14.

The idea of being *holy and blameless* looks to the spiritual and ethical quality of the church (Col. 1:22) with the parallel being the beauty of the bride on her wedding day (Song 4:7). Again, there is a slight difference from the Colossians text. In Colossians, Christ presents them to God; here it is a presentation *to himself*. The condition is the result of Christ's cleansing work and describes the moral state of the church in her position in Christ. She has been incorporated in him and shares the status he gave and provided for her in his love and care.

28. Paul makes the comparison complete: *Even so husbands should love their wives as their own bodies. He who loves his wife loves himself.* The call is for husbands to love their wives as part of their own identity, as if they were physically attached, just like *their own bodies*. Such self-care comes naturally, and so should this kind of love of a husband for his wife. As Christ loved and gave (v. 25b), so the husband should also give care. In fact, the exhortation comes as an obligation: he *should* do this. It is completely right that it should be done. The comparison with Christ's model deepens the obligation: in doing this, they do it like and for him. It is almost a form of worship to live this way, as the connection to Christ drives the point.

The one-flesh idea of Genesis 2:23–24 is present (Eph. 5:31). That passage is often appealed to in the New Testament (see Matt. 19:5–6; Mark 10:7–8; 1 Cor. 6:16). The wife leaves her family and the two become one flesh. In this oneness comes the unity that Paul is urging for the marriage. For a husband to love his wife is an extension of his loving and caring for himself. It also reflects the love he is to have for any person, what Scripture calls one's 'neighbour' (Lev. 19:18). That love most certainly applies to his bride. Plutarch says in *Conjugalia praecepta* 142e,

> And control ought to be exercised by the man over the woman,
> not as the owner has control over a piece of property, but, as the
> soul controls the body, by entering into her feelings and being knit
> to her through goodwill. As, therefore, it is possible to exercise care
> over the body without being a slave to its pleasures and desires,

so it is possible to govern a wife, and at the same time to delight
and gratify her.[117]

Paul's exhortation brings the emotional care and responsibility of
love into this picture; it is not an appeal to ruling and order. The
slight difference in emphasis is important.

This idea of a wife being a part of the husband's self is important. It means that the marriage is not supposed to be a tug of war
for power. As Hoehner notes, explaining that each member of a
marriage is a free agent *before God* who acts for the union, 'It is not
the duty of the wife to tell him to love her. It is his duty to the Lord
to love her.'[118] The same is true in reverse: it is not the duty
of the husband to tell the wife to submit; it is her responsibility
before the Lord to do so. It means that as each partner speaks about
or to an issue, they both are to pursue one voice before the Lord.
That may not always mean agreement, but it will mean harmony
about what does get decided. When I listen to my wife I am hearing
a part of myself and listening for God perhaps speaking through
her. The idea that the couple is a team is expressed in this one-flesh
idea. The identity of the whole working together is the most
important point here. This is not self-love, but a self-giving love for
something greater and more than one's own self. Foulkes notes that
the remark promotes the bride as not lower in social status but as
equal to her husband, even a part of him.[119]

29. Paul explains his seemingly peculiar take on his one-flesh
comparison that to care for another is actually to care for oneself.
He also covers a rationale for how caring should be seen: *For no one
has ever hated his own body but he feeds it and takes care of it, just as Christ
also does the church*. It is here that Paul reveals his core value tied to
the call to love. It involves care and the nurturing of the marriage
as being for the husband like caring for himself. Paul urges the
husband to see his wife as an integral part of who he is. Again, the
example is Christ's care for the church.

---

117. Schnackenburg, p. 252. The citation is from the Loeb edition of Plutarch.
118. Hoehner, p. 764.
119. Foulkes, p. 165.

Paul continues to draw out the point made in Genesis 2:24 about the two becoming one. The term for *body* here is *sarx*, which is an allusion to the idea of 'one flesh' in Genesis 2. This intense sense of oneness breaks down any view of the wife as the 'other'. The incorporation of the perspective of the wife as tied to the husband's own identity and well-being has an impact on all the dynamics in a relationship. The marriage relationship is special, and this is one of the reasons why. The use of the expression 'not hating' alludes to an absence of alienation or hostility one should have about the marriage relationship and the doing of life together. The term *feeds* (*ektrephō*) can mean 'nurturing', like in the picture of raising a child (6:4).[120] The second term, *takes care* (*thalpō*), pictures giving comfort or warmth to someone (1 Kgs 1:2; 1 Thess. 2:7).[121] Best cites a marriage contract that has these two terms in it.[122] Such care is exactly what Jesus gave, not only in his sacrifice in death to cleanse the church, but in all the care he gives to her subsequently to sustain the relationship.

30. Paul then explains another rationale for the Christ comparison, besides the one-flesh picture of marriage from Genesis 2:24: *because we are members of his body*. Paul has equated the husband's role to that of Christ, and the wife's role to that of the bride, that is, the church. This leads Paul to Genesis 2:24, but to make the one-flesh point Paul extends the metaphor of the body he described initially in 1 Corinthians 12:12–27. In fact, the remark here looks very much like 1 Corinthians 12:27. Paul has already made the point that the church is a *body* (Eph. 1:23; 4:12, 16; also Rom. 12:4–5; 1 Cor. 12:12–27; Col. 1:18, 24). We are inseparably connected to Christ. That this connection has ethical implications for how we live is shown in 1 Corinthians 6:15. In that text it has to do with making choices about sex and faithfulness, but in this Ephesians text it is about how the husband relates to his wife, paying careful attention to the example of service and care Jesus provides.

---

120. BDAG, p. 311.

121. BDAG, p. 442.

122. Best, p. 550.

There is another, more subtle point: it is not that the husband or the wife is a member of the body,[123] but that *we* are members of the body.[124] We, including the husband and the wife, share as part of a larger whole. Christ cares for all the members of his body. So husband and wife are connected to Christ and, through their marriage, to each other. The close connection to Christ adds an element of obligation and justification for the picture of being part of the same body and the earlier exhortation that a husband who loves his wife loves himself and follows the example of Christ.

31. Paul now cites Genesis 2:24 to drive home the point of being one flesh: *'For this reason a man shall leave his father and mother and be joined to his wife, and the two shall become one flesh.'* The scriptural definition of marriage serves as the basis of the 'one flesh' remarks (vv. 28–30). The image of marriage drives the discussion and serves as the backdrop for discussing the church as the bride of Christ. The model is that, just as Christ loves his bride, so a husband should love his wife. The text also begins a transition where both partners are in view, as verse 33 will show.

There are three parts to the text. The initial picture involves a man forming a new family unit by leaving *his father and mother*. The reference is more to care and oversight than to location in the ancient world. Then there is the man's *join[ing] to his wife*, which pictures the new unit. Finally, there is the becoming *one flesh*, which in turn makes a twofold point. First, it pictures the unique union that sex brings when a man and woman come together. In 1 Corinthians 6:16, when this kind of physical union is not part of a marriage but involves a prostitute, it is decried as a violation. That kind of union is tied to sexual immorality in 1 Corinthians 6:18, where the general term for any kind of infidelity is used. There is a

---

123. The addition of the phrase 'of his flesh, and of his bones' (author's translation) is unlikely to be original, its support not being as well attested. It was added through the influence of Gen. 2:23, and the idea of the body is how Paul discusses the church. This does make it the harder reading, but in this case it is too hard, as interpreters have struggled to explain its force. The reading makes the image far too physical in force.

124. Schnackenburg, p. 253.

uniting in the sexual act that is not designed to be trivial or casual. It represents a certain giving and attaching of the self that is to be uniquely applied. Second, *one flesh* also portrays the intimate uniting that comes as the marriage brings with it a functioning unit. The verb in Greek for 'joining together' (*proskollaō*) means to adhere or stick to something in the way that glue joins things together.[125] It points to mutual allegiance and connection. Jesus cited the Genesis text when discussing marriage and divorce, stressing that marriage is designed to be a permanent relationship (Mark 10:7; Matt. 19:5, with a non-prefixed form of the verb for 'joined together'). The appeal to Genesis is to divine design and created order. The text also shows how marriage biblically defines a man and a woman. The text in Genesis establishes this, Jesus affirms it and Paul also acknowledges it.[126] In fact, the family is the core unit of creation. It is the context for the stabilizing of all relationships, designed to give a secure place for the raising of the next generation, which is why parents and children will follow in the household code in 6:1–4.

A bridge to the use of the image of Christ and the church may come from the fact that the verb for 'joining' can speak to religious adherence described by a loyalty (Deut. 11:22; Josh. 23:8).[127] Now Paul makes the point that the union of the husband and wife mirrors what God designed for Christ and the church, as verse 32 indicates. How we relate to one another in the world, even in the most basic of relationships, has as its model how God relates to his creation with Christ.

32. Paul affirms the mystery of marriage and then makes clear that he is applying it especially to Christ and the church: *This mystery is great – but I am actually speaking with reference to Christ and the church.* How that which is physically distinct can be seen as a unit is a great mystery, and this is even true of how Christ and the church are united.

Paul argues that marriage is a deep, even profound, mystery, as he is about to show. In contrast to the view of many interpreters,

---

125. BDAG, p. 882.
126. Healy, 'St. Paul, Ephesians 5, and Same-Sex Marriage', pp. 12–21.
127. Best, p. 553.

mystery here is not understood just in its common scriptural sense of some type of revelation now made clear or revealed, although that idea is also present. It also includes its more common everyday sense of something very deep that cannot be completely worked out by human logic or thought. A mystery of marriage is that it binds people together in many unseen, almost indefinable ways. This is part of the reason why divorce is so painful, and part of why divorce is spoken against in Scripture: in a sense we leave a piece of ourselves with the departed spouse. Physical union is more than a mere hookup, which is why it must not be casual. This element of marriage is one of the reasons why Paul condemns sex outside marriage (1 Cor. 6:16). How two people can uniquely be in a one-flesh relationship is profound in itself. It is unique; it is not to be a repeated encounter with many different people. Also mysterious is how two people can become one flesh. Nonetheless, Paul means more than just this, so he calls the mystery surrounding marriage *great* or profound. The end of the verse explains the key point Paul wishes to make and does play on the normal scriptural use of the term *mystery*.

What is surprising about this verse is that Paul declares he is focused on Christ and the church, not just on marriage between people as the citing of Genesis 2:24 might suggest. That also is a part of the great mystery, because beyond the human relationship is the mirror marriage of a connection to God. This shows how profoundly Paul takes every thought captive in Christ. It also indicates how Paul sees life defined by the way God and his plan have an impact on creation. Undergirding how we see the most basic of human relationships as presented in Genesis 2:24 is how God relates to his own community that is also called his body (Eph. 2:16; 5:30). This connection could only be understood once the undergirding model was in place. So the mystery in part includes this element of revealing the parallel between the human relationship and the relationship of Christ to the church, which the human relationship is to model. Paul reveals such an aspect of mystery to marriage.[128] In fact, this mystery – the marriage connection to

---

128. Gnilka, pp. 287–288.

Christ – drives all that he is saying in this section to both the husband and the wife as they are to see Christ and the church as the model for their behaviour and their roles in marriage.

33. Paul now summarizes the call he has made to both the husband and the wife: *Nevertheless, each one of you must also love his own wife as he loves himself, and the wife must respect her husband.* Love from the husband and respect from the wife are to so drive the marriage that it mirrors how Christ loves the church and how the church responds to that love.

The first half of the verse is a summary of the call to love that has dominated the passage from verse 25. The one-flesh idea is also repeated in the call for the husband to *love his wife as he loves himself.* The husband is to lead the home with love. This is an important point, as often the more emotional and relational side of the family is seen to be left to the wife. That is not so here with Paul. The wife is the husband's 'exemplary neighbor' to be loved.[129] The exhortation is individualized as each husband is addressed and so, by default, each wife in the next section is in view.

The new element in the summary is in the call to wives to respect their husbands. The phrase *respect* translates the verb *phobeō*.[130] It refers to a profound respect or regard for someone and is the verb used in the LXX in the statement that the beginning of wisdom is 'fear' of or respect for the Lord (Prov. 1:7). This is about communicating honour to someone and includes an element of deference, so 'respect' could be too soft an idea.[131] One thing that is not meant is 'terror', as is commonly associated with the English term 'fear'. So one could translate the term as 'reverential respect' to show the element of deference. The deference is in part tied to the role the husband has in the family as paralleled with that of the church to Christ. In the passage as a whole, this deference is given in a context where self-sacrificial love is also urged of the husband on the model of Christ, so the ideal is not in the context of a power play but in one of mutual regard. The

---

129. Barth II, p. 719.

130. BDAG, pp. 1060–1062, 'respect'.

131. Hoehner, pp. 783–784.

groundwork for this was laid in verse 21, where the mutual submission of believers appeared. The exhortation is not made with
the proviso that the other person does his or her part, but it is
hopeful of that being the environment to build a solid marriage.
In fact, 1 Peter 3:1–7 assumes a husband who is not a believer yet
who is still to be interacted with through respect. So each person
is responsible for how he or she responds to the exhortations
made to them.

b. Children and parents (6:1–4)
Context
The second section of the household code exhortations involves
children and parents. That parents are in view and not just fathers
seems likely given the citation including both in verse 2 and the fact
that responding to both parents is in view in Proverbs (Prov. 1:8–9;
17:25; 19:26; 20:20). Again, the order starts with the person in the
responsive position and then moves to the person who has responsibility. In distinction from the previous exhortation to wives and
husbands, children rather than their parents get the bulk of the
remarks. The same ordering will be used for slaves and masters.
Obedience and honour are the call for the child, while sensitivity
and nurture are to belong to the parents.

Comment
1. The command to children is straightforward: *Children, obey
your parents in the Lord for this is right.* Colossians 3:20 is very similar:
'Obey your parents in everything, for this is pleasing in the Lord.'
Verse 2 will make it clear that obedience is an extension of
honouring parents. In part, the goal is a stable, orderly home. Part
of the idea may also well be that parents are seen as a potential
well of wisdom, as the Jewish tradition in the book of Proverbs
presents a father who carefully and wisely instructs his son (Prov.
1:8–9; 3:11–12; 17:25; also Deut. 21:18–19). This response is similar
to a description of how Jesus interacted with his parents by being
in submission to Mary and Joseph when growing up (Luke 2:51).
A direct address to children was unusual in the ancient world, as
such remarks normally involved discussion with the parents. It
suggests that the children were present in the congregation when

Paul's letter was read.[132] In addition, the term *children* suggests that both boys and girls are addressed. These children would have been old enough to be able to understand the concept of obeying. The exhortation to *obey* is something they can embrace.

Attempts to suggest that the phrase *in the Lord* indicates that children are full members of the community and that it points to infant baptism extends too far the implications of the child being in the home of believing parents.[133] There is nothing pointing to baptism in the context. This passage is about the way children engage with their parents. The children are to obey because these are the parents the Lord has given them, and the home is seen to be operating before the Lord. That is the only point being made. The term *in the Lord* grammatically goes back to the verb *obey*.

The remark that this is *right* only has the orderliness of the home in view, as the expectation is that children should honour their parents as part of the creation design and an outgrowth of the Ten Commandments. Disobedience of parents is seen as a sign that society is out of whack (Rom. 1:30; 2 Tim. 3:2). Nothing said here is surprising culturally as the same expectation existed in the culture at large (e.g. Dionysius of Halicarnassus, *Roman Antiquities* 2.26.4, who describes the role of the father as the head of the home).

2. The ground for the children's obedience is an extension of honouring their parents: *'Honor your father and mother,' which is the first commandment accompanied by a promise.* The ground comes from one part of the Ten Commandments (Exod. 20:12; Deut. 5:16). The verb *timaō* means to *honor* or have a high regard for someone.[134] The present imperative of the verse points to a continuing attitude. It involves more than merely obeying; there is a personal regard that goes beyond just responding positively to parents. The command appears frequently in the New Testament and is one of the core relational elements in Jewish culture (Sir. 3:8; 7:27; Matt. 15:4; 19:19;

---

132. Lincoln, p. 403.

133. The phrase is well attested in a wide array of manuscripts and so is likely to be original.

134. BDAG, pp. 1004–1005, 'honor'.

Mark 7:10; 10:19; Luke 18:20). Paul sees the importance of the relationship because it is tied to one of the Ten Commandments.

The remark that this is the *first* command *accompanied by a promise* refers to this being the first of the Ten Commandments that comes with a specific positive promise, with the commandments seen as residing at the head of the Torah. In fact, it is the only commandment that comes with such a promise, but it opens the Torah in a sense, being of such importance.[135]

That *promise* resulting from obedience is, in the Old Testament, a long life in the land (Exod. 20:12 LXX; esp. Deut. 5:16). It is the first commandment that treats how we relate to others, as the first four commandments address how we relate to God. Paul broadens the application of the promise by speaking in verse 3 of a long life on the earth, since Gentiles and the now-spreading church are in view. The promise is clearly not automatic, since there are other things that can lead to limiting one's life. The point is that an orderliness to one's treatment of parents leads to a life of peace and longevity (Lev. 19:3; Deut. 21:18–21; 27:16; Prov. 10:1; 11:29; 21:20).

3. Paul names the promise of the commandment: *'that it may go well with you and that you will live a long time on the earth.'* The peace that emerges from a good relationship with parents can yield a long and flourishing life. The promise has two elements. First is that things will *go well*. That is natural as it means the reduction of any conflict in the home. The second is that children may *live a long time on the earth*. This is a variation of the original promise, which looked to long life in the land. The application has been expanded to apply to any believer, Jew or Gentile, and takes account of diaspora believers. It may also be an extension of the first point of having a peaceful, flourishing life. Obviously, obeying this command is not the only thing that results in having a long life. The point is that, all things considered, such obedience has its potential benefits and can make its contribution to such a goal (1 Tim. 4:8). It is important to recall that in the ancient world untimely death of children was common; up to 50% of children had died by their tenth birthday.[136]

---

135. Lincoln, p. 404.

136. Thielman, pp. 400–401.

So the remark is one that very much fits the context. Fowl suggests that it is a 'prudential rule of thumb', and Arnold says that it fits the Proverbs, being a 'general pattern'.[137] This type of thing was often said of the one who kept the law (cf. Deut. 4:4; 5:33). Given the many proverbs that tell children to honour both parents, the advice fits Jewish roots well (Prov. 6:20; 15:20; 20:20; 23:22; 30:17).

4. Now Paul turns to the parents: *[Parents], do not provoke your children to anger, but raise them up in the discipline and instruction of the Lord.* The first question this verse raises is who is addressed by the masculine noun that literally reads 'fathers'. The rendering *parents* is due to the fact that most proverbs dealing with children's relationship to their elders refer to both the father and the mother, with obedience applying to both. The proverbs listed at the end of the commentary on verse 3 all mention both genders. In addition, the children were told to honour father and mother in verse 2. So it is natural to see this advice as extended to both genders, with the masculine simply being a normal grammatical choice in the combination, and with a clear nod to the headship role the father has in the home. In Graeco-Roman culture the father held the authority in the home. This could support the idea that fathers only are meant. A term for 'parents' does exist (*goneus*, used in 6:1), but this is not used here. Still, the thrust of the instruction up to this point has had both parents in view, as verse 2 shows. If the text is seen as only addressing fathers, that would highlight the structure in the home that 5:22–33 indicated. Nevertheless, the application would still extend to both parents as the core relational responsibilities of the mother would not differ from those of the father. What is true of the head of the house would be true of the partner who helps and respects him.

Parents are not to be a provocation to their children. Rather, they are to convey the discipline and instruction of the Lord. Part of this will be seen in how they treat their children, not only in what they say to them. The verb translated *provoke* is *parorgizō*, which means 'to make angry' (cf. Deut. 32:21; Rom. 10:19).[138] Parents should not be

---

137. Fowl, p. 194; Arnold, p. 417.
138. BDAG, p. 780, 'make angry'.

a source of frustration and discouragement to their children. Instead, children should be nurtured. Parents' behaviour towards their children should not involve capricious authority or endless petty correction.[139] The verb *ektrephō* means 'to provide food for someone'. The picture is of caring for someone and giving that person what he or she needs to live and grow.[140] This image was already used in Ephesians 5:29 about how one cares for one's own body. Colossians 3:21 speaks of not discouraging a child.

Children are not to have free rein, but are to be raised in the *discipline and instruction of the Lord*. The combination is probably a hendiadys, saying one thing with two similar words. Guidance in a certain God-honouring way of life is the point. The kind of teaching the father gives to the son in Proverbs is an example. Deuteronomy 6:1–9 also emphasizes this kind of direction. *Discipline* includes the idea of reproof (Prov. 3:11–12; 13:24; 29:15; Heb. 12:5–6). There is an education here that stretches into life and behaviour. It is about teaching wisdom with an eye to God. This all means that although parents possess authority over their children, it is not to be used without sensitivity, self-awareness or restraint. Parents shape children, and the raising up of a child should be intentional in what is modelled and moulded. On the other hand, direction is to be given, so there is not to be a kind of passive withdrawal from a child's life, where the parents are so preoccupied with their own affairs that the children are left to their own devices (a play on words is intended here).

c. Slaves and masters (6:5–9)
Context
The last primary household relationship Paul addresses is that of the slave and master. The presence of the section is amazing in itself as a slave held no authority at all in the house, even though some slaves were seen very much as quasi-family members. Paul acknowledges the reality of a social structure that existed at the time and works for understanding and orderliness within it. Estimates

---

139. Foulkes, p. 170.
140. BDAG, p. 311.

suggest that up to one-third of people in the Roman Empire were slaves.[141] Slavery was not a matter of race but of circumstance and social standing resulting from war, kidnapping, poverty or birth.[142] Slaves were regarded as property, which means that the address of them here as people shows a different approach to who they were. Slaves had very limited rights. They were owned by and controlled by their masters, who could give them many responsibilities, such as helping raise children or handling money. Yet their freedom was limited and the effort to escape could lead to death (see Phlm.). Slaves in this culture often gained a good level of education to perform their duties and could choose to enter this status, unlike the forced indentured status of more modern slavery. Ancient slaves could gain freedman status over time or by their owners' choice. The letter to Philemon about Onesimus shows how and why a slave is to be regarded as a person in a Christian context. Onesimus is promoted to a far higher status as Paul elevates the slave to a brother in Christ *and* equal to Paul as an apostle! So the personal dynamics are being transformed, even as the legal status is left unchanged.

A word about the application of this text: it is often transferred to the work of a labourer in an employment context, yet the analogy is an incomplete one. The employee chooses by contract to give his or her labour and has options to continue that service or not under that contract. That difference is significant. Still, the kind of attitude indicated here for the way work should be done is analogous within that difference. So applications to the workplace, or to prisoners or other contexts where a clear difference in social status is at work in an authority context, is only indirect.

Comment
5. Paul opens with instruction to the believers with lesser authority in the relationship, as he did in the earlier discussions: *Slaves, obey your human masters with fear and trembling, in the sincerity of*

---

141. Best, p. 573.

142. On slavery in this period, see Bartchy, *First-Century Slavery*; Lincoln, pp. 415–420; Hoehner, pp. 800–804.

your heart as to Christ. Once again we get a grammatically masculine address for slaves who were male and female. Obedience to their earthly *masters* is their primary responsibility. The masters are described as 'fleshly' (*kata sarka*) to distinguish them from the Lord. Their obedience is to come with a respect and awareness of the authority their masters possess. That is the meaning of the phrase *fear and trembling* – it does not indicate any sense of terror (1 Cor. 2:3; 2 Cor. 7:15; Phil. 2:12). There is to be respect for the power the owner possesses. The phrase also points to sincerity, not duplicitousness, like the respect one gives to Christ. This means the slave was to carry out his or her duties with integrity and faithfulness. The term *haplotēs* means 'integrity' (cf. 1 Chr. 29:17; Rom. 12:8; 2 Cor. 1:12).[143] The section parallels Colossians 3:22 – 4:1. Responding from the heart before the Lord with faithfulness – that is, with deep integrity – is a core Christian virtue (Col. 3:17).

6. Paul underscores the sincerity that is to come with the work of a slave: *not like those who do their work only when someone is watching – as people-pleasers – but as slaves of Christ doing the will of God from the heart.* The service of a slave is not to be based on circumstances and whether someone is paying attention; it is to be the same whether the master is present or not.

This verse and the next first state the point negatively, then positively, before returning to negative descriptions. Literally, the two negative descriptions present here are as 'eye-service' and as 'men-pleasers'. The meaning is transparent. They are not to do their best only when people, especially their masters, are watching. The terms appear only here and in Colossians 3:22 in the New Testament. Instead, their work is to be undertaken with a genuineness that comes from the soul and reflects the will of God. The note of genuineness reinforces the appeal to 'sincerity' in verse 5 and good intent in verse 7. The description of doing the work from the *heart* means from the soul or from the inside out (Col. 3:23). Sincerity is an important theme for Paul (2 Cor. 1:17–18; 2:17; 4:2; 10:11).

7. Paul completes the thought: *with willingness serving as to the Lord and not to men* (author's translation). As with the wives and children,

---

143. BDAG, p. 104, 'sincerity'.

slaves are to serve with an awareness of their connection to the Christ and in a way that mirrors it. They serve and represent the Lord in their work. This understanding should guide their approach to their labour.

The key term in this verse is *with willingness* ('willingly', *eunoia*). It refers to something done with a good attitude and was often used in diplomatic materials to speak about a person, city or state (1 Macc. 11:33; 2 Macc. 9:21).[144] It has the force of doing something out of goodwill. The term's only New Testament use with this sense is found here. The service one gives is to be given *as to the Lord* and not *to men*, a point reinforcing the service as slaves of Christ of verse 6. The virtual repetition serves to drive the point home. Would what is done be good enough to show the Lord?

8. Paul gives a motive for such obedience, namely, accountability to God: *because you know that each person, whether slave or free, if he does something good, this will be rewarded by the Lord.* The Lord is watching what we do and rewards those who do it well. So the service is rendered not only *as if* to the Lord but actually *to* the Lord.

Every person is accountable to God. This is noted in texts like 1 Corinthians 3:10–17, which says that the quality of each person's work will be tested (Matt. 16:27; 25:14–46; Luke 6:35; 2 Cor. 5:10; Gal. 6:8; 1 Pet. 1:17; Rev. 22:12). There is no social class in this test, for it applies to each person, whether slave or free (Rom. 2:11; 1 Cor. 12:13; Gal. 3:28; Col. 3:11). It means that at that time justice will also be done to correct any injustice. What a master might miss or leave unexpressed, the Lord will see and reward. The emphasis is on what is done well, as it is the rewarded good that Paul notes. The call to live by doing good is common in Paul (2 Cor. 9:8; Gal. 6:10; Eph. 2:10; Col. 1:10; 1 Thess. 5:15; 2 Thess. 2:17).[145] God sees everything and will sort it out (Luke 12:7). Colossians 3:24–25 makes a similar point, but also adds the negative possibility. The reward in Colossians is also described as the inheritance (Eph. 1:14, 18; 5:5).

9. Now it is the masters' turn: *Masters, do the same to them, giving up the use of threats, because you know both you and they have the Lord in heaven*

---

144. BDAG, p. 409, 'willingness'.

145. Best, p. 579.

and there is no favouritism with him (author's translation). The call to the masters is that they should have the same respect and awareness that the Lord is watching how they act in their use of authority. This awareness matches the sense the slaves are to have as they serve their masters. The idea of doing good in verse 8 is likely a point of comparison. The use of threats is to be abandoned out of an awareness of the status of a slave as a person. Such advice would be counter-cultural. Abuse was common in the cultural context, but that is prohibited here (Plautus, *Amphitryon* 291–349; Suetonius, *Claudius* 25, notes laws to curtail such abuse; Pliny, *Epistles* 3.14).[146] The presence of *the Lord* is the great leveller. He has no favourites and will treat everyone the same. In fact, all are the same before him (Deut. 10:17; 2 Chr. 19:7; Acts 10:34; Rom. 2:11).

We see evidence of this in how Philemon is told to treat Onesimus in Paul's letter. There the status of Onesimus is elevated to that of a brother and even of the apostle Paul, as Philemon is to consider how to treat this slave who had fled the home of his master. Mercy was to be a driver in that response, rooted in an appreciation of the mercy Philemon himself had received from God (Phlm. 16–19).

The teaching here has a parallel in Colossians 4:1, while another note about there being no favouritism is found in the word to slaves in Colossians 3:25. Colossians 4:1 speaks of masters treating slaves justly and fairly. The remark here is like the response of John the Baptist to soldiers when he addresses the issue of a potential abuse of power in Luke 3:13–14. No matter what the social status of people may be, the response that honours God respects other people as those made in God's image. There is a hint of the mutual submission of 5:21 here because the point is that all submit to the Lord.[147]

Theology
The household codes reveal a core Christian relational ethic. It is framed in a mutual respect such that mutual submission is how all

---

146. Hoehner, p. 814.
147. Thielman, p. 409.

believers are to engage with each other (5:21). That does not prevent Paul from seeing roles for people in relationships that give families a structure within which to work. However, these roles are defined in a way that has an impact on their traditional power relationships. So the wife is to be submissive, but the husband is called to serve sacrificially and to treat his wife as if she was a part of himself. Children are to obey, yet the parents are not to exasperate them. Slaves are also to obey, but their masters are not to use threats as their standard way to motivate. There is to be orderliness but also a level of human concern.

Just as important, if not more so, is that these relationships are not seen to be private and isolated; they are driven by how both parties relate to and are to be responsive to the Lord. So the ethical responsibility is seen as part of the relationship and accountability each person has to God. He models the wife's and the husband's response. Accountability to him is at the centre of what is said to the child, the slave and the master. The call to be aware of the instruction and discipline of the Lord accompanies what the parent is to teach. All of this reconfigures the relationships in ways that make the exhortations distinctive. A Christian home is to be a unique place where all are aware that God sees how these relationships are being conducted. This feature is probably the one most ignored when these texts are taught or preached and the only concerns are the roles and how they function. When they are taught with this dimension missing of the connection to the Lord, they are inevitably taught in a direction that undercuts this point. God cares about relationships, especially those in the home. When love, care and service abound, the presence of the Spirit can shine in the relationships God gives to us.

B. The armour of God (6:10–20)

Context
The final exhortation section of the letter addresses the fact that life in a fallen world is a battle. It builds off of the call to walk in unity, in holiness, in love, in light and with wisdom (4:1, 17; 5:1–2, 7–8, 15). There are forces that seek to derail those aligned to God from this path. The struggle is pictured as hand-to-hand combat.

What is distinctive here is that the battle is seen as being not between people but between believers and spiritual forces (6:12). To survive, one must be prepared for this battle and engage with it at the level at which it is being fought. That means drawing on the spiritual provisions God has given us and not being focused on the circumstances. This is the most explicit 'cultural war text' we have in the New Testament epistles, but it defines that battle in ways that are distinct from most of the ways the church engages in that battle today. That is because it is the spiritual forces that are the concern. It is resisting their efforts that Paul stresses, not our material circumstances. Today's approach is often dedicated to fighting people, who actually are a goal in mission, as Paul suggests at the end of the unit.

The section is sometimes described as a *peroratio*, a rhetorical part of ancient speeches that seeks to bring the speech to a conclusion that rouses the emotions, much like a pre-game speech by a coach.[148] The point is debated. What is clear is that Paul issues a final call that makes clear that all he has urged comes with an intentional dependence on God and the power made available to us in Christ. Without it, defeat looms. One more point is important: the exhortation here is not individual, but corporate. The text says the struggle is 'ours' (v. 12), and the second person references in the verses are plural.

Paul summarizes the unit with a general exhortation in 6:10–11. The principal battle is defined in 6:12. Then the armour is presented in 6:13–18. The model comes from a Roman soldier; it could well be that Paul's jailers are the basis for the imagery. Paul then asks specifically for prayer for himself as a prisoner and for his mission in 6:19–20 as he closes the unit and transitions to the end of the epistle.

The background for the armour image appears to be Isaiah 59:16–17, where the Lord is described in armour much like that in this Ephesians text, with reference to the breastplate of righteousness and the helmet of salvation. There also is a picture of justice as a belt in Isaiah 11:5. The mouth as a sword alludes to Isaiah 11:4. In other words, the prophet of old is in the background, a theme

---

148. Lincoln, pp. 432–433; Thielman, p. 414, is sceptical of that connection.

that Second Temple Judaism also developed in how it spoke about the armour (Wis. 5:17–20). The one difference from Isaiah is that what was described as belonging to the Lord we now share as believers. The tone of 1 Thessalonians 5:8 is similar to that of this text in Ephesians.

Comment

10. Paul begins with a call to be strong: *Finally, be strong in the Lord and in the strength of his might.* Life in this often hostile world requires endurance and strength, but not the kind we give ourselves. Rather, to resist at a spiritual level requires the *strength* supplied by God rooted in his *might.* What Paul has urged in the letter does not come easily. So he closes by noting how the distinctive path of the church requires God's enablement. The present imperative (*endynamousthe*) points to a continual need to *be strong* in this way (Josh. 1:7; Rom. 4:20; Phil. 4:13; 1 Tim. 1:12; 2 Tim. 2:1; 4:17). The exhortation is passive. It is a strength supplied from elsewhere, so can be translated 'be strengthened'. However, even though the strength comes from elsewhere, it is to be actively sought. There is an imperative to act here and to give space for God to work.

The theme of the strength of the Lord takes us back to the prayer in 1:15–23 and the call to understand the power of God that is available to us. Ephesians 1:19 is especially in view. The power in 1:15–23 was said to be from God yet was exercised through the Christ; it was like that which raised Jesus from the dead. In our position as God's children in Christ, believers have access to that power and we apply that understanding in our lives, drawing on the spiritual resources it provides. The text is an expansion of 1 Corinthians 16:13–14 with its call to stand firm in the faith (cf. Rom. 13:11–14; 1 Cor. 15:58). Paul made a similar point but without the full call in Colossians 1:11, and then closes with a more general exhortation in Colossians 4:2–6. Fowl compares the text to the point of John 15: one must be connected to the vine and abide in Christ.[149]

11. Paul calls for the wearing of armour: *Clothe yourselves with the full armor of God so that you may be able to stand against the schemes of*

---

149. Fowl, p. 203.

the devil. Paul commences his metaphor, calling for the putting on of armour for a battle. However, ground is already won, so standing firm is the position from which we battle (see v. 13 as well). The ground that has been won needs to be held, but that can only be accomplished with intent and commitment.

The imperative formulates the putting on of the armour as an urgent call. The *panoplia* or *full armor* is detailed in verses 14–17 and describes an infantryman. The response here is primarily defensive, but the idea of going on the offensive is also possible for Paul, at least in terms of the spiritual weapons believers have (2 Cor. 10:3–5). 'Weapons of light' are mentioned in Romans 13:12. The purpose of the armour is to resist whatever the *devil* throws at us. The devil's methods include anger and division (4:27). A lack of forgiveness can be a reflection of succumbing to him (2 Cor. 2:11). These schemes may suggest something subtle as it takes being alert to face up to them (2 Cor. 11:14; 1 Pet. 5:8). The threat is real because of the power the devil possesses to control people (Eph. 2:2). He can take advantage of a lack of self-control (2 Cor. 7:5). Everything urged in the good walk of Ephesians 4 – 6 is designed to prevent the devil's success. Note the repetition of being clothed with truth and righteousness from 4:24.

12. Paul explains why such armour is necessary: *for our struggle is not against blood and flesh but against the rulers, against the authorities, against the cosmic powers of this darkness, against the spiritual forces of evil in the heavenlies* (author's translation). The battle is not against people, but against an array of spiritual forces. This is not a normal battle, nor should believers think of the opposition in normal human terms. To think in human terms is a mistake of cosmic proportions.

The core image is of a hand-to-hand battle, up close and personal. The term *palē* refers to such intense battle.[150] The fact that we are to have armour on also pictures hand-to-hand combat in the struggle for turf. This is the only place where this term appears in the New Testament. Paul identifies whom the battle does not involve and whom it does. The battle is not against *blood and flesh*, that is, people. The unusual order reflects the Greek expression,

---

150. BDAG, p. 752, 'struggle against'.

while English translations normally have 'flesh and blood'. The enemy in this spiritual struggle is not people. People and circumstances are not the key to such battles; it is a far more subtle and serious struggle.

This battle is against real but unseen *spiritual forces*, named with various descriptions to show that no matter how anyone thinks of them, this is the enemy. Paul writes of *rulers, authorities*, the 'cosmocrats' (*kosmokratōr*) of *darkness* and *the spiritual forces of evil in the heavenlies*. The first two of these terms already appeared in 3:10. The term 'cosmocrats' or 'world rulers' may well refer to powers associated with the cosmos (*T. Sol.* 8:1–3; 18:2–3).[151] It is another New Testament term that is used only here. Part of Jesus' work was to defeat such forces (Col. 2:15). Such an intense, up-close battle with transcendent forces requires deep and strong spiritual resources. Wrestling is normally about who has the greatest strength, so the previous exhortation to be strong in the Lord makes sense. Even though these forces are in our face, the strength to stand exists. In a place like Ephesus, where Artemis was such a dominant presence, the remark vividly fits the context. False worship of the gods is tied to demons elsewhere (1 Cor. 10:20–21). Paul has already made clear that victory is possible because of the power at work in believers (Eph. 1:19–21; 2:6; Col. 1:13).

13. Paul repeats his main exhortation before he begins to enumerate the pieces of armour: *For this reason, take up the full armor of God so that you may be able to stand your ground on the evil day, and having done everything, to stand.* What such a battle requires is clothing oneself for battle with the *full armor of God* (Rom. 13:12; 1 Thess. 5:8). This armour offers both protection and weapons for attack. With both available, one can stand up to the struggle that is a part of the *evil day*, which is the present evil age (Gal. 1:4; Eph. 2:2; esp. 5:16). Taking all it provides and doing all one can in preparation, one can face the battle with the hope of standing. The expression *having done everything* looks at what has taken place already as one takes up the armour. To face the battle successfully one must see it coming, understand what it takes and be prepared.

---

151. Lincoln, p. 444.

The imperative here is another urgent call like the exhortation in verse 11. In that verse, standing against the devil was the point. Here it is the possibility of victory. The term *panoplia* refers to *full armor*.[152] Only the use of all the spiritual resources will allow believers to resist in the day that is full of evil. The goal is to survive the battle, and that takes doing all one can in the fight. Bruce refers to doing 'all that your duty requires'.[153] The idea of eventual victory is part of the point of the section.

14. Now Paul begins to enumerate the pieces of armour in a listing that extends to verse 18: *Stand therefore, having girded your loins with truth, and having put on the breastplate of righteousness.* There is possibly no correlation between the noted characteristic and where it is located in the armour; it could be merely a function of creating the imagery of a full set of armour (Isa. 59:17; Wis. 5:18–22). Whereas these images apply to God in the texts just cited, in Ephesians this armour is now applied to believers, showing a transfer of characteristics to us as a result of God's work in Christ. Still, it is the imagery as a whole that serves the point, more than the location of the individual pieces. For example, in 1 Thessalonians 5:8, faith and love are the breastplate, while here it is righteousness, showing flexibility in the imagery. The challenge of these verses is considering whether we are looking at position,[154] virtues, or both, with one built on the other.[155]

A spiritual battle requires spiritual resources. That is what Paul begins to list here as part of the armour. Standing strong, as verse 13 already called for, becomes possible because believers have these attributes at their disposal (1 Cor. 16:13; 2 Cor. 1:24; Gal. 5:1; Phil. 4:1; 1 Thess. 3:8; 2 Thess. 2:15). In the references just cited, the exhortation to stand firm often comes in the section closing a discussion on how to live, and it does so here. This shows that the context pushes in the direction of application and virtues. The imperative *stand* is another urgent call. There is nothing optional about this exhortation. One is not wise to go into battle unprotected.

---

152. BDAG, p. 754, 'full armor'.

153. Bruce, p. 407.

154. So Best, pp. 598–599.

155. So Hoehner, pp. 839–841; Arnold, pp. 452–453.

The *truth* here is tied to being armed with God's message about Jesus and what is provided through his work on our behalf. The girding of one's *loins*, or waist, allows for manoeuvrability to engage in the fight. Ephesians 1:13 and 4:21 have already noted how the gospel is tied to truth and how Jesus is truth (also 4:5: 'one faith'). It reflects an understanding and personal embrace of what God has done in and through Jesus and so points from what one understands to integrity. We stand on and are to be directed by such truth, reflecting it in how we live.

Righteousness cannot exist without the righteousness Jesus has given to us. Obviously, the *breastplate* protects the core of the body from injury. It was made of metal and often tied together by rings connecting the parts. We can be warriors because Jesus is a warrior (Isa. 11:5; 53:12; 59:17). What he has given us enables us to be what we are called to be (Rom. 1:16; 3:21–22; 4:3, 5). *Righteousness* can also describe the quality of being righteous (1 Cor. 1:30; 2 Cor. 6:7; and esp. Rom. 6:13–14; Eph. 4:24; 5:9). What God rains down on us allows us to reflect who he has made us to be (Isa. 45:8). So the sanctified life coming out of the righteousness of God acts as a protection in the preparation for battle.

These characteristics are both objective and subjective. One leads into the other. However, the stress is on the product in our lives, that is, the virtues we show growing out of what God has done for us.[156] Being prepared for battle means having both access to and appreciation for what God has done and what that means for who we have become and how we are to live.

15. The armour imagery continues: *by fitting your feet with the preparation that comes from the good news of peace.* Here the allusion is to Isaiah 52:7. Part of the battle is reflecting the gospel not only in what we preach or teach but also in its lived-out application as *good news of peace*. This assumes the reconciliation so prominent earlier in the book (2:11–22). One aspect of this battle is overcoming the prejudice that often poisons human relationships between people of different backgrounds. Here the beauty of Jew and Gentile

---

156. Arguing for virtue over imputation is Wenkel, '"Breastplate of Righteousness"', pp. 275–287.

coming together has been highlighted; it is the gospel 'appropriated and proclaimed'.[157]

This verse is connected to verse 14 and its description of what it takes to 'stand'. One's *feet* are to be *fitt[ed]* or shod with the gospel. Military sandals or half-boots were called *caligae* and were sometimes reinforced with hobnails to give them an ability to grip the ground. It is significant that Paul highlights the gospel's connection to peace. The goal of the gospel is not conflict and vengeance, but peace.[158] It is not only about forgiveness, grace or salvation, as important as these are; it is about the peace the gospel eventually produces between people and God, and among people themselves (2:14). The picture is of battling conflict in the pursuit of peace, an odd picture for battle, but appropriate for people influenced by the gospel and its distinctive way of life. In other words, the pursuit of reconciliation and peace in the message about Christ is the ultimate antidote to a world full of dissension and division (1:10). The idea of *preparation* of this gospel means that its goals direct and guide us in our engagement. We live in such a way that we show we are grounded in the gospel of peace. This is not just about preaching the gospel or engaging in missionary activity (though the passage does point to that), but also about living out that gospel by showing what the message incarnated looks like.

16. Paul continues to list the elements of the armour: *and in all of this, by taking up the shield of faith with which you can extinguish all the flaming arrows of the evil one.* Yet another element tied to taking up and standing in verse 14 is *the shield of faith*. *Faith* is a crucial part of the armour for it cancels out danger by extinguishing the most threatening of all the weapons the devil throws at us, namely, those arrows aimed right at us. Ephesians has noted faith several times (1:13 ['believed in Christ' = faith], 15; 2:8; 3:12, 17; 4:5, 13; 6:23). In 1 Thessalonians 5:8, faith is a breastplate. The point is that faith gives protection. In 1 Peter 5:8–9 there is a call to resist the devil by faith. The call to faith echoes Ephesians 3:16–17 and the idea of being strengthened by it. Again, we have a combination of the faith

157. Bruce, p. 408.
158. Schnackenburg, p. 278.

in terms of its objective content and its subjective application of trust in God in the midst of the circumstances. It is not self-confidence, but reliance on God, as these are spiritual resources tied to what God has done for us in Christ. In the Old Testament the fear of God is a shield (2 Sam. 22:31; Ps. 18:30).[159] Threat becomes capability with the shield of faith. The fact that Paul lingers here to describe it is another indication of its importance.

The ancient shield was made of wood planks covered with metal and canvas, trimmed in metal and often dipped in water to douse any flames. The damage the devil seeks to cause is pictured as *flaming arrows*, with faith being the protective shield that blocks them. The shield could be as much as 4 ft high, 2½ ft wide and an extra palm's length in breadth (Polybius, *Histories* 6.23.2). So it was long and thick. The arrows were known as *malleoli*, and were dipped in pitch, lit and then shot at the enemy (Herodotus, *Histories* 8.52.1). These arrows were up to 7 ft long and had an iron tip that could be as long as 2 ft. Such arrows could travel up to 33 yards.[160] The threat of fire could cause panic among the troops, as a flaming shield would be thrown away, exposing that soldier and the other troops to the fire (Livy, *Histories* 21.8.12). The shield protected the soldier and prevented such panic, especially as soldiers often stood next to each other and locked their shields to protect the group (Josephus, *War* 3.259).[161]

For Paul, faith stops the challenges of the devil. The shield is the most flexible piece of armour; with faith, nothing damaging gets through. It is seen as especially important with the additional note *in all of this*, 'in all circumstances', highlighting it as the protection required in every event.

17. Two pieces remain. They form a joint exhortation: *And take the helmet of salvation, and the sword of the Spirit, which is the word of God.* Here another urgent command is present. Less obviously, the gospel is again invoked with the promises of the Scripture to which the command is tied. So we have the *helmet of salvation* that protects

---

159. Arnold, p. 456.
160. Hoehner, p. 847.
161. Foulkes, p. 181.

our head and the *word of God* that can be wielded in close combat. Salvation and the word are related because the word is about salvation. Both must be embraced in order to fight the battle. In the New Testament, the *word of God* is often not the Hebrew Scriptures but the word of the gospel; Luke–Acts often uses it this way, and the tie to salvation makes that likely here (Luke 8:11; 11:28; Acts 4:31; 6:7; 8:14; 11:1; 12:24; 13:5, 46; 17:13). So that is where the reconnection to the gospel exists. Bruce argues that victory is implied because *salvation* is already accomplished (Eph. 2:5).[162] Salvation is a protection against serious damage (Ps. 140:7), perhaps even from attacks from spirits given the tight association in Ephesus with idolatry and a prominent pagan temple. In 1 Thessalonians 5:8, the helmet is the hope of salvation. Perhaps what is intended here is the idea that our secure identity in an already possessed salvation means that we have no reason to be fearful. The helmet was a padded metal bowl-like shape with a short guard for the brow. The padding was of either leather or cloth. It also had a neck guard. Imagery like that in Isaiah 59:17 may be present, only there it is God who wears the battle gear.

The word as a *sword* is a common biblical image (cf. Isa. 11:4; Heb. 4:12; Rev. 19:15). The *machaira* was a short sword that fits the hand-to-hand combat in view.[163] It was about 2 in. wide and 2 ft long. The word is energized by the *Spirit*, a reference to the power of this word. This word can be seen as an offensive weapon that protects through being the truth or as a defensive weapon in applying that truth.[164] The example of the latter is Jesus' response to the devil in the temptations (Matt. 4:1–11; Luke 4:1–13). Salvation and the gospel are key protections against the evil day.

18. Paul concludes the active equipping with a call to surround all activity in prayer: *With every prayer and petition, pray at all times in the Spirit, and to this end be alert, with all perseverance and requests for all the saints.* We share in this battle, so our prayers are not just for us as individuals but also for all believers, who all fight in the struggle.

---

162. Bruce, p. 409.

163. BDAG, p. 622, 'a relatively short sword'.

164. Arnold, p. 462.

Prayer is to be our mode of existence, a constant feature in facing the conflict. The term 'to pray', although not a main verb in the Greek, functions like one,[165] but most likely is tied to the idea of standing and of the armour as a whole. Prayer frames all that is done in taking up the armour. It is not part of the armour but is to come along with it. The present tenses of the participles 'praying' and 'being alert' point to this constancy as well. We are to be vigilant in prayer.

Paul uses two words for prayer to suggest that all kinds of prayer should be lifted up to God. The first term, *proseuchē*, is a general word for prayer, while the second, *deēsis*, is focused on specific requests or petitions (cf. Phil. 4:6). He also refers to the need for a constancy in prayer by calling for it *at all times* or at every opportunity. Given the participle 'praying', Paul mentions prayer four times in the verse, as it also ends with a note about petition (*requests*). This prayer takes place in connection with *the Spirit*, as a spiritual battle requires spiritual resources through dependence and seeking of guidance.

We should be connected enough to what is taking place in the lives of other believers that we can pray for them, since we are to be *alert* with *perseverance* and *requests for all the saints* (Rom. 12:12; Col. 4:2). The term *agrypneō* means 'keeping careful attention to something', being aware of what is happening (1 Cor. 16:13).[166] Luke 21:36 might be an example of such a prayer. Paul will present himself as an illustration of it in the next two verses. He repeats the term for petition used at the start of the verse here (*deēsei*). Bringing others before God in the context of the battle is part of what the community is to do, since it is a body. Armed with salvation, the gospel and prayer, the church can face the battle.

19. Paul presents himself as an example to be prayed for: *Pray for me also, that I may be given the message when I begin to speak – that I may confidently make known the mystery of the gospel.* Paul asks for the strength to proclaim boldly the gospel and its mystery.

The idea expressed by *confidently* suggests speaking in a difficult situation, something his imprisonment was. His appeal might even

---

165. Thielman, pp. 432–433, though we prefer to see it as a frame for the armour as opposed to making a new paragraph.

166. BDAG, p. 16, 'to be alertly concerned about'.

lead him to speak before Caesar, if not an important deputy. This is not about being brash or insensitive, but about being clear.[167] The phrase *when I begin to speak* is literally a reference to the 'mouth' and is a rhetorical way to refer to speaking (Exod. 4:12; Isa. 59:21; Luke 21:14–15). In particular, Paul wants to focus on *the mystery of the gospel*, the idea raised in Ephesians 3:3–10 of the role of Gentiles in the plan of God. Colossians 4:3–4 makes a similar request. Paul often made a request for prayer (Rom. 15:30–32; 2 Cor. 1:11; 1 Thess. 5:25; 2 Thess. 3:1). One often thinks of Paul as being bold in sharing the gospel (1 Thess. 2:2), but even the apostle needed such prayer. It is interesting that he does not pray for a change in his circumstances, nor for judgment on his enemies, but rather that he might be faithful, just as the church prayed in Acts 4:23–31.

20. Paul details his situation: *for which I am an ambassador in chains. Pray that I may be able to speak boldly as I ought to speak.* His service for the mystery of the gospel has placed him in this situation. He wants his calling as an ambassador to drive him (2 Cor. 5:20). He desires to be a faithful representative of Jesus. The verb for 'speaking boldly' matches the noun 'confidence' in verse 19.

The expression *ambassador in chains* would normally be a cultural affront, describing as it does ill-treatment of an emissary, but Christians did not have any social status yet.[168] The term *ambassador* points to a legate in the Roman world, showing that Paul sees himself as acting on behalf of God as a representative of Christ's kingdom, a heavenly kingdom that transcends all earthly allegiances (Phil. 3:20–21). He has already noted that he is a prisoner (3:1; 4:1). Paul's attitude can also be seen in 2 Timothy 1:8 and 2:9, and how he accomplished this before his trial is described in Acts 28:31. A gospel triumphant in terms of being proclaimed is what the answer to this prayer will bring. The issue for Paul is not his circumstances but his being faithful in them. He had received a call to declare the gospel wherever that might be, so he is following through faithfully (Acts 9:15; 27:24; 1 Cor. 9:16). Later, he seems to have sensed that this prayer had been answered (2 Tim. 4:17).

---

167. Arnold, p. 467.
168. Barth II, p. 782; Smillie, 'Ephesians 6:19–20', pp. 199–222.

This section would seem very strange if the letter was pseudonymous. The claim that it is included for verisimilitude is weak, as
the real question is why an author would include such a note if Paul
had long been dead.

Theology
Paul knows that he lives in a fallen world where people are easily
misled as to what should drive life. He describes this life as a spiritual battle requiring spiritual resources. Those resources are tied to
drawing dependently on the truth and enablement that come from
a new identity in Christ. The battle is not against people, but against
real yet unseen evil spiritual forces. They lead people astray and take
them into their invisible clutches. The gospel and the faithful
preaching of it provide the way out of this danger, one people
caught in those spiritual forces rarely grasp. So the mission of Paul
and those like him who believe is to proclaim this gospel in the
midst of a world that often seeks the solution in a million other
places. Paul asks for prayer for the saints to persevere and for
himself in his current imprisonment. Key to all of this is taking up
these resources and drawing on all they have to offer. This is how
we can stand our ground and survive the confrontation. It means
not just knowing that we are God's, but actively taking up the virtues
noted here. Those virtues are rooted in truths that fill them and
make them real, worth drawing on for victory.

C. Closing remarks (6:21–24)

Context
Paul closes the letter noting that he is sending Tychicus to give them
more news so they may be encouraged despite Paul's imprisonment (vv. 21–22). He then closes with blessings of peace and grace
(vv. 23–24). The way he closes shows the personal connection Paul
wishes to maintain with the recipients of the letter.

Comment
21. Paul has more to let them know so he sends an emissary on
his behalf: *Now that you also may know how I am and what I am doing,
Tychicus the beloved brother and faithful minister in the Lord will tell you*

everything. Tychicus will be that messenger. He is commended to the Ephesians with the twofold description of being a *beloved brother* and a *faithful minister*. They can trust his report; Paul is confident that he will be a trustworthy messenger. Such letters were often carried by a friend or entrusted to a stranger, a risky undertaking. Finding a faithful messenger to deliver a letter was sometimes a challenge in the ancient world. Cicero, in *Letter to Atticus* 1.13, spoke of his hesitancy to send an epistle for lack of a trustworthy courier.[169]

Paul marked out a few people as *beloved*. He described Onesimus as a 'beloved brother' (Phlm. 16), while Timothy is described as a 'beloved and faithful child' (1 Cor. 4:17). Epaphras was also called *faithful* (Col. 1:7). The phrase *how I am and what I am doing* covers all the news tied to Paul, including a more positive perspective on things connected with his imprisonment. Paul had earlier hinted that the Ephesians were discouraged about his situation (3:13), but he does not want them to remain there. It is suggested that words very much like those in Philippians 1:12–18 may reflect the direction of this encouragement.[170]

Tychicus was with Paul at one point (Acts 20:4). He was Asian. Paul also contemplated having him advise in Crete as either he or Artemas was sent there for that task (Titus 3:12). He also was the messenger for the letter to Colossae (Col. 4:7). This likely explains the presence of *also* in the verse as Tychicus is on a trip to inform many churches, including Ephesus and its region. The trip's purpose is to update and encourage the churches there with information sent directly from the apostle and a messenger who knows him. He may also have carried the letter to Philemon. What is said here is parallel to Colossians 4:7–8, with only the idea of his being a fellow slave omitted in Ephesians. The idea of Tychicus being sent from Rome, as Paul's co-worker, to Ephesus is noted in 2 Timothy 4:12. It is important to appreciate how different and difficult communication was in the ancient world in comparison with our own. Accurate information about Paul is the point here.

---

169. Thielman, p. 442.

170. Thielman, p. 440.

What is lacking is a list of personal greetings. Some contend that this is significant in the dispute over authorship.[171] It does not fit Paul's usual pattern. This was covered in the Introduction under point 29 of section 5b ('Theological differences'). Paul is leaving a legacy as he writes from prison unsure of his long-term fate. There are many in Ephesus he does not know as they arrived after he left and he is providing direction for the future. Another point is that the letter is one for the region, not just for Ephesus, so this may also help to explain the lack of direct personal notes that would not make sense for the other locations. That may explain the difference. As Tychicus is heading to both Colossae and Ephesus, it may be that he is planning a longer stay in Ephesus; this may then explain the lack of greeting, as he will bring it personally. It makes sense that he might have had a longer stay there since Paul was more directly tied to that church.

22. Paul now describes the mission of Tychicus: *I have sent him to you for this very purpose, that you may know our circumstances and that he may encourage your hearts.* Two goals come with Tychicus's arrival: to update and to encourage them. The update will be about Paul and those with him (*our*). No-one else has been explicitly mentioned in the letter up to now, but Paul often had people around him helping him. The reference could be to news about the church in Rome, as a courier like this was the closest thing the community had to an ancient Internet that could share information about how others were doing.

Paul's imprisonment could well have been discouraging, but Paul trusts God in it. In fact, it is amazing how little Paul writes about his predicament. He is more concerned about them. Paul also spoke of encouraging the hearts of the Colossians (Col. 2:2; 4:8; also 2 Thess. 2:16–17). Tychicus will 'continue what the letter was intended to achieve'.[172] He wants to strengthen them (Eph. 1:18; 3:16–17). Colossians 4:9 noted that Onesimus was sent with Tychicus, but Paul gives no mention of that here.

23. Paul closes the letter with the first of two blessings: *Peace be to the brethren, and love with faith, from God the Father and the Lord Jesus*

---

171. For example, Schnackenburg, pp. 286–288.

172. Best, p. 617.

Christ. Three core virtues drive the church. A goal of the gospel is *peace* (Gal. 6:16; God of peace: Rom. 15:33; 16:20; 2 Cor. 13:11; Phil. 4:9; 1 Thess. 5:23; 2 Thess. 3:16). Peace was a theme in 2:14–18; 4:3; and 6:15. *Love* and *faith* are relational keys – that is, faith in God and love for the saints. Faith was noted in 1:15; 2:8–10; 3:17; and love in 1:4, 15; 4:15–16; 5:2. Paul closes with a return to a brief mention of these virtues as he sends his wishes of peace and love with a shared, active faith, virtues that are the fruit of the activity of *God the Father* and the *Lord Jesus Christ.* 'Grace' and 'peace' were raised in Ephesians 1:2, while here we have 'faith' as well. The address is to the *brethren*, not to the usual Pauline 'you' (Rom. 16:23; Col. 4:18; 1 Thess. 5:28; 2 Thess. 3:18). This is a hint that the letter was to circulate among both those known and those not known to Paul.

24. A final benediction closes the letter: *Grace be with all of those who love our Lord Jesus Christ with incorruptibility* (author's translation). This is a benediction that looks to eternity, given the reference to grace and the love it produces. Grace came from love (2:4) and yields love. Paul closes the letter praying that the believers might have a continued experience of that which is their salvation.

Grace is the core word of salvation. It was developed vividly in 2:1–10, appreciating how God gifts his people life, enablement and power, and it leads to peace, faith and love, which is the theme of Paul's close to the letter. *Love* is a major theme of the letter (love of God: 2:4; of Christ: 3:19; 5:2, 25; of the husband: 5:25, 28, 33; and tied to the believer: 1:4; 3:17; 4:15–16; 5:2; 6:23).[173] The key word here is *aphtharsia*, which means 'incorruptible' or 'undying' (1 Cor. 15:42, 50, 53–54; 2 Tim. 1:10).[174] There is discussion as to whether it best connects to 'grace' or 'love'. Either is possible, but the emphasis on grace yielding love is probably at the core here. The objection that the term 'grace' is too far removed in the Greek sentence is countered by the awareness that the verse is a bracket, a package whereby grace is the box in which love is found. The eternality suggested by the reference to incorruptibility has an impact on both ideas if grace is in view. That connection seems

173. Lincoln, p. 466.
174. BDAG, p. 155, 'incorruptibility, immortality'.

likely here given that Ephesians 2:1–10 is the core illustration of power that Paul wants the Ephesians to grasp. This is a grace that does not fade and is pure. That is the last word lingering eternally at the end of the letter as the product of grace. It includes riches that never end (2:7). The sun never sets on such grace.

Theology
The letter closes seeking connection and fellowship with those to whom Paul writes. Tychicus will update them. Then comes a waterfall of blessing that has been expounded in the letter as a whole: peace, love and faith, all tied to the grace from which they emerge, a grace that never ends – simply amazing.

Conclusion

Ephesians is an amazing summary of Paul's view of God's blessings, his plan, the enablement believers have access to and the reconciliation God has achieved in bringing Jew and Gentile together in Christ. In creating the church, God brought all of these wonderful heavenly blessings in Christ. He also gave a full enablement by his Spirit to experience these riches. Paul's ministry has been about making this work of salvation known. That work of divine grace is to reshape people and their lives. The giftedness they possess allows them to work collectively alongside one another to represent God as lived-out light in a dark world. That life looks different from that of the world, being enabled by a Spirit that allows them to live in ways people are otherwise incapable of following. This enablement allows for transformation in marriage, with their children and in their social relationships. Equipped with this enabled righteousness, they can face the spiritual battle that is a part of life in a fallen, broken and troubled world. Utilizing those spiritual resources allows them to stand in the midst of that battle. In being made into God's workmanship by the grace of God, they are equipped for every good work God calls them to. What is left is to apply God's word as Paul has revealed it and, in so doing, to show forth the way of grace. This drawing on spiritual resources results in a life lived in community that also reflects what God had in mind when he made us in his image. As such, the collective life they lead is a mirror not only of what was but of what is to come, pointing to the wisdom of God. A life so lived results not only in a demonstration of reconciliation but also in an existence that extends praise to God for the realization of hope it reflects. All of this makes Ephesians a real gem of an epistle and a genuinely unique contribution to the canon of Scripture.

Finding the Textbook You Need

The IVP Academic Textbook Selector
is an online tool for instantly finding the IVP books
suitable for over 250 courses across 24 disciplines.

---

ivpacademic.com

TYNDALE COMMENTARIES
FROM INTERVARSITY PRESS

Tyndale Old and New Testament Commentaries are
designed to help you understand what the text
of Scripture says and what it means.

Find all the volumes and join the Tyndale Commentary program
at **ivpress.com/tyndale-commentaries-complete-series.**